PRAISE FOR AUGIE

"I enjoyed the book greatly. The author ⬚⬚⬚ ⬚⬚⬚⬚ ⬚⬚⬚⬚ was a man of courage."

⬚pire 35 years

"Augie was one of the best all a⬚⬚ ⬚⬚⬚ ⬚⬚⬚⬚⬚⬚ ⬚ was great on the bases and also behind the plate. You'd have to rank him as one of the great umpires."
— Andy Olsen, NL Umpire 13 years

"In umpiring circles, Donatelli is a legend - this is a terrific book for baseball fans and aspiring umpires."
— Rich Garcia, AL Umpire 25 years

"Regrettably, John Bacchia's masterful and compelling biography of this multi-faceted man comes posthumously, some two decades after his death. Yet we are grateful to him for bringing Donatelli's story to light."
— Author Phil Pepe

"Good book, but Harrelson is still safe!"
— New York Yankee Legend, Hall of Famer Yogi Berra

Augie, by John Bacchia, pays tribute to one of the finest umpires ever to call balls and strikes. It's the story of a boy who escapes the dangers of the coal mines to fly B-17s during World War II, only to be shot down and captured by the Germans. After enduring unspeakable hardship, Donatelli returns home, enrolls in umpire school, impresses everyone with his integrity and class, and starting in 1950 for the next 24 years arbitrates disputes with such Hall of Famers as Leo Durocher, Jackie Robinson, Stan Musial, and Yogi Berra. The passion, the love of the game, and the great stories are all here. Read *Augie*, and you'll be safe at home.
— Peter Golenbock, Author

New York Mets Manager Yogi Berra and outfielder Cleon Jones
disagree with Augie Donatelli's 10th-inning call in Game 2 of the
1973 World Series in Oakland. Donatelli had called Mets shortstop
Bud Harrelson out at home plate in one of the longest games in
World Series history. Photo Courtesy of Associated Press.

AUGIE

Stalag Luft VI to the Major Leagues

John Bacchia

iUniverse, Inc.
Bloomington

Augie
Stalag Luft VI to the Major Leagues

iUniverse books may be ordered through booksellers or by contacting:

iUniverse
1663 Liberty Drive
Bloomington, IN 47403
www.iuniverse.com
1-800-Authors (1-800-288-4677)

ISBN: 978-1-4620-0724-0 (pbk)
ISBN: 978-1-4620-0725-7 (cloth)
ISBN: 978-1-4620-0726-4 (ebk)

Library of Congress Control Number: 2011904434

Printed in the United States of America

iUniverse rev. date: 8/17/2011

Cover Photo: Yankee manager Casey Stengel and Augie Donatelli standing toe-to-toe during an exhibition game, April 13th, 1951. Copyright Bettman/CORBIS.

To those who prevail during troubled times.

Contents

FOREWORD

I first heard the name Augie Donatelli when I attended the 1955 World Series between the Dodgers and Yankees at age 12. My father and I stood in line in front of Ebbets Field in Brooklyn for 12 hours to get to see those games. Of course, I saw great players such as Berra, Snider, Robinson, and Campanella, but I recall that my father made sure I knew all the umpires. I remember he mentioned Augie, and I never forgot the name. Years later when I was an aspiring young umpire myself, I was thrilled to first meet him in 1971. It was during spring training, when the young umpires could meet the major league umps. Later, I would go to games just to see Augie umpire. I remember how hard he worked during spring training games. He always hustled, and that set a tone for the younger guys; his efforts didn't go unnoticed. As a former Marine myself, I could see the discipline that he had. I'd go to spring training games just to watch Augie, Shag Crawford, and Al Barlick. It was great. Their life was umpiring.

All the young umpires back then knew how Augie really stuck his neck out to get the ball rolling on the Umpire's Association. The guys from my era were always very grateful for his sacrifices for umpires. The young umpires of today don't really know much about the history, but in the fifties, guys were paid a modest sum per game and worked with very few benefits. Back then, umpires only got paid six months out of the year. Sometimes they would have to take an advance. They didn't make much money, so they borrowed on their salary for the following year to make ends meet. It wasn't easy, but you umpired because you loved the game.

I remember how gracious Augie was to the young guys. He was interested in what we had to say, and was always willing to help. He gave me encouragement and advice. He was a tough guy. A no-nonsense guy, and he had a military work ethic. He saw a lot of heavy action during World War II. He was a helluva tail gunner. Some umpires today have their fingers in a million different interests, but the old-school guys were true umpires. Augie was very passionate about his profession. He worked hard, he hustled and he had a strong-fisted way about handling situations. He was a very, very strong umpire. In umpiring circles, he's a legend.

Rich Garcia, Major League Umpire (1975 - 1999)

PROLOGUE

In *The Greatest Generation*, television journalist and author Tom Brokaw wrote about individuals who endured the Great Depression and World War II. The book documented the sacrifices and travails of men and women who survived daunting challenges. They lived through problem plagued times, survived and later flourished, but never thought of themselves as anything special. They modestly felt that they did what they had to do, and they followed in the footsteps of others who did the same. The story of August J. Donatelli might have fit in snugly within the pages of that landmark book. Donatelli found himself in the thick of the action as a tail gunner aboard a B-17 and like many World War II survivors on both sides of that conflict, he somehow managed to emerge from countless dire experiences with his energy and spirit intact. He did the same as his friends, neighbors, and brothers.

Augie was a first generation son of Italian immigrants, a man destined to a coal miner's life. However, his restless personality led him to umpire the national pastime at its highest level. To say he was a tremendous umpiring talent was true. Most people don't normally think of umpires in that light. But perhaps that's a fallacy. It's a rare individual who can stand before unrelenting managers, loudmouthed ballplayers, and harshly vocal crowds and render judgments with complete conviction. And it takes a unique personality to absorb the complaints of athletes, who never accept an umpire's split-second decisions with anything less than extreme prejudice. Legendary Dodgers' General Manager Branch Rickey, who was best known for breaking baseball's color barrier by signing Jackie Robinson, also had an eye for umps. Rickey, who served as an officer during World War I, was a man of deep Christian beliefs, who also had strong beliefs in the scarcity of good umpires.

"Where do you find such a man," Branch Rickey wrote. "A man involved in a game who has the authority of a sea captain, the discretion of a judge, the strength of an athlete, the eye of a hunter, the courage of a soldier, the patience of a saint and the stoicism to withstand the abuse from the grandstand, the tension of an extra inning game, the invective of a player and the pain of a foul tip in the throat? He must be a tough character with endurance and the ability to keep his temper in self-control, he must be unimpeachably honest, courteous, impartial, and firm, and he must compel respect from everyone!"

It was Rickey himself who scouted Donatelli during a minor league game, and promptly relayed his opinion of Augie's abilities to the league office. For Donatelli to jump out of the woodwork to impress hardboiled baseball men such as Rickey and also umpire Bill McGowan, there's little doubt that he had a special gift. He was a natural. It's little wonder that in the 1984 motion picture *The Natural* starring Robert Redford, the umpire is named Augie. If there ever was a natural when it came to making calls, Augie Donatelli was it. His uncanny and quick rise to the major leagues had nothing to do with any sort of extraordinary politicking. It's safe to say that he was the antithesis of a politician. In fact, he also had a talent for rendering his opinion, on any subject, right squarely between the eyes. Writer Jerome Holtzman once branded Augie with the nebulous title "most diplomatic," after an informal poll of major league players. Holtzman subsequently wrote in an October 12, 1990 article in the *Chicago Tribune*, "The grizzled Mr. Donatelli hit the ceiling. He almost grabbed me by the collar and asked me to write a rebuttal. "I'm no diplomat in striped pants," he shouted, "I'm an umpire!"

He *was* an umpire. In fact, Donatelli was an umpire's umpire. He spearheaded the formation of the umpire's union. Yet despite the heavy burdens he voluntarily flung on his own substantial back, and despite the oftentimes bitter disputes, both on the field and off, he always displayed a love for the game, and a humble realization that he was lucky to be part of it. Augie, the Bakerton, Pennsylvania coal miner, maintained a special secret signal to his fellow major league umpires. He used it when times got exceptionally tough on the diamond. After a long and heated on-the-field rhubarb had died down, he might sneak a glance over to one of his fellow umpires and mimic the motion of shoveling coal. No one would notice, except his fellow comrades in blue. The inference was that no matter how rough things got on the baseball diamond, it was still infinitely more palatable than the long hours of shoveling coal during those brutally difficult hand-loading days of the 1930s.

As an umpire Donatelli plied his trade during a magical time. He watched firsthand as Willie Mays and Hank Aaron streaked onto the baseball scene. He was behind home plate when Stan Musial stroked his 3,000[th] career hit, and he stood steps away as Jackie Robinson dashed around the bases at Ebbets Field. During his career he engaged all of those men with conversations of various tones. He argued nose-to-nose with Casey Stengel and Leo Durocher, and he called balls and strikes for pitching icons such as Warren Spahn, Bob Gibson, Sandy Koufax, Tom Seaver, and Don Drysdale.

In the winter months during the late 1980s, I spent several weeks interviewing Mr. Donatelli. The grand lion of umpires confided his life story to me. Not because I was a prolific writer, but because his son Pat told him that I was a good guy. It wasn't long after those many interviews and candid conversations that he was diagnosed with cancer. He died in May of 1990. For various reasons, interest in his life-story waned. The notes and partially completed manuscript sat on a dusty shelf like a time capsule. Decades later I decided to mine them for their tales. Mr. Donatelli lived through some very turbulent times as a coal miner, tail gunner, and major league umpire, and hopefully I did justice to these previously untold stories. I should make it clear that Donatelli, like many men of his generation, wasn't very interested in sharing the details of his war experiences. He finally shared them with me very late in life. While the book documents his many harrowing incidents during World War II, it is not intended as any sort of glorification of his sacrifices. Donatelli would not have been interested in that. It is a representation of events that made him the man he was: a decent citizen and a very good major league umpire. Many POWs, Augie included, never fully escaped the haunting memories of those many terrible days and nights in combat, and also his many trying times as a prisoner of war. From a personal point of view, I have close relatives who survived traumatic experiences directly related to the war. In the mountainside of present day Croatia in the shadow of Trieste, Italy, my grandfather was whisked away by Nazi soldiers, while his children (my mother and uncle) followed in a successful teary-eyed protest of his release. My father – at age 16 – was forced to brandish an unloaded rifle and trudge through rain-soaked forests with live rounds cascading from all directions. I had another uncle who lived in a cave for months to escape detection. My father-in-law, Erich Fischer, innocently watched as his house and town were destroyed by Allied Forces on the march. Another German friend foraged through the rubble of his decimated city. World War II had millions of victims on both sides of the conflict, and almost unanimously those who experienced it directly don't wish it portrayed as anything other than a tragic time.

There were many who offered guidance and encouragement throughout the writing of this book, including the Donatelli family, who welcomed me into their home time and time again, including Augie's wife Mary Louise Donatelli and her children, Pat, Dave, Barbara, and Carol. There were also many who offered their expertise and support in the writing of the book. Ken Samelson who edited the manuscript. Ken was editor of *The Baseball Encyclopedia* and has authored and edited many books. Broadcaster and friend Warner Fusselle also lent his baseball and editorial expertise to the project as well as access to his baseball library. Rick Wolff, broadcaster and executive editor, also offered generous guidance to the project as did legendary sports writer Phil Pepe, and public relations executive John Cirillo. I would also like to thank the many former Major League umpires who offered their time for interviews, including Rich Garcia, Jerry Crawford, Andy Olsen, and the late Ron Luciano and Al Salerno.

World War II veteran Donald Kremper, and author Dawn Trimble Bunyak also offered their invaluable expertise and photographs. Bunyak's book, *Our Last Mission* served as an important compass for me as I delved into Augie's interviews. Through Bunyak, I was able to locate Mr. Kremper, a World War II POW whose experiences nearly mirrored Donatelli's. Although he never actually met Augie, he knew who he was and later attended major league games in New York City and watched Donatelli umpire from afar. Some of the photos provided by Mr. Kremper were taken by a German guard, who traded the photos for contraband. They were brought back to the U.S. after the war. Sgt. Frank Paules, a camp spokesman, carried many of the photos back with him. I'd also like to thank the highly professional staff at the A. Bartlett

Giamatti Research Center at the National Baseball Hall of Fame. Most importantly, I thank my family for their patience, love, and support, including my wife Erika, and children Christian and Kimberly, and to my own parents Carlo and Dora, and also to Thomas Bacchia.

John Bacchia
Leonia, New Jersey
December 2010

ONE

Holy Hell

Augie Donatelli umpired his first organized game while he was a prisoner of war. The story seemed so implausible. How could such a scenario have unfolded? Little in his wildest dreams might Army Air Force Staff Sergeant Donatelli have imagined that he was testing out his future profession. The prison camp games were laced with so many disagreements and so much verbal sparring from spirited young American POWs, that Donatelli's umpiring was a welcome solution. The contests he umpired ran so smoothly that the players insisted he work all of the games. So it was in the midst of war, suffering, and destruction that men played softball to keep sane and to kill time, and the career of one of baseball's most respected umpires of the fifties and sixties had taken its first fledgling steps.

As fate would have it, had Donatelli not been injured while parachuting out of his doomed B-17 during the first daylight air raid on Berlin, he would have most certainly been playing and not umpiring. When healthy, he was a talented athlete, and a minor league caliber baseball player. Had it not been for his experiences during World War II, it's entirely possible that he would not have entered the world of umpiring at all. He might never have discovered that he had a knack for making calls. And his war record, no doubt, made him an attractive candidate for those who hand-picked him to join the National League in 1950. Donatelli was certainly perceived as a man who could handle himself and also deal with the complaints of raging managers, players, and fans. He entered Major League Baseball during a volatile era that featured the breaking of baseball's color barrier. The first black umpire wouldn't arrive until Emmett Ashford made it to the majors in 1966. But in 1950, baseball's umpiring priorities seemed focused on finding individuals capable of handling the pressures of a changing game, and Donatelli's war record proved that he was capable of shouldering tough challenges under pressure. In retrospect, his war experiences were probably very significant to his umpiring experience, and some might say he umpired with the command of a staff sergeant.

"I loved the guy, but he could be tough," recalled John Kibler, a National League umpire for 27 years. "One time, he's got the plate, I'm working in the infield, and just to check the count, I said to him, "What's the count? 'He stepped in front of the batter and shouted so that everyone in the ballpark could hear, 'What game are you watching?'"

During a game between the San Francisco Giants and Montreal Expos, Montreal had a sizeable lead when the Giants' Chris Speier hit a solo home run. It was seemingly clear to most at the ballpark that the ball had sailed foul by a substantial margin, but the inexperienced third base umpire had mistakenly signaled that Speier's shot was a homer. After a volatile reaction from the Expos, the young umpire looked towards Donatelli, who was umpiring behind the plate.

Donatelli barked, "Don't come back here, don't come back here unless you want me to make the call!"

The umpire closest to the play was expected to make the call, but the confused young umpire continued to amble towards Donatelli, and Augie made good on his comment and decided to reverse the call. "FOUL BALL," he bellowed! The Giants' manager came charging out of the dugout towards Augie, followed by Speier. Augie later told the young umpire, "Don't change your mind because sooner or later they'll hammer you."

Donatelli showed little tolerance for disrespectful tirades from ballplayers, and occasionally dispatched them as if they were cadets at Air Force Basic Training boot camp. The no-nonsense military mind-set made him unpopular with the combative spirits who seemingly never grew tired of challenging umpire's decisions. It also led to disputes with hard-headed managers. Augie never expressed his opinion in uncertain terms.

When a manager pleaded his point to vehement extremes, Augie would sometimes counter with the phrase, "What are we talking about here?" as if to infer that no man's life was in jeopardy based any umpiring decision. Donatelli realized he was an important keeper to the integrity of the sport, but never lost perspective that the game was light years removed from some of the cruelty he experienced during World War II, yet when a player or manager crossed the line he showed little tolerance.

In the early seventies, Montreal Expos shortstop Tim Foli displayed an unusual amount of vitriol towards umpires. Between games of a doubleheader in Montreal, umpires Satch Davidson and Bruce Froemming complained about Foli's aggressive temperament to Donatelli.

'Hey Augie, you're the crew chief, you've got to control this guy.'

When Expos manager Gene Mauch brought the lineup card out for the second game, Augie told him, "Hey, if I see Foli move his lips, he's gone." Mauch, himself a very prodigious umpire-baiter who had his share of run-ins with Donatelli, stood up for his emotionally charged player.

"Augie," Mauch replied, "you don't understand. He's just a high-strung competitor."

Donatelli shot back, "I'm not a doctor, I'm an umpire."

"All of us busted out laughing," Froemming recalled. "Mauch didn't have an answer for that one. Augie was great, just great."

Donatelli wasn't timid about putting a man in his place, and didn't take verbal retributions too lightly, and he certainly wasn't shy about ejecting a player if they disrespected a decision. But it wasn't necessarily his own judgment that he was defending; according to him it was the respect that should be accorded for his role as a major league umpire. Presiding as if he were both judge and jury, he led the National League in ejections four separate times, including a career high 13 ejections in 1953. Some thought that he carried a chip on his shoulder. Others said he that he had the courage of his convictions. Which was it?

Leo "The Lip" Durocher, a notorious umpire baiter, was incessantly going toe to toe with Donatelli. Leo was thrown out of games a total of 95 times during his managerial career. The two men went nose to nose with the frequency of ballroom dancers, but with the impassioned vitriol of hated rivals. Augie tossed players and managers out of games a career total of 103 times in 24 years. By comparison, Hall of Fame umpire Bill Klem ejected 251 over the course of 37 years. Donatelli came within a whisker of ejecting bombastic Oakland A's owner Charlie Finley from a World Series game, and he once ejected two different players during the same at-bat.

While his military background might have played a role in his on-field approach, his background as a coal miner also played a not so subtle role in his pro-union views, and that was partially the impetus that led him to spearhead the formation of the National League Umpires Association in 1963. It was very apparent that coal mining and war experiences were significant to his baseball career on many levels. He emerged from a rugged past during a bellicose time filled with war and anti-union violence, and ended up in a profession that required him to draw on that toughness

As Bob Uecker conveyed in *Catcher in the Wry*, "Let's face it, umpiring is not an easy or happy way to make a living." It's been said that the umpire's life is that of a loner. He is a friend to few, and more often he is thought of as an enemy by all around him – including the irate fans in the stands who openly threaten his life. "Kill the ump!" If you stop to consider that umpires didn't enjoy homestands as players do, and that back in the 1950s, before the union existed, the pay grade was hardly the draw that it is in 2011 when umpire salaries climbed well into the low-to-mid six figures. There was a time when most umpires needed a second job to help make ends meet. From Augie's perspective, the pressure, long road trips, occasional mayhem, and confrontations were simply part of the job that put him at the heart of a game he loved. He never disguised the fact that he lived through some difficult moments as an umpire, especially when the league decided to demote him from crew chief status. They informed him that they did so because of inadequacies in the field, but he believed that the reasons had more to do with his pursuit of forming an umpire's association. This is not to say that Augie was a victim of the umpiring life. His moxie was the driving force behind the formation of the Umpire's Association. While he often fought ballplayers and managers, he was a unifying force for umpires. Under his leadership, they coalesced and fought tooth and nail for a pension plan, and they gained basic benefits that were absent in the 1950s. They fought and negotiated for hospitalization improvements, death benefits, and benefits for widows. They also managed to increase the starting salary and compensation for working postseason and All-Star games. These were perceived as massive advancements in the umpire's work condition. During his time as a negotiator, he sat across the table from league presidents and lawyers and gave them a rough go.

"Augie's the man who made all the good things possible in umpiring today," said former National League umpire Harry Wendelstedt. "And he did it at a great personal price. They stripped him of his crew chief status." Yet the good, the bad, and the ugly of union negotiations was only one part of the Donatelli story. The union also helped draw the umpires closer together. As umpire Larry Goetz related in his autobiography, written by Jerome Holtzman, "The fans probably don't realize this, in the old days the umpires never saw each other after spring training, and even in spring training we didn't always meet. We could go a full season and the only umpires we ever talked to were our partners. The Umpire's Association changed all of that. It became a fellowship."

"Augie loved to get up early in the morning," umpire Ed Vargo recalled. "He told me to meet in the lobby of the hotel at 6:30. I meet him. He's got two knives and two brown bags. And I said, 'Augie, what are you going to do? He says: 'never mind, let's go.' And we go across the street into the park and start digging up dandelions. He loved dandelion salad. A squad car comes along and they want to arrest us. Augie told them we were umpires. I can still see that one cop walking away and scratching his head."

When Donatelli spoke, umpires usually listened. But the high regard with which he was held had as much to do with his work as it did the force of his personality. Those who understood the mechanics of umpiring believed that he was among the best ever. Even those who disagreed with his judgments couldn't deny that he always hustled. In his prime, he was much more mobile than the average umpire and had an uncanny knack for being at the right place, with the correct line of sight, at the right time. He was also thought of as a first rate arbiter of balls and strikes. As a National League umpire for 24 seasons, he called the game in atypical fashion, getting down low on one knee and signaling with a unique flair. At one point during his career, he discovered that by stabilizing himself so low and on one knee, he could get a truer view of certain regions of the strike zone. It was said that his style was reminiscent of the way coal miners swung their picks in the crunched up confines of their work space. On major league diamonds, he punched out calls as if his life depended on it. Yet his dramatic style wasn't as much a conjured up byproduct of a theatrical imagination as it was a reflection of his personality. There was no ambiguity to any of his decisions – on or off the field. Throw the name Augie Donatelli out to veteran major league umpires and the adjective "legend" oftentimes entered the conversation. To the umpiring fraternity of his era and to most of the men in blue today, he is thought of as a renowned figure from the past. Initially, I had a slightly different perspective. Donatelli first made an impression on me during the 1973 Fall Classic. I was a 13-year-old Mets fan and watched in great angst as he called Bud Harrelson out at the plate in the 10th inning of a 6 – 6 deadlock during Game Two of the World Series between the New York Mets and Oakland A's. I remember jumping up and down in disbelief and stamping my foot down loudly on the carpeted floor of my parent's home; kicking over a plastic covered foot rest and throwing myself headlong onto the sofa. After watching the replay, I fired a pillow across the room that accidentally grazed my uncle's head.

"No way," we all yelped.

The '73 Mets of Tom Seaver, Jon Matlack, Jerry Koosman, and Tug McGraw were my heroes. "Ya Gotta Believe!" – only this time I couldn't!

Watching the replay over and over again, I was convinced that the call was dead wrong. Flash forward nearly a decade.

Through a quirk of fate, I'm standing in the same room as Pat Donatelli, Augie's son. Pat and I had both landed entry level summer jobs as "viewers" at Major League Baseball Productions. The job entailed going through footage of recently played games and logging shot descriptions of events as they transpired on the screen. Young Donatelli was also a talented artist, a carefree sort, who had the remarkable ability to contort his face into the intimidating features of actor Clint Eastwood portraying Dirty Harry. Not surprisingly, broadcaster Warner Fusselle nicknamed him Dirt.

Standing near a soda vending machine, Pat Donatelli flipped a coin behind his back. It popped up into the air and rattled directly into the coin slot; an achievement for the ages. My luck wasn't nearly as good. Later that day, young Donatelli pulled out a video copy of the 1973 World Series film and decided to analyze the famous play involving his father on my behalf. He hit the pause button the moment Ray Fosse slapped the whisk of a tag on Harrelson's hip. Augie, lying flat on the ground, gave the out call. It was still impossible to judge, even in slow motion, but everyone who saw it pronounced a definitive opinion. To every Mets fan, he missed him. To A's fans, Fosse brushed a fiber of Harrelson's uniform.

I was interested in meeting the umpiring legend; attracted to him like a moth to a flame. Not long after, I found myself sitting in Augie's Florida condo, at the invitation of Pat. Augie had just returned from a golf outing and was sitting in his living room preparing to go out for dinner. After barely being introduced, Pat excused himself and went into the next room to make a phone call. "Dirt" left me sitting alone with his father, who no doubt had his suspicions about me. I knew some baseball related facts about him, but he knew very little about me. Of course, I knew he was the very same man who sent Willie Mays up in arms, and enraged Yogi Berra and the entire Mets team – all with one demonstrative call. But I also knew that he was the same guy who went toe to toe with fierce competitors such as Leo Durocher and Jackie Robinson.

Umpires are hard to rank. There are few statistics to substantiate an opinion of their excellence – nothing such as a "correct call average." Generally, fans only notice umpires when they are perceived to have made a mistake. Augie ended his career with a controversial call on a very big stage. Many casual baseball fans probably never heard of him, and there are only nine umpires who have been inducted into the Hall of Fame: Bill Klem, Jocko Conlan, Al Barlick, Tom Connolly, Billy Evans, Cal Hubbard, Nestor Chylak, Bill McGowan, and Doug Harvey. No doubt, umpires such as Conlan, McGowan, and Barlick considered Donatelli in their rank. Stars of the fifties and sixties looked at him with great respect: men like Bob Gibson and Dick Allen. It was implied by more than one player that when Donatelli umpired, he had the game by the throat. Ten years after his death, and many years after he made his last call, Augie Donatelli was placed on the top ten list of modern-day umpires compiled by a survey of members of the Society for American Baseball Research. At his peak, he was a tremendous umpire.

According to veteran umpire Jerry Crawford, "Augie had a tremendous ability to get from one place to another. He always knew where the ball was, and what direction it was coming from. He was able to move to the right spot. In the umpire's eyes, Augie Donatelli ranks very high."

Augie Donatelli is on top of the call at home plate in 1954 as Gene Baker of the Cubs is tagged out in the ninth inning at the Polo Grounds in New York. Copyright Bettmann/CORBIS

As I sat with Donatelli, I stared quietly at his face. He reached down to put on a pair of black shoes that he had carried into the room. He engaged me with some small talk about golf and the weather. Then out of nowhere came a can of shoe polish and a brush. He intended to shine his shoes. I immediately thought of Nippy Jones and the famous moment from the 1957 World Series between the Milwaukee Braves and New York Yankees. A pitched ball skipped past Nippy's ankles and bounced to the backstop. After retrieving the ball, Augie, like a crime scene investigator, inspected the evidence, found remnants of shoe polish and awarded Jones first base. It became a significant play in World Series lore because not long after making the decision on the hit batsmen, Eddie Mathews smashed a game-winning home run. The call proved to be a pivotal point in a Braves Game 4 World Series victory over the Yankees.

I pondered whether I should bring that up. The details were a bit blurry in my mind. The play had occurred before I was born. I certainly didn't want to talk about the call at the plate during the 1973 World Series. I began to feel the silence weighing heavily on my shoulders. My thoughts raced back to my recollections from the Yankees - Braves World Series. I remembered reading that he had changed his mind on that call after discovering shoe polish on the baseball, but was it something he cared to talk about? Pat's voice could be heard from the adjacent room as he continued chatting on the telephone. A few more seconds of awkward silence passed as I coyly studied Augie's face. I was surprised that it lacked the fierce quality that I had anticipated. I wondered if he could squint with the aplomb of his son. Was he thinking to himself in Clint Eastwood fashion, "Make my day." I pictured myself being unceremoniously thrown out of the apartment. Surprisingly, his voice had a humble and calm tone to it. As I came to understand by this point in his life, the heavy lifting was done. Augie's eyes studied this 20-something kid from New Jersey who sat in his living room. But just as I was about to utter the name Nippy Jones, Augie inquired about my background. He wanted to know about me. I told him that both of my parents, Carlo and Dorina, had been born in northern Italy. They grew up in a small country-side farming village east of Trieste. Suddenly he revealed that he didn't really care to talk about baseball. He began talking about his favorite Italian dishes. He told me he'd make his specialty dish for me if I hung around town. I decided to take him up on his offer. There were quite a few things I was curious to ask him about, including that play at the plate during the '73 World Series. To say that this book was born over a plate of lasagna wouldn't be far from the truth.

The first thing I realized was that Donatelli had a down-to-earth attitude towards his baseball accomplishments and experiences. It was a surprising facet to his personality that I did not expect. He never forgot his humble beginnings, and he wasn't much affected by accolades. I asked him his thoughts about being pictured on the cover of the first issue of *Sports Illustrated* with Eddie Mathews of the Milwaukee Braves and Giants catcher Wes Westrum in 1954. His only comment was "magazines come and go." When I attended a game with him at Shea Stadium in New York, he walked amongst the fans and enjoyed observing the attitudes of young kids as they marveled at their baseball experience. Even though they had no clue who he was, they seemed to run up to him for no apparent reason. He was happy to exchange a kind word. A young boy approached him with a baseball, asking "You think I'll get someone to sign this?" Donatelli ran his hand across the kid's head and said, "You betcha!" When I accompanied him to his home town of Bakerton to participate in the celebration of its 100th Anniversary, he hobnobbed with the town folk as if he had never left. When we sat in the El Cap, a St. Petersburg eatery owned by his stepbrother Steve Bonfili, he proudly pointed out a work of art that hung on its wall. It was a color montage of Augie. He wanted me to see it because his son had created it, not because he was the focal point.

During the course of my many conversations with him, Augie often uttered the phrase "holy hell." It was the closest thing to an off color remark I ever heard him utter. He used the expression for emphasis in describing a thorny or precarious scenario. One could tell how strongly he felt about something simply by being tuned-in to his intonations of the phrase. The holy hell of war was one thing. The rigors that a coal miner endured were a different kind of holy hell. If he emphasized the words in a certain way, you understood how much of a burden or challenge he felt something was. He often prefaced a tale by using the expression. I learned to use it as a gauge. If he drew out the letter "O" and extended the letter "L" in the words "hoooo-leee", you knew it was going to be a weighty anecdote.

He told about his experience during the first daylight bombing of Berlin, and described the bird's-eye-view of a B-17 bursting into balls of black smoke and fire, consuming men's lives in the blink of an eye. Donatelli witnessed those things from point blank range. He described his own near brushes with death. He talked about his escape, and also about wandering unarmed through German occupied territory by foot.

He told of his POW death march, and being forced to bury corpses at gun point. All of a sudden the baseball aspect of Donatelli's life drifted to the background. I knew the umpiring stories would have to take a back seat as he delved into his life before the world of umpiring. Was Harrelson safe or out? That question would have to wait. By this point I was certain of only two things. His lasagna was way above average. And his stories had me hooked. *Holy hell*, I thought.

TWO

Coal Miner's Son

You load sixteen tons, what do you get.
Another day older and deeper in debt.
St. Peter don't you call me 'cause I can't go.
I owe my soul to the company store...

Song writer – Merle Travis

"Sixteen Tons" was written by Merle Travis in 1946 and later made popular on a national level by Tennessee Ernie Ford, who made the song a number one hit in 1955. Whenever anyone asked Augie Donatelli what a coal miner's life was like, he'd reply, "Just like the song."

Donatelli was born in Heilwood, Pennsylvania in 1914 and raised in nearby Bakerton, a coalmining town whose very name was derived from two English mining bosses: Col. Robert B. Baker and his colleague John Holton. Coal was the life-blood of Bakerton, yet life in its lush green hills was just as sufferable as the life of desperation described in the Merle Travis song.

A casual observer who knew nothing about coal mines could wander through the modern-day roadways and heavily forested mountainous territory and not notice that mining was what sustained most families. During good times and bad, the front doors to most homes remained unlocked, and the people were friendly and cordial. Yet there were pressures that prevailed in an environment where there were precious few ways of making a living; as the saying went, you either worked in the mine, sold moonshine, or took it down the line. When the coal mining industry suffered, those who chose to tough it out in Bakerton suffered two-fold. Demand for coal weakened, labor discord worsened, and people scrapped to get by. During the early 1920s, Augie was only a youngster attending grade school, but the hardships were impossible to ignore.

The Arble Grammar School was a small two-story building. Grades one through four were situated on the ground floor, and grades five through eight on the second. Not much for education, he fondly recounted the day that formal schooling came to an abrupt end in Bakerton. Sparks from a passing train caused a fire. To the delight of most of the students, the old school burned completely to the ground. A temporary schoolhouse was eventually built, but as a result of the fire the students enjoyed a half-year of vacation time. However, this did not disturb Augie in the least. He was a self-described "terrible" student. His restless personality contributed to that. The many A's that mounted next to his name in the teacher's grade book stood for absences and not academic achievement. He was often compelled to escape the classroom any way that he could. When the teacher turned her head, he stood up and quietly tip-toed directly out of the building. He did this time and time again, becoming so proficient at his escape techniques that the teacher rarely noticed until he was miles away. For Donatelli, school was a den of boredom, but occasionally a spectacular stage for antics. He recalled how many of the songs the class sang during music period were patriotic in nature. During the rendition of Yankee Doodle, the teacher always blew a tiny mouth organ to let the class know what key they were to sing in. When the organ blew, and the class began to sing, one student's voice was particularly horrific. As Augie described it, it was a sour sound that twanged like a "croaking frog." Whenever the boy sang, young Donatelli laughed uncontrollably, and the entire class unfailingly followed.

"Gus, please control yourself!" ordered the teacher.

Eraser fights often ended in fisticuffs, and once a student ducked out of the way of an eraser propelled at his face. In doing so, banged his head on the corner of his desk, and a fight ensued in front of the classroom. One of them grabbed an ink bottle off a desk and flung it at his tormentor. With the comedic timing akin to a scene from a Little Rascals episode, the ink splattered against the wall precisely as the teacher walked into the classroom. Somehow, amidst the tumult and skipped classes, Donatelli managed to pass the quizzes and advanced grade after grade. When it came time for high school, however, his parents seriously came to the conclusion that it might be best for him to drop out of academics to begin his career as a coal miner.

"We were the children of coal miners and laborers. The opportunity for college was only there for the best students," Augie said mater-of-factly nearly a half-century later. It was Augie's siblings who convinced their parents that he should attend high school. It was an important decision. He matured greatly, improved his class work, and sharpened his skills in both baseball and basketball. He was destined, however, to eventually work in the mines, and after graduating from high school in 1932 that's exactly what he did. Bakerton was only a mere two-hour drive from Penn State University, but Donatelli thought of it as light years away.

His attention turned to coal. He entered the world of coal mining at age 18, during the midst of the great depression. His first job in the mines involved coupling and dumping coal out of heavy steel cars as they emerged from the mines. He and his fellow laborers were also responsible for preparing the cars for a return trip. Once 30 or so cars were connected, a motorcar powered the heavy load of metal and wood down into the mine. Each day began at 6 AM with a one-mile walk, often side-by-side with his four brothers and his stepfather. Augie arrived at the mine at seven o'clock each morning after his mile long walk from home. Long lines of similarly dressed miners arrived like clockwork, and each man, chiseled with a stoic demeanor, briskly stepped into rail cars called a "man trip" to be carted deep inside the mountainside. The temperature darted downward quickly the deeper they traveled. The iron wheels of the rail car made a loud clatter that was amplified by the walls of the long narrow tunnel. If the temperature was 75 degrees outside of the mine, it was closer to 50 in its deepest section. This non-mechanized era of coal mining, made the job brutally physical, and was carried out in dark and malignant surroundings.

The heading or the main corridor was six to eight feet high so a miner could simply get off the rail car and walk a hundred yards or so to get access to the particular "room" he worked in. The area was usually approximately 20 feet wide and the roof was four feet high. But the sizes of the rooms varied. Occasionally miners were forced to work in rooms that were significantly smaller. Donatelli sometimes worked in a space that was only 28 inches in height. He dug with pick and shovel while lying on his side most of the day. The sounds of metal pounding into the rocky coal echoed loudly in the area and throughout the mine. Oil burning carbide lamps were the only thing that generated light. Two men were assigned per each room and often spent most of the day in the close confines and on their knees. It was difficult to make out the features of a coworker's shadow covered face. Socialization was about as far-removed from a coal miner's reality as a line from a Robert Browning poem might be. There was very little talking that took place. The motivation was simple. Shovel as much coal as possible, and get out of the mine alive.

The 1930s were an era of pre-automation, but there was mechanized equipment that didn't exist only a decade before. "We used a machine to cut the room, but we would do the rest by hand," recalled Donatelli. "First you loaded the bug dust, or the coal that was pulverized by the machine. We shoveled the black "bug" dust into the cars, then used dynamite to make the room bigger after the dust was loaded. You couldn't start using the dynamite until all the bug dust was shoveled out, because it would have been blown out all over the mine."

The dust was composed of tiny particles of stone and was a major contributor to black lung disease. Breathing particles was inevitable but oftentimes the men avoided using explosives until the end of the day, so that the dust could settle over night. They fashioned their own explosives with black powder, drilling holes deep within the rock with a long hand drill. There was a special fuse called a "squib" that was used to light the powder. It burned for a few seconds, giving the miners enough time to seek cover, but there were instances when the squib went out before igniting the powder, a common scenario that often created nerve-wracking situations. Someone would invariably have to make the attempt to relight it. There were often stories of deadly accidents that occurred when this happened. A miner would approach, and as luck would have it, the explosive went off, maiming or killing him.

Safeguards were few. To protect themselves from deadly gas, the miners' only reliable precaution were live canaries. If a bird died, it was a signal that too much gas had accumulated. The miners also used wood props to keep the room from collapsing on them. Augie and his partner shared the task and responsibility of properly installing the props, but many life-threatening hazards still remained.

"You always felt like you were in danger and sometimes the roof would growl as if there was a tornado above you."

There were occasions when a lamp went out because it ran out of fuel, and all that remained was utter blackness. It was an eerie experience to be trapped a few hundred feet under the ground without any light and without a clear sense of orientation. The only method of pointing one's self in the right direction was by grabbing a car rail and following it to safety. Augie recalled a trick the men used to avoid these blackouts, "A miner used his own urine to replace the evaporated water necessary to keep the lamp burning."

Donatelli and his partner, usually one of his brothers, loaded approximately 30 tons of coal per day, which amounted to 12 cars. The cars were six feet wide and mounted on iron wheels. They held two tons but they were usually intentionally overloaded to two ton six. It was common knowledge that when the coal reached the top lip of the car it amounted to two tons, but Augie and his partner always liked to pile at least 600 additional pounds on top of that.

He later said, "The more coal you shoveled, the more money you made. The more you could get in a single car, the better off you were."

Smaller hand carts slid into the room, and were filled by bouncing the coal off the low ceiling and into the cart. Then that coal was dumped into the large steel car.

The miners always hoped to have empty cars on hand, so that once a car was filled and carted off, an empty car was there to take its place. There was little time or energy to talk, and the only time they stopped work was when they were hungry. The men alternated between standing up with their back pressed against the roof of the room and working on their knees. To keep things interesting, Augie liked to turn things into a competition between himself and his partner to shovel as much as they could. It was a day-long foray into madness. A constant rumble of pick and shovel. At times the task became so boring as to render the mind numb. The first meal of the day came after the duo loaded four empty cars. Then while they waited for more empty cars to roll into position, the coal miners took a little break to eat. It was more like wolfing down whatever happened to be inside one's lunch pail or "growler" as it was sometimes called. Once those empty cars got into place, they'd put the food down and got back to work. There was no official lunch break in those early days.

"While eating, you could feel the air pushing towards you once those empty cars were on their way down…you could physically feel it. Once the cars came in you put your lid on the bucket right away because there were rats. Big ugly rats," recalled Augie. " Sometimes you'd have to kill them with your shovel. It wasn't unusual to see a rat crushed by a passing coal car."

While working Augie rarely spoke to his partner, because he wanted to conserve his energy, and the noise of the pick and shovel generated more than enough noise to make small talk difficult. There was also the issue of dust and dirt circulating in the air. However he recalled one subterranean conversation that occurred while he was still a rookie coal miner.

"Hey, Gus," Augie's brother Hugo called out. After you finish eating, don't forget to cover your lunch pail."

"Why?" Augie asked while chomping down on a chicken leg. When I'm done with this there won't be anything left."

"That's what you think," Hugo shot back, "when you're done, those rats there will want to inspect the bone."

Augie turned his head toward where his brother was pointing and saw a pair of five pound rats scampering around.

"Holy hell!" Augie yelped. "If you think they're big you should have seen that rat I saw a few months ago," Hugo boasted. "Must have been two feet long. And you should have seen what he looked like after they ran across the track and got splattered by a car filled with two tons."

It wasn't uncommon for a miner to kill a rat if he wandered too close, but often the men tolerated the rats for one simple reason. They gave advanced warning when a cave-in was imminent. Rats had a keen sense for vibrations, so if they began to scamper for the surface, it was a not so subtle signal for the men to follow.

Other than lunch, which was timed to happen while the filled up coal cars were being motored to the surface, the only other time that a man stopped working was to go to the bathroom. The miner usually ambled to an old part of the mine to relieve himself.

By the end of the day, the Donatellis retraced the mile walk back the house, oftentimes trudging step by step, feeling as if they were tethered to ball and chain, after hour upon hour of exhaustive physical labor. Inevitably, their faces were covered with soot and sweat. Before dinner they went into the basement and scrubbed the blackness off their bodies, drying themselves off with old burlap cement bags. It was an inviting moment, a chance to cleanse the body of the black filth of coal dust, and gave the Donatelli men a chance to shift their collective moods to a less somber tone. The burlap was much more durable than regular cloth towels, but once they were boiled for a long period of time they became nearly as pliant as towels.

Then came the jokes, and the thoughts of food, wine, and baseball. Amidst their daily drudgery of life in the coal mines, the national pastime continued to be a major topic at the dinner table. Augie and his brothers relegated much time arguing over game situations. Admittedly, Augie was quick to correct his older brother's mistakes; a habit that often created quite a fuss around the kitchen table.

As Augie pondered many years later, "I was pretty darn good at making people angry at me."

Brother Hugo later recalled, "Gus was always a leader, but he was lousy to play baseball with if you made a mistake."

It was clear that the kid they called Gus loved baseball and had aspirations of becoming a professional player. Black coal gave him his livelihood, but baseball fueled his soul. The entire family, with varied degrees of interest, listened to the games on the radio. Tuning into the Pirate broadcasts, Rosey Rowswell was the pied-piper of Pittsburgh baseball. His play-by-play and commentary was often repeated and mimicked by the Donatellis, catch phrases such as, "Get upstairs, Aunt Minnie, and raise the window! Here she comes!" Then came a sound effect of a big crash like the sound of a window breaking. "That's too bad," Rosey sobbed. "She tripped over a garden hose! Aunt Minnie never made it."

Roswell also carried a slide whistle, and when a member of the home team connected on a pitch, the announcer would blow on the whistle and add, "Hurry up, Aunt Minnie, raise the window!" At that point his fellow broadcaster would drop a tray filled with an assortment of noise makers to the ground to simulate the smashing of Aunt Minnie's window. The diminutive Rowswell, whose previous occupation was as a secretary at Pittsburgh's Third Presbyterian Church, delivered the games with a gaudy yet completely infusive and cheerful style. He was the ultimate homer. At first, he followed the team as a fan, attended many games and even traveled with the team. He was so appreciated as a fan that the 1925 World Champion Pirates gave him a gold baseball charm as a reward for his support. The Pirates were Rosey's "Picaroonies" and he worshiped the home team as if they were his extended family.

There was genuine affection for a generally hapless franchise. The team's appearance in the 1927 World Series became an endearing trademark. It attracted a special following and Augie proudly admitted that his mother, Vincenzina, often sat near the radio and paid very close attention to Rosey's colorful style. She enjoyed his poetic sounding descriptions of things like the uniforms, which at the time were blue and red.

"It was amazing to me how an Italian born citizen who never even heard of baseball until after coming to the United States became such a big fan," said Augie. "She always wanted to meet Rosey Rowswell."

Little did Vincenzina know that she would eventually meet Rosey at Forbes Field on a day when the Pirates honored her son, Major League Umpire Augie Donatelli. Back in the 1930s such a notion would have seemed like a feckless daydream, a moment of ridiculous mental relief during a strenuous day in the coal mines. Equally fantastic would have been the idea that Rosey's eventual broadcasting sidekick, Hall of Famer Bob Prince, would years later become a regular friendly visitor to the Donatelli household.

The entire Donatelli family worked in the mines all day, and found diversions like baseball to keep their minds off their dangerous subterranean work. It was a life devoid of most luxuries, but they did make it a point to enjoy whatever entertainment came their way. Augie's siblings also attended as many concerts as they could. The big bands made their way to nearby Sunset Park to play; well known performers such as Glenn Miller, Benny Goodman, Harry James, and Cab Calloway. When Guy Lombardo played there, Augie's brother

Joe managed to get Guy to taste the family wine. The report was that Lombardo enjoyed it so much that he nearly missed his cue to go on stage.

Such moments were few and far between, and the struggles of a coal mining life nudged Augie's father into a battle with alcohol, which eventually led to the end of his marriage with Vincenzina.

"When I look back, I realize how strong my mother was, both emotionally and spiritually. My father wasn't mean to any of us, but he was an alcoholic. Later in life, there were many times that I tried to understand the hardships he went through. But he could not cope"

The saving grace for the Donatellis stemmed from the fact that his mother eventually remarried, and the entire family, four boys and one girl moved in with their new stepfather and his family. Mr. Bonfili had two boys of his own from a previous marriage. All totaled, it was a loud and lively household. In addition to his own family, Bonfili had regular boarders who lived in the home. One of those tenants was Augie's father. Vincenzina eventually forgave her ex-husband's excess drinking, and they remained on cordial terms. In essence, Augie enjoyed the presence of two male father figures, additional male boarders, as well as his brothers. To say this was a testosterone-driven household would be an understatement. Yet each evening the dinner table was much more than a poor-man's banquet. Family members, and oftentimes tenants, gathered for a meal prepared by Vincenzina. From the Donatelli side there was Joe, Guido, Hugo, Mary, and August – or Gus, as Augie was then called. From the Bonfili side there was: Aldo, Steve, and Bernetta.

Family conversations often drifted from local gossip to baseball. The Bakerton hometown team was the Pittsburgh Pirates. Bakerton was less than 100 miles away from Forbes Field, the Pirates' famed stomping grounds built in 1909. Augie recalled some of the most prominent Pirates memories from his youth, including the hitting accomplishments of the Waner brothers: "Big Poison" and "Little Poison." Paul was known as "Big Poison" because he owned a stockier frame than his brother. Paul played 15 seasons in Pittsburgh from 1926 to 1940, won three National League batting titles, and was a Hall of Famer. Brother Lloyd, also a Hall of Famer, hit .355 as a rookie in 1927 with a league leading 133 runs scored. The Waner brothers practiced their hitting in

Oklahoma corn fields by belting corncobs with sawed-off broomsticks. Augie and his brothers practiced their hitting wares with chucks of coal and stone.

On most nights the entire combined family gathered at the dinner table. It was the only time during the day, other than Sunday mass, when the entire family was together. Augie's favorite dish was polenta. A massive pile of golden-yellow cornmeal was placed at the center of the table, and drenched in rich tomato sauce. It seemed as though the large portion took up most of the table. Elbow room was a precious commodity, but there was always space for a bottle of wine. On one occasion, Vincenzina asked her son Hugo to go into the basement to siphon more wine into the empty half-gallon bottle that sat on the table.

"Mom, send Gus or Joe," complained Hugo.

After a stern look from his stepfather, Hugo reluctantly rose from his piping hot dish and loudly descended down the basement steps. He despised going into the basement alone. Hugo fumbled around in the darkness and decided not to light a candle. He squatted down in his catcher's stance and hastily filled the bottle with the wine and made a quick retreat up the stairs and back to his meal.

"Here it is," exclaimed an out-of-breath Hugo as he slammed the thick glass bottle onto the table.

No one thought more about it until the next morning when Mr. Bonfili went down into the basement to get dressed in his mining gear and discovered that one of the spigots was left partially open and the contents of the barrel had poured over the floor and transformed into a murky purple liquid. Hugo suffered a handful of rather severe slaps to the head and body as a result of his carelessness.

"He was punished, all right," recalled Augie, "but if anyone could take a punishment it was Hugo. He was a tough cookie. He was a boxer."

Augie proudly recounted how Hugo had entered the Golden Gloves competition at Motor Square Garden in Pittsburgh. The competition involved six three-round bouts over three nights. For Hugo, the fights came after a full day of work in the coal mines. After the workday concluded, the men piled into a car and drove to Pittsburgh. As Hugo put it, "I was pretty sore at the end of the week, but I could take it, and I never did mind taking a punch in the nose."

The brothers often sparred with each other and held their own impromptu boxing matches to hone their skills and Hugo proved to be a natural. Hundreds of fans gathered into the building for the championship brawl.

Augie recalled the battle with a gleam in his eyes, "Bang, bang, bang! Punches landed from every angle; the roar of the crowd; what a fight! Both my brother and his opponent, who happened to be from Pittsburgh and was the crowd favorite, went toe to toe. They didn't coast for one second."

The fight was settled in a tiebreaker round, where Hugo delivered a combination that sent his exhausted foe to the canvas. The scene played out like a prequel to a *Rocky* movie; the Donatellis overflowed with excitement. This hard-nosed family, filled with pride, had made its mark in Pittsburgh and Hugo was the reason. During an era when pride and hope were regularly drained from people's lives like clockwork, this was a psychological kick-start. Not only for the Donatellis, but also for the entire town of Bakerton. In a half-crazed state the family sped back home to spread the word that it's town borders held a champion in its midst. Yet this was not a generation that long dwelled on accomplishments or hyperbole.

To say that the Donatelli boys were tough was an understatement, Augie's brother Joe developed a reputation for his bar room brawls. According to Joe, he never started a single fight, but was proficient at ending them.

One of the brothers' favorite summertime spots was a reservoir hole owned by one of the mining companies. The boys loved to practice diving off a 25-foot high ledge. One day the Donatellis and a group of other Bakerton boys were coming up with dives that were much wilder than normal and the fun evolved into a competition. Augie's brother Guido was preparing to dive when someone shouted a false warning.

"Hey, Guido. Duck!"

Guido sensed that one of the boys was about to deliver a roundhouse punch to the side of his head. The boy feigned the punch and Guido ducked. In doing so, he lost his balance off the ledge and plunged into the water at an awkward angle. He landed at a perpendicular angle and generated a loud splat. When he hit, the potential for serious injury seemed very real. Guido drifted motionless for what seemed to be an eternity as the boys held their collective breath. Suddenly he came to life, swam to shore, climbed up the bank and delivered a series of lively punches that sent the sorry young pranksters running home.

It wasn't long before Augie found himself in the center of a fight of his own. This one would be a precursor to the baseball unionizing battles for which he will be forever known. Set amidst the sometimes violent and cruel history of the coal miners union came a scenario which tested Augie's mettle. In some ways this was perhaps a sterner challenge than the one Warren Giles and the lords of baseball plopped in front of him decades later, but in this instance the young coal miner had much less to lose. The fight would come from a historic backdrop that was filled with extreme anti-union sentiment.

The following description originated from a government committee report that was presented as a first-hand account of the life of a coal miner. "The influences of all the years of meager living and struggle for mere existence among these barren hills, had left an imprint on these miners and their families, that amounted almost to despair. Their women folks become old and hollow-eyed before their time. The children were found undersized and with supplicating eyes begging for help."

According to records of Bethlehem Mines Corporation, there were four patrolmen and a captain for the area of Heilwood, Mentcle, and Brownstown, whose job was to help keep unions from spreading. One unnamed resident quoted in the book *Pennsylvania Mining Families: The Search for Dignity in the Coalfields* remembered the following:

The coal company had an iron hand and ran the company towns like a prison camp. There was a searchlight mounted on a tower at the end of the village. It was turned on after 9 PM curfew. A whistle blew and the Coal and Iron Police would patrol the town on horses. There was no freedom of assembly. The Coal and Iron Police would stop people getting on and off the train and interrogate them: "Do you have permission? Where are you going? Who are you seeing?" They would pull men out of the houses and hit them with clubs.

During these bellicose times, the work schedule for coal miners became sporadic. On weeks when demand picked up, miners worked five or six days a week, but when it slowed down they were sent home without pay. The Miner's Union also experienced massive amounts of turmoil and change. During the Great Coal Strike of 1927, coal companies battled for cost reductions, and pressured unionized miners to accept cutbacks. Powerful companies even gained support from politicians at the state and local level, and when they demanded a 25 percent reduction of wages, a long and drawn out labor war resulted. Scabs were asked to operate the mines for non-union wages, and private police were hired to keep the financial pressures strong. They became so effective at disrupting the lives of coal miners that they were reviled. And by doing their cold-blooded work so well, they perpetuated good paying jobs for themselves. As the battle raged, the strike of 1927 evolved into a campaign to break the solidarity of miners. The Coal Company evicted some of the most outspoken strikers from their mine-owned homes. When this happened, makeshift barracks were erected on the east end of town. Augie recalled stories of how some families lived in plywood structures for as long as a year. They endured the harsh Pennsylvania winter and certainly faced unyielding hardships. Donatelli was not too young to notice. Breaking the miner's spirit was a brutal and heartless business. Evidence of the rigors families faced was visible in the tattered clothing they wore. The self-sacrifices were so very evident. It wasn't uncommon to see youngsters walk alongside the railroad tracks with the hopes of finding pieces of coal that had fallen from railroad cars during transport. They eagerly retrieved the precious black rocks and guardedly hid them under their jackets for the walk home. Once safely inside, the coal could be stoked for its life-giving heat.

The harsh working environment of the coal mines helped Donatelli develop some strong pro-union ideas. Especially since some of the men whom he respected most, including members of his family all shared similar views. Coal mining men were paid based on the amount of coal they dug each day, yet it was oftentimes common for the weight to be computed inaccurately at the weigh stations or "cheatin' houses" as they were commonly called by the miners. The mining bosses had long since forged a reputation for trying to cheat workers out of every penny they could. Each miner was supposed to be paid an extra amount of money when he exceeded expectations. The company had workers called weigh men, whose responsibility it was to weigh the total amount coal each group of miners shoveled each day. As a way to deter the "cheatin' house," the union assigned a man called a check weigh-man to make sure that everything was done fairly. Ironically, none of this had any effect on Augie Donatelli's salary at that point. Working outside the mine, he was paid $2.50 per 10-hour day, but Donatelli felt a strong urge to help the men who toiled inside, especially since those men included his stepfather and brothers. Management also stubbornly held onto a common practice of keeping the miners in the mines until every single coal car was weighed and accounted for. The logic of keeping the men in the mines longer than necessary made no sense. After all, they had toiled all day long, and were anxious to escape its depths as soon as possible. According to Donatelli, the men were told that the mine had no interest in changing this long-standing policy. This was the lighting rod that forced the men to fight for fair treatment. It was here that Donatelli and his fellow miners drew the line in the sand.

As a form of protest, the union leaders told Augie and the other men who worked outside the mine not to dump the coal out of the final group of cars until management allowed the miners out of the mines. They wanted to force management's hand. As Donatelli told the story, "At the end of the day, all hell broke loose when we refused to unload the coal. One of the foreman said flat out, 'if you don't dump that coal, then you're ALL out of jobs.' "

Augie said that the warning was effective because two of the men who worked alongside him decided to resume work. They were older than Donatelli and both had families to support. For them no job meant great hardships. A threat to take away their job was nearly as appalling as threatening their lives. He recalled cases of entire families being forced to live in cold makeshift homes for months. Donatelli had no family to support, and had no intention of jumping at the command. The blunt order made Augie even angrier. The foreman refused to back down and ordered Augie to resume unloading the coal. Donatelli felt the eyes of the other men peering at him to see how he would react.

Augie responded directly, "Sorry sir," he said respectfully, "I'm not budging until you order the men out of the mines."

The foreman barely hesitated before he informed Augie that he was out of work. Donatelli's stomach sank to the ground. He had nothing else to say. He decided to turn and walk away – never once regretting his decision.

Said Augie, "Some of the union fellows looked at fighting the mine bosses like warfare." This was Donatelli's first battle and his first tough setback.

Management played an exceptional game of hardball, fighting tooth and nail on every single issue. Donatelli was out of a job, but not for long. The company coveted Augie's ability as a coal miner, but just as importantly, they liked his talents on the baseball diamond. Augie, the plucky shortstop, was one of the best ballplayers on his company team. He was a member of the Barnes number 15 mine in the Cambria County Industrial League, and had forged a reputation as a slick fielder. Although he wasn't a long ball hitter, Donatelli was a good contact hitter, and often batted over .300. The significance of this was not to be understated, because the games were so popular that hundreds of people attended. The crowds that these semi-pro games often attracted were especially impressive when you consider that the entire population of Bakerton was no more than a few thousand. Local baseball had become a form of entertainment. Other than an occasional trip to the movie theater or town dance, baseball was one of the few forms of local entertainment that existed. There was baseball on the radio, but live baseball at the local field generated much more excitement. It cost very little to attend the local games and fans were guaranteed to run into friends, which turned the contests into social happenings. The games were taken so seriously that some of the teams in the league searched for college players to occupy their rosters. Donatelli jealously recalled how the mine bosses didn't require them to work their summer jobs at the mines on game days. To keep an important player fresh, a foreman might tell him to spend the day at home to rest for the big game. It was also common knowledge that a miner who belonged to the company baseball team was less likely to be dismissed or laid off.

Donatelli enjoyed the competitive nature of the games and the colorful camaraderie that existed among the players. There was no shortage of nicknames among his teammates: Goose, Flip, Ike, Spud, Bruno, and Butter. Remarkably, two of the 14 members of that ball club were talented enough to play in the minor leagues. In 1938, Donatelli went on to play for the Beaver Falls Browns, the Paducah Indians, and the Pennington Gap Lee Bears.

The bad blood that existed when Augie was fired slowly dissipated. Eventually management relented on their policy of forcing the men to dwell in the mines until all the coal was weighed and dumped. Augie's popularity among his fellow miners had reached new heights, and upon being rehired he was asked to take a spot inside the mine. Donatelli quickly accepted the offer because it gave him the opportunity to earn more money.

Major league baseball continued to provide an important diversion; Augie had turned 13 just prior to the 1927 Series, and was mesmerized by the larger than life personality of Babe Ruth, and the hitting skills of the Waner brothers. The Pirates had captured the heart and soul of Bakerton after they won the 1925 World Series when they miraculously charged back from a three game to one deficit against the defending champion Washington Senators to win in seven games. One play from the '25 Series received great scrutiny, and became a subject of conjecture and conversation across the country. In Game 3, Senators outfielder Sam Rice ran after a line drive hit by catcher Earl Smith that sailed into right center. Rice, a star of his day who played for 20 seasons with a career .322 batting average and was voted into the Hall of Fame in 1963 appeared to have made a tremendous diving catch that sent him careening into the temporary stands at Washington's Griffith Stadium. The problem came when the outfielder remained out of sight for more than ten seconds. The Pirates contested the play with the contention that a fan recovered the ball out of view from the umpires, and most fans in the ballpark, and stuck it back into Rice's glove as he remained on the ground. Umpire Cy Rigler called it a fair catch, and as Augie mused, "all hell broke loose." Irate Pirates owner Barney Dreyfuss propelled himself onto the field and participated in a protracted argument with the umpires. The overflow crowd of more than 36,000 plus fans watched as the heated exchange continued. The call stood, however, and Washington won the game 4 to 3. When Rice was questioned about the play after the game by Commissioner Kenesaw Mountain Landis, he only said, "The umpire said I caught it." Of course, Pirates fans still had their doubts, but astonishingly, Pittsburgh stormed back to win the final three games of the Series, making Rice's mystery catch less significant in baseball lore. But the play still remained a mystery up until the day Rice died when a sealed letter he left at the Hall of Fame was finally opened in 1974. In the letter Rice blandly stated, "at no time did I lose possession of the ball." The excitement surrounding the game no doubt made a lasting impression on young Augie. Not from the perspective of the umpiring, but rather the excitement and interest that the game generated.

It's not a major revelation to say that baseball enjoyed a newfound burst of popularity because of Ruth's 60 home run season in 1927, a year in which he single-handedly hit more home runs than any other American League team. The phrase Ruthian became part of American culture in describing things that were bigger than life. The '27 Yankees were so dominant that history still regards them as one of baseball's best teams ever. They never fell out of first place a single day and won 110 games by season's end. Their exploits generated interest in Bakerton, especially when the Pirates and Yankees opposed each other in the '27 World Series. Legend had it that the Pirates were dumbfounded by the Yankees display of power during batting practice on the day prior to the Series opener. Ruth alone had out-homered the entire Pirates team, but the Pirates managed to outhit the Bronx Bombers in the opener - nine hits to six, but the Yankees still emerged victorious 5 to 4. Donatelli recalled following some of the games by listening to the voice of Graham McNamee on the NBC radio broadcasts, and carefully combing through the newspaper accounts. It was a disappointment, however, when they couldn't muster a fight against New York, losing four straight in the Fall Classic. It would be Pittsburgh's last Series appearance for 33 years. However, the Pirates subsequently fielded many competitive ball clubs, but each year seemed to end with a letdown. Particularly in 1938 when the Pirates finished a heartbreaking two games behind the Chicago Cubs for the National League pennant. The Pirates had what seemed to be a comfortable lead, but the Cubs overran them by winning 21 of their final 26 decisions.

As the years went by, the Donatellis were loyal listeners of Pirate voices Al Helfer and Rosey Rowswell. The colorful Rowswell reached remarkable popularity in the thirties and forties especially among the Donatellis.

Those who knew his baseball vernacular knew that a "doozy

marooney" referred to an extra base hit, "a dipsy-doodle" was a strikeout by a Pirates pitcher, and "oh my aching back" translated to a loss for the home team.

During an important head to head series between the Cubs and Pirates that began on the final week of the season, the Donatellis held their hopes high. At the time, the Pirates were in first place by a game and a half. They listened on the radio as the Cubs won the series opener on the strength of Dizzy Dean's pitching. Chicago had purchased the sore-armed Dean from the St. Louis Cardinals for a shockingly hefty price of $200,000 along with three players. Dizzy came through when they needed him, and the Cubs found themselves a half-game out of first. The next day, Cubs player-manager Gabby Hartnett belted a clutch ninth-inning home run to help Chicago win and gave them a half-game lead in the standings. Then the Cubs broke the Pirates' back the next day with a 10 to 1 demolition.

As a youth, Augie also admittedly admired the St. Louis Cardinals, nicknamed the Gas House Gang. He reveled in their feisty style. He also confided that the only thing about baseball that he had no interest in was the umpires. He never paid attention to them, except when they made an incorrect call.

"I was good at giving 'em hell."

Ironically, as a youngster, Donatelli thought of umpires as a necessary evil. They were men clad in ties and stuffy black suits; in his youthful eyes umpires were akin to mine bosses – voices of authority whose judgment was inevitably meant to be questioned.

"I was the type of youngster who was always full of vim and vigor and never even considered umpiring as a career opportunity; and to think of a career as a major league umpire? You might as well have told me that I'd become a United States Senator. That's how far umpiring was from my thoughts."

Not only did he become an umpire but he was to become one of the National League's most prominent arbiters. Yet back in the 1920s, he was a student whose sole future pointed towards the coal mines. In his heart, he had tightly-held aspirations of becoming a professional baseball player.

As the years went by, Augie's future drifted away from playing professional baseball to the life of a full-time miner. His playing talent wasn't Major League caliber, and things changed drastically after the bombing of Pearl Harbor in 1941. When he enlisted in the Air Corps at age 28, the thought of soaring through the air on a bomber seemed glamorous. It was the antithesis of working in the dark shaft of Barnes number 15. Little did he know that he would undergo the type of flying missions that made the coal mines seem like a safe haven.

THREE

Tail Gunner

Donatelli was scheduled for a night-bombing practice mission over the Mojave desert on a SBD (scout bomber diver), a rugged two-seater that was often used to bomb navel vessels. The mission was to locate a target within the heart of the desert and hit it with a practice bomb. Donatelli was the tail gunner. For this particular mission he was paired with a pilot who was just as inexperienced and nearly as cocky. Donatelli never thought to apologize for his brashness. The title "gunner" fit his personality. His flight partner was younger than Augie, a tall Scandinavian- looking blond-haired man with a slight California twang. Augie had never spoken to him prior to the mission, but that was nothing out of the ordinary. The only time a gunner associated with a pilot was during the actual test flight. They rarely, if ever, socialized. Prior to the assignment, it was usually a major or sergeant who paired the flight team off on the ground only minutes before the flight mission.

"Donatelli, you're flyin' with Bentson!"

The teams assembled for breakfast at 2 A.M. during a night run and fell in for assignments at 3 A.M. As usual, some of the men were half asleep while the flying orders were being handed out. Some of the younger guys actually fell asleep while standing, and collapsed to the ground in a heap. Donatelli didn't have that problem. The military experience was so stimulating for him that he had to regularly remind himself of the dangers. Escaping the toil and drudgery of the coal mines was as implausible as playing shortstop for his beloved Pittsburgh Pirates. The idea had a wildly liberating aspect to it. It was an instant metamorphosis from a subterranean world to a soaring one.

It's certainly no secret that the objective of war is to kill the enemy. For young soldiers the enemy is a faceless adversary. As one looks back at the travails through the filter of time, soldiers sense their experience from a very different perspective. War is as dissimilar from sport as possible because it encompasses life and death and also complete brutality, but the parallels to sport do exist. In a strange way we almost expect it. Close ballgames are described as battles; the football term blitz is taken from the German word blitzkrieg or lighting war; there's sudden death, the battle in the trenches, and the long touchdown pass in football, called the bomb. Combat pushes men to their extreme limits both physically and emotionally. In some ways it supplies the survivors with a deep satisfaction. According to famed fighter and test pilot Chuck Yeager, "I don't recommend going to war as a way of testing character, but by the time our tour ended, we felt damned good about ourselves and what we accomplished." Entire books have been devoted to the subject. In 1984, former Marine and editor of the *Texas Monthly* and *Newsweek,* William Broyles, Jr., explored some of the contradictions inherent in telling war stories. With the familiar, authoritative voice of "one-who-has-been-there," Broyles asserted that when combat soldiers were questioned about their war experiences they generally said that they did not want to talk about it, implying that they "hated it so much, it was so terrible" that they would prefer it to remain "buried." Not so, Broyles continued, "I believe that most men who have been to war would have to admit, if they are honest, that somewhere inside themselves they loved it too."

For most men who survive the harrowing experiences of war, the only redeeming qualities to the stories are the fact that they survived. When they think of the many friends and colleagues who died on the battlefield, their expressions turn forlorn and distant. They find the emotion difficult to express. Augie was clearly proud of his military service record, but as he shared these experiences Donatelli often paused. They were long thoughtful pauses. Firstly, to recall details and secondly to fight back the emotion that the storytelling brought back. Although he never verbalized the thought, it seemed as though an occasional smile from Augie revealed that he considered it a miracle that he himself had survived the war.

Lowry Field proved to be Donatelli's home for nearly two months. The Air Force base was situated not far from Denver, Colorado. It was used as a technical training ground for Air Force bomber crews. This was not only his first taste of flying, but also his first extended stay away from Bakerton. The men flew practice missions during various times of the day, from the crack of dawn to the middle of the night. The school operated three shifts; the night shift was over at 6 A.M., lights out at seven, and the actual practice missions usually ran for no more than two or three hours. The regimentation, odd hours, and drills were designed to prepare the men for the rigors of war.

Donatelli had butterflies in his stomach as he and Bentson prepared to take off from Lowry Field in Colorado several minutes after being given clearance. He described the feeling as being twice as intense as the nervousness he felt when stepped into the batter's box in a key situation. He was still very much a rookie flyer. Prior to joining the Air Force he had never stepped aboard an aircraft, now it was to become a daily part of his existence.

"SBD 112, you're okay for takeoff," was the command from the control tower.

The plane was a thick, low-wing two-seater with a large propeller up front. The SBD became legendary in the Pacific as a Navy ship-borne dive-bomber. It had a great ability to pull out of vertical dives after releasing bombs, and was known for its ability to absorb punishment. Its top speed, however, was only 252 miles-per-hour and it had a range of 1,000 miles. The single prop engine whirred loudly as the plane climbed quickly into the night sky. Augie described the sound as deafening. Seconds after takeoff the plane escaped the runway lights and was completely shrouded in darkness. The only thing providing illumination were the lights that ran across the cockpit dashboard. It reminded Augie of how the old carbide lamps shed light in the dark mines. Donatelli felt around for the triggers of his two .30 caliber heavy machine guns. They rested in front of him on a flexible mount. The pilot had two .50 caliber guns of his own. A swinging bomb cradle beneath the fuselage could accommodate a single 1,000 pound bomb. The wings could hold two additional 100 pound payloads. The SBD rose to about 12,000 feet.

Augie's responsibity was to scan the skies for enemy aircraft, and assist the pilot in locating the ground target for the simulated drop. The plane was headed towards Rice, California, on what would be considered a short range practice mission.

Approximately halfway to the target the bomber experienced a problem.

"Pull the waddle pump!" was the command from the pilot.

Donatelli pulled the lever in an effort to spark the motor, but to no avail. The engine had come to a complete stop.

"Keep pumping, damn it!" ordered the pilot.

The only way that pilot and co-pilot could communicate were by hand signals, or by screaming over the roar of the engine. Augie came to the strange realization that there was no need to scream because the engine was silent. A ball of fear erupted in his gut. It was the first time he had experienced such a shock. The only noise in the cockpit was the sound of air rushing past the canopy. The silence prevailed as the SDB dropped two hundred feet. Five very long seconds passed before Augie pulled on the pump again. This time, as if by miracle, the engine restarted. An extreme feeling of relief filled the cabin.

After radioing what had happened back to base, the command came back for the plane to be taken to Blythe Air Base to have its engine checked.

Augie recalled many years later, "After the plane landed safely I was so happy that I started telling everyone in sight what had happened. I found a pair of GIs who happened to be good listeners and gave 'em every detail. More than once."

Donatelli was shocked back into reality when he saw Bentson beckoning him back towards the hanger where several mechanics were working on the engine.

When Augie walked back to within earshot Bentson said, "Okay, here we go again, Donatelli."

Augie couldn't believe his ears. He had assumed that they would be assigned another plane, or be whisked back to Lowry on another flight. He had assumed wrong. A nervous sense of quiet uneasiness descended over the two men. Augie had no desire to reveal to Bentson that he was panic-stricken over the prospect of taking off in the same plane. It was only later that he had admitted that he was scared. The SBD took off smoothly, but only eleven minutes into the return flight the engine began to sputter. Again, Donatelli began working the pump, this time to no avail. The plane dropped like a brick and began screeching as it plummeted towards the desert floor.

"Let's get the hell out of here!" Augie shouted.

"Hold on," replied Bentson, "She'll start up again. Just hold on."

Donatelli gripped the sliding canopy so tightly that his knuckles turned white. He thought by grabbing the canopy there was less of a chance of it decapitating him when the plane slammed into the ground. Bentson was able to level off, but the engine remained silent. It was too dark for Augie to determine how far off the ground they were, but he sensed that it couldn't have been more than a few hundred feet. The canopy was shrouded in blackness. Both men anxiously bobbed their heads, hoping to get a sense of the terrain; Augie imagined that Bentson was flying directly into a mountainous sand dune. It was at that point that he realized they were most likely well below an altitude that might have been considered marginally safe to bail out from. There was no other decision to be made but to ride the plane into the ground.

Augie decided it was best to ask, "How close are we?"

The question was answered by a jarring thud. The plane vibrated wildy and Augie's body slammed forward into his harness strap. He braced for the anticipated conclusion to the flight. But it didn't come. A few more seconds passed and Augie sensed that the bomber was still gliding through the air.

"Holy hell," he mumbled to himself.

He looked back and could see the outline of a rather imposing ridge. He realized that the sudden jolt was the result of the tail of the plane slamming into the back edge of a sandy ridge. A few more seconds passed before the inevitable. The plane seemed to bounce off the sand. Again, Augie's body pressed violently into the seatbelt. He could see debris bounce off the canopy as the bomber's wings plowed through the terrain. Augie braced himself, clenched his teeth, and closed his eyes in anticipation of the worst.

He expected to die.

The plane continued to plow through the desert terrain.

For thirty more yards, it smashed through shrubs, dirt, stone, and sand. The upheaval seemed to continue for an eternity until the plane buried its way into the sand. Finally, it skidded to an abrupt stop and Donatelli was jostled violently as if he were a rag doll. The entire front of the plane and part of one of the wings was covered with sand. He couldn't believe that he was still alive and conscious. In a partial daze, he frantically unbuckled himself as quickly as possible, and crawled out of the wreckage.

"Bentson," muttered Augie.

No reply.

Donatelli dragged himself back towards the front of the plane.

"Bentson, you okay?" he repeated.

When he got to the wing, he saw through the darkness that Bentson was slumped over the controls. He appeared unconscious. Donatelli worked his way to the front of the cabin and began undoing the pilot's belt. He fumbled for the latch just as Bentson regained consciousness. Augie helped him out of the cockpit and dragged him from the plane. The danger of an explosion still remained, but luckily there was no fire. As they crawled from the wreckage, Augie felt a sharp pain in his leg. When they were about twenty yards away from the plane both men collapsed to the Mojave sand. They were amazed at the mangled propellor, and amazed that they were alive.

The Mojave occupies some 22,000 square miles of territory, no water anywhere in sight. During the winter months temperatures can drop to below 20 degrees, and during the summer months it can soar to 120 degrees in the valley. It's a climate of extremes, filled with creatures such as rattlesnakes, tarantulas, and cougars – not very hospitable.

The men were supplied, at best, with a two days of water, and decided that their first course of action was to fire their flares. After that, there was nothing to do but wait. The temperature was cool in the early morning hours, but would most certainly climb substantially by mid-afternoon. Augie built a fire from some of the dry tumbleweeds and brush that he found in the area.

"Donatelli," said Bentson, "Wait here and guard the plane, let me find some high ground to get our bearings."

Augie expected to receive orders, after all he was a subordinate, but the bizarre thought of guarding a wrecked plane in the middle of the Mojave desert brought a sour grimace to his face.

"Now, who the hell do you think is going to come along and swipe a busted plane that's buried in the sand?" Donatelli asked sarcastically.

Bentson glared at him and went on his hiking expedition, while Augie plopped to the ground near the fire; he also quietly second-guessed Bentson's decision to go back up in the SBD after their first experience with mechanical failure. He also questioned himself for not barking out his opinion. Being a good soldier required more than blindly following orders. It required judgment. He promised himself he would never withhold his opinions again.

Hours passed, the flares had proven futile, so all that remained was a long quiet wait. Bentson returned to report that they were deeply ensconced in the midst of an endless bounty of sand, stone, and juniper trees for miles on end. They fed the fire until the early morning when the early dawn offered a welcome break from the darkness. As they sat in silence they noticed a faint rumbling in the distance. It was the unmistakable sound of engines. Augie and Bentson jumped to their feet and began waving frantically until they were certain they had been spotted. They were soon back at Lowry Field counting their blessings.

Years later, Augie admitted to pondering what his future luck in the war might be if a simple training mission proved to be near fatal. A few weeks after the crash in the Mojave, Augie was assigned to test oxygen tanks with another pilot. The tanks were experimental, and they needed to be tested under actual flight conditions. The flight went without a hitch, everything went according to schedule, and after a two hour flight the plane set down and Augie went to the mess hall for lunch. He recalled not being particularly tired or hungry, and when the captain looked for another tail gunner to continue the testing, he again volunteered his services.

"No, Donatelli, you go grab a bite. We'll round up another guy."

Augie tried to change his mind, but the captain was already looking for another man.

The man he chose never returned from the mission. His plane crashed due to pilot error and neither pilot nor tail gunner survived.

"It could have very easily been me on that plane," recounted Augie. "I often thought about those close calls at Air Gunners School. I wanted to get on with the business of fighting the real war rather than putting my life on the line at a training facility."

It wasn't long after that Donatelli was reassigned to Dalhart, Texas. It was there that he met the crew that he'd be flying with for most of his combat missions in Europe. It was also there that he met Lieutenant William C. Hendrickson of Danville, Illinois. It was Hendrickson who gave Donatelli the nickname that stuck with him throughout the rest of his life. Up until this point he had been known as August. Most of his friends and acquaintances called him Gus, but the Lieutenant changed all of that. When Gus reported for duty for the first time, Hendrickson had some other ideas.

"Tail gunner Gus Donatelli reporting for duty, sir!"

Hendrickson saluted him back, "At ease sergeant," he said in a firm voice. Then he asked, "What do they call you back home?"

I answered with much resolve, "They call me Gus, sir."

Hendrickson let out a laugh, "Well, that's not gonna be your name here. My radio gunner's name is Gus Hauser, and my top turret gunner's name is Gus Ball. If I yell out a command for Gus nobody's gonna know who the hell I'm talking to."

He paused for a second and said, "August, from now on your name is Augie."

Recalled Donatelli, "there were a lot of names he could have pinned on me, but I sort of liked the sound of it – Augie."

The crew stayed at Dalhart for a number of weeks for some additional training with aircraft carriers, and then it was on to New York where they boarded the Queen Mary to begin a two week voyage to Greenock, Scotland, a small port city located on the south bank of the River Clyde. It was a major assembly point for the Atlantic Convoys, and the river town was Augie's very first taste of Europe. It's modest stucco front buildings and surrounding green mountains made the town inviting, but Augie recalled his first experiences there as being rather awkward. The Air Force thought that the men were due for some morale boosting recreation after the long ocean voyage, so they arranged a dance hall engagement.

By Augie's description, "They brought in approximately 100 or so English girls, dressed in sharp looking blue military uniforms. They lined up all the GIs on one side of the room and all of the ladies on the other. The idea was to get us to dance. They played three records, but nobody budged even an inch. Of course, the girls were waiting for some of the men to break the ice, but believe it or not, we were all either

Photo of tail gunner Augie Donatelli. It was at a military base in Dalhart, Texas that "Gus" Donatelli picked up the nickname for which he would be forever known. Photo Courtesy of the Donatelli Collection.

too shy or too hyped up for fighting action to think about having fun. I'm sure if one of us made the slightest of moves, he would have been flooded with women. And some of those ladies were lookers, too. Of course, there were a few less than desirable girls as well. Come to think of it, most of the men were fairly ugly." He continued, "Eventually, they all filed out of the room, bored to death. I don't blame 'em for leaving. What the hell kind of a way was that for soldiers to behave?"

The next destination was an air base in Kimbolton, England. It was the staging ground for many long range bombing missions throughout Europe. Augie and his crew were assigned to the 379th bomber group, squadron number 527. It was December of 1943 and the weather had turned very cold. After a breakfast composed of powdered eggs, the men went back to their barracks, where a radio kept them apprised of the action. They monitored all the available channels for radio messages from bombers as they flew in, reporting information such as their status and fuel situation. Augie listened intently to get a taste of the war. It was in Kimbolton that the crews were assigned to their B-17s. They flew their missions aboard several bombers, including "Rocky" and also a bomber called "The Fickle Finger of Fate," a plane whose painted insignia was a hand with its middle finger extended into the air. Donatelli's first mission, however, was on the B-17 Judy.

The Judy was the B-17 aircraft that tail gunner Donatelli boarded for his first combat mission on December 13th, 1943. Photo Courtesy of the 379th Bomber Group World War II Association.

The Boeing B-17 bomber quickly became one of the United States' most important weapons during the Second World War, and its accolades and missions made the Flying Fortress a legendary piece of American aviation history. The bomber carried four powerful 1200 hp Wright R-1820-97 prop engines that generated a throaty snarl. The B-17s cruised at approximately 250mph with a ceiling of 35,000 feet and a range of 2,400 miles. It weighed 36,000 pounds when empty and 72,000 pounds was its maximum weight, while carrying up to eight 600-pound bombs, and at least 10 powerful .50 caliber machine guns.

Donatelli was in charge of two .50 caliber Browning machine guns in the tail of the plane. One of his main responsibilities was to make certain that no enemy fighter swooped down through the formation without repercussions; he also called out the location of fighters over his headset to alert the rest of his crew as the enemy came barreling in. On occasions when an assignment opened up aboard another B-17, members of other crews were asked to volunteer. It was termed, "flying spare." Augie was often quick to volunteer because it counted towards the 25 missions that were required to complete one's tour of duty. The officers stood near a stone fireplace in a large open area where all the crews assembled. Augie usually tried to make a point of leaning against the stone while awaiting his assignment, perhaps the ballplayer in him clung to a superstitious ritual. When flying spare, the officers picked the crew alphabetically. There was only one gunner whose last name began with D that was ahead of Donatelli. The young man was from Johnstown, Pennsylvania, located only a matter of miles from Bakerton. Augie never revealed his full name. After missing the call to be aboard the flight, Donatelli cursed his bad fortune. He wanted to be aboard that plane. Luckily for him, he was not. The bomber became caught in a holding pattern, just circling in the air space near London. It was waiting to join a formation when an accident occurred. The plane collided with another bomber. Nearly 20 men died over friendly soil without even firing a single shot. The boy who died in what could have been Donatelli's place was only 22-years-old.

While at Kimbolton, Donatelli bunked with an airman from Indiana, Pennsylvania. His name was Ed Dugan. Ed had returned from a difficult mission the day before and was sound asleep in the barracks. It was five o'clock in the morning when a sergeant stormed up the steps, yelling obscenities and throwing stones at the door. He violently pushed the door open and stormed into the room.

"Okay, listen up 'cause you're flyin' spare!" he screamed.

Then approximately halfway down the list he barked out the name Dugan.

The first thought that crossed his mind was that they must have been short men, because Dugan deserved ground time after what he had been through. He remained motionless in the bunk.

"Listen, Ed," Augie said as he poked him, "C'mon, get up now."

He just moaned and moaned. He didn't want to go up again so soon. Donatelli sympathized with his bunkmate, but he later said, "When they bark out your name you'd better jump, or have a better excuse than, 'I don't feel like it.'"

Seeing that Ed was having such a tough time, two of the guys lifted his mattress and dumped Dugan to the ground.

It wasn't long after that he was 25,000 feet up in the air.

Bombers flew in groups of four, and for this mission The Rocky was the lead plane. Dugan was a gunner on one of the wing planes. A fourth plane flew towards the rear. Each plane held a crew of ten men, and he knew every member of the crew very well. There was pilot, 1st Lieutenant, William Hendrickson and Co-Pilot John Moore. The gunners were Gus Ball Jr., Sam Bishop, Rance Webly, Thomas Grange, and Augie. The navigator was Harry Wolodka, the bombardier, Jim Moore, and the radio gunner was Gus Hauser. Hauser was the artist who painted the symbol of the bomber prominently on the side of the plane. He was also responsible for marking the back of the leather flight jackets after each successful mission.

One of Augie's most dangerous missions involved the bombing of German occupied positions in France. The Rocky approached its target with some strafe from the German fighters. The entire crew heard pilot Hendrickson's voice over the radio.

"They're comin' in, we've got company."

Just then, what seemed like a swarm of thirty German Focke-Wulfs swooped down on the four plane formation of American Bombers that included Rocky. The Focke-Wulfs were much smaller than the bombers, and were built to make speedy attacks. Their job was to weave through the formations to harass and destroy as many bombers as possible. The B-17s were big targets with almost no cover – but could absorb lots of punishment. Shells from the ground exploded all around as a maze of cloud and vapor trails engulfed the plane. Augie desperately tried to shoot down the first two Focke-Wulfs with his guns firing like mad. He was off his seat and squatting down on his knees as he squeezed the gun triggers. Rocky began to tremble violently. After he saw the first enemy fighter smoke and burst into flames, he turned to the second plane and sent it down smoking. Both Focke-Wulfs flamed-out a safe distance from the Rocky. From his position he could see hunks of debris and fragments fly helter-skelter through the air, as scores of enemy fighters whizzed by.

Then the words from the radio blared out a warning.

"There's too many of 'em. They're raining on us!"

Augie looked at the plane on the wing of the Rocky and saw it get pummeled. Large holes in the fuselage became visible. Donatelli remained calm and kept firing from his knees. He realized that it was possible to accept death without experiencing panic. Seven more Focke-Wulfs cascaded in and hit the bomber with all guns blazing. As Donatelli glanced to his left, he saw the site of Dugan's plane spiraling downward. He kept firing but couldn't take his eyes off Dugan's plane and followed it down as far as he could. He saw no one bail out.

The confluence of exploding shells, bullets, and vapor trails filled the sky and created a confusing jumble. The strong smell of burnt powder and fuel permeated the entire cabin. Augie scanned the sky looking to find an approaching target. He spotted one at 11 o'clock and promptly squeezed the triggers, but his right gun had malfunctioned. He continued firing his left gun, which continued to "work like a beauty." Suddenly, a new set of Focke-Wulfs swooped in. Augie swiveled his guns. Just then, he felt the bomber nose jolt downward. For a brief moment he found himself looking up into the sun. The Rocky was heading lower, but the barrage of fire from the determined Focke-Wulfs went unabated. Donatelli felt he was nose to nose with the enemy. He could make out their faces as they chased Rocky towards mother earth. Three German planes pulled to within 50 yards distance, a swirling mass of clouds, smoke, and flak served as the backdrop. Augie stopped firing and worked on un-jamming his machine gun. He frantically pulled the mechanism, and then gripped his guns tightly and continued to fire. Rocky was now descending at a steep 40-degree angle. He pressed his oxygen mask tightly against his face. He squeezed his right finger against the trigger of the gun, and his left hand pressed against the metal of the fuselage. As he tried to pull it away, he discovered his skin pulled against the sub-freezing cold metal. A voice over the headset reported that Hendrickson was unconscious, and the Rocky dropped like a brick. The captain and co-pilot were slumped forward as if they had been fatally hit. The bomber roared downward from 25,000 feet to 14,000 feet to 8,000 before two of the German fighters finally pulled off their deadly attack. The flak from the ground fire remained heavy; a shell ripped into the door of the ball turret compartment and left the turret gunner hanging onto the plane by his guns alone. Somehow, he pulled himself back into the plane. Another shell banged through the top turret and blew the helmet off the man there and knocked him violently to the deck. The last of the German fighters pulled off as Rocky continued its deadly descent. A few more seconds passed before the B-17 began to level off. The plane was well below 2,000 feet.

The radio crackled to life, "We're okay. They're off us."

Little did Donatelli and the rest of the crew know, but Hendrickson had decided to play dead… and the strategy worked. The bomber appeared so seriously damaged that the Germans had stopped the attack as a hailstorm rose from the ground. The term flak was derived from the German word **Fl**ieger**a**bwehr**k**anone, or aircraft defense cannon. Once the plane leveled out, Augie crawled back into the main compartment and could see that the fuselage was laced with gaping holes, and there were at least nine, 20-millimeter live rounds still rolling around inside its hull.

Augie later said, "I don't know how that plane kept in the sky. At least we were headed back to Kimbolton, still in one piece; but I couldn't help but think about poor Dugan," Donatelli lamented. "I thought about how we dumped the poor guy out of bed. I considered him a friend. I prayed that he had gotten out, but his chances were slim to say the least. That's the way war was, you lived minute-to-minute, not knowing whether you'd survive to see the next day, or whether the guy standing next to you was going to be the next to die."

Rocky's brush with disaster received attention. Captain Hedrickson was later quoted as saying, "If there's any credit to be given, give it to Augie. He saved the day." He was referring to Augie's apt shooting from the tail gunner position which fended off the attacking Focke-Wulfs. Donatelli continued to fire his machine guns skyward at the German fighters as the smoking B-17 sped towards the ground.

When the plane landed, all ten men were able to walk away. As they inspected the battered bomber, they marveled at the fact that the top turret gunner's chair was physically embedded in the metal tail of the plane.

"All I could say was, holy hell," said Augie. "Only a miracle and the grace of God saved us that day."

The B-17 bomber Rocky caught fire following a maintenance accident. Weeks earlier, Donatelli nearly perished aboard this aircraft during one of his 18 combat missions. Photo Courtesy of the 379th Bomb Group World War II Association.

When the fighting ended, the topic of baseball flashed in Augie's mind.

He loved to chide his fellow crew members about their favorite ballclubs, and he was always quick at recounting his own diamond triumphs.

"Any of you guys ever see Honus Wagner play ball? Greatest shortstop ever. The guy played for the Pirates for 18 seasons and won the batting title eight times," boasted Augie.

"Big deal," a young airman shot back, "the Iron Horse was 10 times better, and I got his autograph. Besides I think you just shot down Wagner's third cousin."

"Ya don't say," answered Donatelli. I'll give you MY autograph right now, if ya want it." He then held up his right fist.

"What the hell is YOUR autograph worth, you ain't no major leaguer. You're way too old to make it to the majors. By the time we get back no scout is even gonna sniff at ya."

Donatelli did indulge the whim that he might have been a major league ballplayer, and he was described in a local newspaper as an "accomplished ballplayer." He also enjoyed a brief fling at the Class D level. He later claimed that he never played or practiced enough, and that his time working in the mines limited any chances he might have had to hone his skills. Back at Lowry Field, Augie excelled at the competitive baseball that was played, and he played so well at shortstop that the officer in charge offered him a higher technical rating at the school just for playing on the team. Baseball had a significant presence during the war. It was a morale booster to those that followed the boxscores and standings in *Stars and Stripes*. There were many big name players that contributed to the war effort directly: Ted Williams, Joe DiMaggio, Bob Feller, Johnny Mize, Johnny Pesky, Warren Spahn, and Stan Musial were all in service. Williams saw well-documented action as a Naval aviator. More than 500 major leaguers, including 35 Hall of Famers, and 4,000 minor leaguers served in the military during World War II. Of that group, only two men were killed. From the 1939 Washington Senators, Elmer Gedeon was Killed In Action at St. Pol, France in 1944. His career consisted of five games in the outfield with a .200 batting average, and the other casualty was Harry O'Neill from the 1939 Philadelphia Athletics, who was Killed In Action at Iwo Jima on March 6, 1945. His career consisted of one game at catcher without an at bat. And pitchers Hoyt Wilhelm and Warren Spahn earned Purple Hearts and both participated in the Battle of the Bulge. Spahn also earned a Bronze Star and was lucky to escape with his life when the Ludendorff Bridge over the Rhine River in Remagen collapsed. Ralph Houk who was an Army Ranger, rose to the rank of Major. He too was at the Battle of the Bulge and Bastogne and was awarded the Purple Heart, Bronze Star, and the Silver Star.

There was some talk of the national pastime being put on hold for the duration of the war. Commissioner Judge Kenesaw Mountain Landis wrote a letter to President Roosevelt asking for advice.

Replied Roosevelt in his Green Light Letter, "I honestly feel that it would be best for the country to keep baseball going. As for the players themselves, I know you agree with me that the individual players who are active military or naval age should go, without question, into the services."

It was determined that even in its subpar state and minus many of its stars Major League Baseball kept morale high among civilians and soldiers alike. One St. Louis beer company, Alpen Brau, even took out an ad that linked the war effort to a ballgame.

Sure Adolf, you got off to a flying start! That foul double play
combination, Hitler to Hirohito to Benito
worked like a charm in the early innings…
What you didn't count on, was the fact that a fighting spirit can
overcome any lead. You're starting to realize that now. The
United Nations are hitting their stride. They have started smashing
your pitchers all over the lot… putting men on bases everywhere.
Soon they'll be scoring on your home plate!

Donatelli's 18th mission on March 6, 1944 was to be his most dangerous. It was described in the briefing room as a deep penetration raid: the assignment was the first U.S. daylight bombing of Berlin. The target was to destroy armament industries in and around the Nazi war capital. It was approximately a 1,200 mile round trip flight, by far the longest range mission that Augie had ever participated in. This made the task even more perilous because there was very little margin for error. Every gallon of fuel had to be accounted for in order to safely make the return flight, and if a bomber was forced to expend a lot of energy during combat the chances of making it all the way back to base were drastically diminished. For this mission, Augie was assigned to a B-17 fresh off the assembly line. It was silver and without paint, a factor that was a plus for such a long range mission, since the lack of paint made the bomber more fuel efficient. It required much paint to cover a bomber, and so it would burn less fuel without it. The plane didn't have a name, just a number. The final three digits were 555.

The tail gunner position was a lonely one. He was isolated in a cramped space. During the course of a long flight, he had to continue to man his position and report back to the pilot over his interphone. He would report any change in condition or any sightings of enemy fighters. Donatelli occupied some of his time in the tail section by scraping the ice off the bullet proof glass shield to give himself an unobstructed view. He kept his helmet with him for just such a purpose. By using its brim, he chipped away at any icy buildup. The temperature at 30,000 feet was 60 below zero, so the ice reappeared quickly. The cold was distracting.

Augie sat on what amounted to a modified bicycle seat, but when it came time to man the guns, he leaned forward into a kneeling position. There was a constant draft that poured in and Augie fought the cold and potential frostbite by keeping himself in constant motion. Donatelli felt it was important to stay alert because part of his duties included passing along any pertinent information to the pilot, such as enemy planes swooping in for an attack. During combat he often barked out bombing results to the bombardier since he had the best view to determine whether or not a target had been hit.

The tail gunner was an important line of defense for any B-17, and German fighters respected the damage that a tail gunner could muster. They often approached their targets from above – 12 o'clock high – to avoid the tail gunner's storm of bullets.

The site of hundreds of bombers in formation was breathtaking. The B-17s left long steaming trails of vapor. From the vantage point of the tail gunner's seat it appeared that the entire sky was flooded with devastating machines that had the destructive force to cripple a city. At certain points the bombers flew directly into solid cloud banks where visibility diminished to nearly zero - all that could be seen from the tail position was a tiny piece of the trailing ship. This lack of visibility made formation flying difficult.

By this point, Augie was only seven missions shy of ending his tour. The war had long since lost its luster as some romantic adventure. He saw it for what it was: a dangerous undertaking that was a call of duty. In quiet moments he wondered whether the bombs would reach their target, and whether or not he would survive a mission deep within the heart of the Nazi war machine. The flight route took the formation over the Northeast shore of Germany. The first few hours of the trip was uneventful until the initial entrance into dangerous air space over German soil. Then, over the radio, came the first warning from the ship's navigator.

"Here comes our escort," the voice said matter of factly to warn the rest of the crew.

Donatelli peered through the shield and there at 11 o'clock, he spotted a formation in the distance. They appeared as small specks. They were too small to be bombers. A rush of adrenaline charged through his system and he hastily rechecked his machine guns.

"It didn't take much to energize those babies," Augie later recalled. "After a light squeeze of the trigger, out sprayed a long string of bullets across the sky. We knew the planes coming in were Focke-Wulfs and Messerschmitts. We also knew all of us gunners would have to do a hell of a job to fight those planes off. Our job was to buy enough time to position ourselves over the target."

As Augie kept his eyes on the incoming planes, the bomber experienced a sudden jolt. They had flown into a barrage of cannon fire from the ground. The German fighters zeroed in on the B-17, and the bomber responded with a return barrage from every gun position. The ferocity of the German attack was overwhelming. The German fighters efficiently cleared the entire left side of the bomber formation in a matter of minutes. The air was heavy with flak, and the frequency of black bursts made it difficult for the gunners to zero in on target. Scrap metal the size of jellybeans cut into the bomber at a rapid rate that Donatelli hadn't before experienced. The Messerschmitts whizzed by above the bomber and unloaded their .20-millimeter cannons with deadly accuracy.

"They're hitting us so hard, we're gonna bust open," came a warning over the radio.

Oil was spurting from one of the engines, and there was smoke everywhere.

The vibration got so intense that it was difficult to hold onto anything, and firing on target seemed impossible. Augie held his position. He clenched his teeth and squeezed both triggers, but had only a vague clue where the bullets were flying.

It wasn't long before two of the four engines gave out under the heavy fire. The pilot couldn't feather the prop, and the bomber continued to shake violently. Augie turned his head and looked back into the main cabin as he heard the pilot bark out instructions over the headset. It wasn't an easy task to move from the tail gunner position back into the main part of the plane. The gunner had to negotiate his way past center vertical struts that were part of the tail wheel retraction system, and with the plane bouncing around so much this crawl to the main cabin would prove to be an even bigger challenge. The alternative was for him to jump through an escape hatch in the back of the plane. He could open that and dive out, but he opted to climb back into the cabin.

"Jump!" was the command, "Tell 'em to jump!"

Donatelli stayed in his position and continued to fire off shots as if he had gone mad.

Said Augie, "As soon as enemy pilots discovered you were a cripple, they'd gang up on you and knock you out of the sky, so I wanted to show them we still had plenty of fight in us."

The other gunners came out of their turret positions – the two waist gunners and the top turret gunner were standing near the escape hatch, holding on for dear life as the plane continued to bounce violently. Donatelli fired again, turned back and saw that everyone was standing around and holding on to whatever they could. He was surprised that no one had made a move towards the door. No one wanted to jump into the hell-storm that was churning outside. There was so much noise that no verbal communication was possible. Augie looked back and saw that the radio operator was pointing his thumbs downward. He was signaling for the crew to bail out on the command of the captain. At this point the bomber was bouncing so violently that it seemed ready to split open. He began to stagger and crawl towards the cabin's exterior door. He later said, "It was the longest 20 feet of my life."

In the time it took him to make his way to the hatch no one had jumped. Donatelli reached for the door, kicked it open, and backed his way out.

"Bingo, I was out of there," he said.

As he tumbled, he shut his eyes tight, half expecting to be sprayed by bullets or blown into pieces. He tumbled through the sky. Peering through his windblown eyes, it seemed impossible to distinguish sky from terrain. In training camp he was told that once you jumped from the bomber your body would be tumbling at 210 miles per hour, but it was necessary to resist the temptation to pull open the chute too soon. The men were instructed to count to 100. Once he achieved some separation from the B-17, Augie still expected to be impaled by a shard of flying debris. After the chute opened, the harness jerked forcefully into his shoulders, but he was relieved to finally have some of direction. He scanned the horizon for enemy planes. Looking up, he discerned a glimpse of another crew-member bailing out. He realized that he was an easy target, and that there was nothing he could do to protect himself. In the distance he saw another B-17 burst into flames, spin out of control, and plummet downward. He thought perhaps it might have been his bomber, but he was in no way certain. It was later tallied that a total of 68 bombers were lost that day. Augie continued his descent. He began to focus on the ground and noticed that he was drifting towards a dense forest. The tree-tops were approaching rapidly as he braced for a rough landing.

"Holy hell, I'm done," he thought to himself.

Augie smashed through the first few braches easily, but halfway into the tree his chute caught a limb and he subsequently swung sideways into another heavy branch. He came to an abrupt stop and was dangling some ten feet above the ground. Donatelli tried to work his way free of the harness, but the branch broke and he plummeted to the soil like a sack of potatoes. He groaned with pain and covered his face with his hands. He felt cold snow that had worked its way down the back of his neck. His head was still spinning from the insanity that had just transpired. After a few seconds he slowly collected his composure and dragged himself to the foot of the tree he had just fallen from. There was no one in sight. He looked up and watched as bombers continue to fly into the distance.

Augie was in the middle of a forest somewhere on the outskirts of Berlin and was seriously hobbled by an injured ankle. The trees were densely packed and snow covered the ground. In the distance, he could hear that the sky battle continued to rage. Eventually a German patrol was going to pass through the area, so he knew it would be wise to gather and hide the parachute, but he knew the snow would make it difficult for him to cover his tracks. Then as he pulled himself along the ground in search of something he could use as a crutch. It wasn't long before a lone figure approached from a distance. The shadowy figure had probably been spying on his actions for quite some time. As he ambled closer, he raised his right hand as if he were cautiously greeting a new visitor. The middle aged, heavyset man wore a frumpy mid-length coat and hat. Donatelli assumed he was a local of some sort, perhaps a farmer. The man gestured above his head trying to communicate what he was after. It suddenly dawned on Augie what the farmer wanted. He was interested in the parachute, so Donatelli decided to reveal where he had hidden it. The nylon from the parachute was a valuable commodity during a time when all materials were difficult to come by.

As the farmer gathered his spoils, Augie stood to his feet and began limping in the opposite direction. He realized that his ankle was most likely broken, but continued to drag on in pain for another 20 yards before he collapsed. It was getting colder. Donatelli hoped he might stumble upon a barn, or crawl underneath some heavy brush; anything that might protect him from what was certain to be a frigid night.

Augie knew that the forest would be littered with debris and airmen – both dead and alive. Perhaps he would stumble on a crew member who could assist him.

Then came a sudden crackling of branches. Augie turned, and just then a voice cried out, "HALT!" There was a gun barrel pointed directly at his face. Holding the weapon was a German soldier peering at him with cold, hard eyes. Donatelli raised both of his hands above his head as the soldier moved closer.

"Pistola," he shouted!

"No," replied Augie, "No gun."

He walked to within a few feet of Donatelli who felt more helpless than he ever had before.

Englander," asked the soldier?

Donatelli shook his head, "No, no – I am Americaner"

The Germans stared at Donatelli with a skeptical look. The soldier waved the barrel of his gun in the direction he wanted his newly found prisoner to walk. Donatelli limped ahead of him.

"Los," he ordered.

They walked for a mile and a half with Donatelli dragging his leg the entire way, until finally they reached a point in the road where another soldier waited with a motorcycle equipped with a sidecar. The foot soldier got in and motioned for Donatelli to sit in front of him. The motorcycle accelerated down the dirt road, and the cold wind plowed into Augie's face. He gripped onto the sidecar the best he could as he imagined himself being thrown through the air should the motorcycle hit a bumpy spot in the road. Donatelli knew that he would be interrogated upon arrival. All captured Allied airmen were interrogated at a transit camp before being assigned a permanent prison. The airmen had been schooled on how to react during interrogations, and the implication of revealing even small bits of seemingly harmless information. The Germans responsible for the interrogations were often times highly educated officers who held occupations such as professors prior to the war. Some were even educated in the United States and knew the nuances of the language and popular culture.

The motorcycle burst into an open clearing, where Augie could see an expansive military air base. He was taken aback by the site of row upon row of German Focke-Wulfs. Augie couldn't help but stare at the familiar swastikas on the tale of the parked planes as he whisked by. He was not accustomed to being in such close proximity to the enemy. Swastikas were everywhere he looked.

American POWs were often processed through a camp located north of Frankfurt called Dulag Luft. It was there that they were photographed and stripped of their various possessions and often thrown into solitary confinement. Large white stones covered the front lawn of the camp spelling out the words: "Prisoner of War Camp," and the same identification was painted on the top of each building to discourage an Allied bombardment of the 500 acre facility. Watchtowers were spaced around the camp at regular intervals, and guard dogs patrolled the perimeter.

For captured Allied airmen, the stay here was destined to be a brief one. It proved to be an orderly method for the Germans to identify and document their captives and also served as an opportunity for them to garner as much information from the men as possible. In addition to serving as a transit camp, it also had a more dubious purpose. It was a psychological testing ground. If a prisoner displayed any sort of nervousness or weakness and was perceived to have any strategic knowledge, then there was a good chance that the interrogation would be elevated to include rough treatment. The interrogators were fishing for any strategically pertinent information or technical details. POW Donald Kremper told of being interrogated about the American bomber's ability to accurately deliver its payload through cloud cover. The new system was called Pathfinder and code named Mickey Mouse. It was a piece of airborne radar equipment positioned in a dome underneath the lead bomber. Kremper stated that he knew very little about the system, yet he was very surprised when the interrogator pulled out a folder that contained information about his entire crew. He had clippings from Kremper's hometown newspaper, and he also had a group picture of his bomber crew which had only been taken the month prior.

At his rank, Augie also did not possess privileged information, but the debriefings continued like clockwork. Sergeant Donatelli was treated for his ankle injury and then led through a doorway and ushered into a plain-looking room with a table and a single chair. The guard motioned for Augie to take the seat. Moments later a German officer walked into the room and pushed a pack of cigarettes in front of him. Augie displayed no interest.

The interrogator initiated the conversation in English, "You come from Italy?"

Donatelli responded by giving his serial number.

Interrogators often tried to engage the prisoners in small talk, or any type of banter that seemed insignificant.

"Your mommy comes from Italy?"

Once again, Augie answered with his name, rank and serial number.

Then, "Your father comes from Italy?"

Donatelli maintained his poker face, but glanced up at the German. He was an average sized man with a block like face; his manner was sharp, loud, and direct. He spoke with a staccato rhythm; quick bursts followed by silence. Augie maintained his stare. Donatelli's eyes widened when he saw the interrogator pull a knife from his belt. He read anger in his interrogator's face.

Augie decided that he should speak.

"Name: Donatelli, August J, Sergeant, serial number, 13047431."

He knew he was only required to give name, rank, and serial

number, but he also sensed that the German was not in a mood to play cat and mouse.

"Your name is Donatelli," he bellowed, "That is Italian… someone from your family comes from ITALY!"

No answer.

With that, the interrogator raised the knife high and jammed it into the table with great force within inches of Donatelli's hand.

Augie's body stiffened as the interrogator pulled the knife from the wooden surface.

The German then pushed the table away and called for the guard.

"Get this pig out of here," he commanded in English.

Demeaning as it was, they were words that Donatelli was relieved to hear because it meant that he would survive what seemed to have been the longest day of his life. Subsequently he was reunited with Lt. Hendrickson and learned of the details of what transpired aboard the bomber after Augie had bailed out. Co-pilot John Moore had declined to parachute from the plane, and was the only crew member on Donatelli's bomber to perish that day.

Augie Donatelli is standing, second from the right. He is posing with the B-17 bomber crew that he flew most of his World War II missions. Photo courtesy of the Donatelli Collection.

1. Your name *August J Donatelli*   Rank *S/Sgt.*   Serial No. *13047431*

2. Organization *379 Gp* Commander *Preston* Rank *Col* Sqn CO *Carlam* Rank *Major*
              (full name)   (full name)

3. What year *1944*   month *March*   day *6*   did you go down?

4. What was the mission, *Berlin*, target, *Bearing Factory*, target
    time, *between 12.30 + 2*, altitude, *24,000 ft*, route scheduled, *straight*
    in + out, route flown *same*

5. Where were you when you left formation? *In Vicinity of target*

6. Did you bail out? *Yes!*

7. Did other members of crew bail out? *I learned later at Du Lag*
Luft (Frankfort) from Lt. Hendrickson (Pilot) that Lt. Moore
(copilot) did not leave plane

8. Tell all you know about when, where, how each person in your aircraft for whom no
individual questionnaire is attached bailed out. A crew list is attached. Please
give facts. If you don't know, say: "No Knowledge". *After we received*
orders from Pilot to bail out. I took the advantage
of the first person to bail out — Plane was on fire — when I
bailed out — I have no knowledge of Lt John Moore copilot

Air Force casualty questionnaire with hand-written answers filled
in by August J. Donatelli shortly after the war had ended. Courtesy
of the 379th Bomb Group World War II Association.

at the Prison Camp Du Lag Luft
Frankfort Germany, I learned from the
Pilot (Lt. Hendrickson) that the copilot
Lt. Moore would not leave plane
Our Pilot Lt. Hendrickson tried to Put
Parachute on copilot Lt. Moore - the latter
resisted. All the way on the mission
since we hit the coast of France our crew
knew that Lt. Moore (copilot) was unnerved
the way he acted + talked over inter
phone — as matter of fact he did not talk
he screamed of inter-phone — the plane was
in such condition that we were forced to
bail out for fear of exploding any moment,
not only was right wing on fire but also
the plane was vibrating so badly you could
not stand in position without holding on to something
Other than that fatal mission I would say
our crew was one of best in operation - including
Lt. John Moore - co-pilot.

Detailed casualty report written by Donatelli in 1946.
Courtesy of the 379th Bomb Group Association

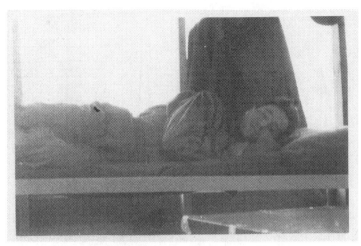

Donatelli napping in his bunk. He flew most of his missions from Kimbolton Airfield in England. Courtesy of the Donatelli Collection.

Tail gunner Augie Donatelli reporting for duty.
Courtesy of the Donatelli Collection.

FOUR

Prison Camp

It was a difficult five day train ride from Dulag Luft to a prison camp that would be his new home. The trains were nothing more than wooden boxcars with straw covered floors and an overflow of 50 men packed side by side. Locked inside the cars the POWs endured a cold March wind cutting its way through. Donatelli looked to shield himself from the unrelenting stream of air. From time to time he caught a glimpse of the countryside which was riddled with cumulative signs of damage that all the Allied air strikes had caused.

The destination was Stalag Luft VI in Heydekrug which was located north of Poland, near the city of Memel. It is currently part of Lithuania and was eventually renamed Klaipeda. At the time, however, the area was part of German controlled territory in East Prussia. Stalag Luft VI was located in the outskirts of a small town named Heydekrug, not far from the Baltic Sea. It was the farthest north POW camp, and the port city eventually proved to be a battleground for the advancing Russian Red Army

As the men filed off the boxcars they became the object of attention of local inhabitants who gazed at the collection of American airmen as they stumbled and hurled themselves off the boxcars. The soldiers gave the men ample opportunity to relieve themselves in the open area near the train yard, and in full view of passing trains and a scant collection of local citizens. The airmen could care less about the public spectacle, and were completely satisfied to relieve themselves after the painfully long train ride.

The prison camp itself was in a forested area in the outskirts of the village. From a distance, Stalag Luft VI appeared as a rectangle shaped collection of elevated rows of barbed wire fences, surrounded by multiple guard towers. The foreboding colors of weathered wood and grayish brown brick surrounded by menacing fences gave the place a forlorn and cold appearance. Lush green pine trees served as a backdrop to the camp, but the only speck of color within its fences was a large red Nazi flag which flew on a tall pole at the heart the compound. Jutting up from behind two rows of barbed wire fences was the outline of four large barracks made of brick, each having a capacity of nearly 600 men with 60 prisoners housed in each subdivision or unit. There were also 10 or so smaller wooden buildings within the confines of the campground. As the exhausted men soon discovered, the brick barracks were laid out in four long rows at the center of the camp. Two layers of wire fences surrounded the grounds and just behind the fences stood eight intimidating well armed guard towers evenly spaced on the camp exterior. A short warning fence surrounded the interior of the camp ground and served as a danger zone. POWs quickly learned that wandering behind the low wire border would be cause for the guards to open fire.

Inside the large open quarters, there was a stark collection of double-decker bunks, stools, and tables. The perimeter of the living area was surrounded by nearly thirty beds. In the far corner was a tiny room that housed buckets for the men to relieve themselves. At one point during the war there were more than 10,000 men encamped there; including a swath of American, British, Canadian, and Russian POWs. The true capacity of the prison was estimated to be more in vicinity of 6,000, but the Germans accommodated the overflow of POWs in the wooden structures.

The food was scarce and light, and often six men were forced to share one loaf of bread for an entire meal, or watered down potato soup. They also sipped powdered coffee and were given the contents of Red Cross parcels, which contained items like canned meat and proved to be vital sources of sustenance. The commandant was Oberst Von Hoerback, who was demanding, but fair. According to Augie, most of the American and British were treated correctly under Geneva Convention guidelines, provided they did not attempt any circumvention of the rules. Russian POWs, on the other hand, were treated with much less regard, partly because the Soviets had abstained from signing the Geneva pact during the conclusion of World War I. As the months wore on, the total number of American prisoners of war in German occupied territory nearly tripled to in excess of 90,000.

The men had their assigned chores at Stalag Luft VI, including cleanup and toilet duties. There were also crews assigned to burying men who died. The men were only able to shower every few weeks, and those lasted for no more than a few minutes. The Guards marched Augie and some other prisoners into a shower room, six men at a time. Moving slowly, Donatelli positioned himself under one of three shower heads in the room. They were given less than a minute to bathe. Augie angrily recalled how the soap often burned his eyes when the water was shut off. He yelped his displeasure to the guards but to no avail.

During the summer months the men diverted their attention from their growling stomachs by generating their own sporting endeavors. Since they didn't have much in the way of food, the energy levels were sustainable for relatively short periods, but the competition was lively. On the 4th of July, the airmen organized boxing matches that were very popular with the POWs as well as the German guards. The summer of 1944 was the sixth anniversary of the Louis vs. Schmeling rematch, the boxing battle of the ages that pitted Germany's champion, Max Schmeling against America's Joe Louis. The fight symbolized the battle between democracy and fascism. Louis avenged his loss to Schmeling in 1938, two years after he suffered a 12th round knockout. Augie had become a boxing enthusiast ever since watching his brother capture the Golden Gloves championship in Pittsburgh. The Louis vs. Schmeling heavyweight rematch garnered worldwide focus. The historic fight was broadcast over the radio and millions listened around the globe. As Augie remembered it, listening on the radio in Bakerton, PA, it was a humid night in June of 1938 and a crowd of 80,000 packed Yankee Stadium in a fight that was perceived as a showcase for Aryan physical supremacy. The rematch only lasted only two minutes, and Lewis won on a knockout. It remained one of the major sports events of the 20th century.

Schmeling had enlisted as a paratrooper, but was wounded during a battle in Crete in 1941, and was relegated to more mundane duties. By 1944, Schmeling occasionally gave boxing exhibitions to German troops in prison camps with the intent of raising the morale of German soldiers. Surprisingly, his presence even boosted the spirits of Allied POWs, especially when he told them that he admired Louis and considered him a powerful opponent, a great champion, and a friend. He left the POW camps to the sound of cheers from the men imprisoned there.

The boxing exhibitions at Stalag Luft VI were obviously far less consequential than the Schmeling vs Louis fights, but they maintained their own drama. The matches were held in a spot at the camp that could accommodate the most onlookers. The boxing ring was positioned near a barbed wire fence that divided the compound so that British RAF could observe the fisticuffs. Hundreds of men peered on and cheered as the three round fights took place. The men didn't have enough energy for the fights to go much longer. The fights featured American against American, American against British, and American against Canadian. POWs encircled the ring, and even the German guards gathered around and watched with as much interest as the POWs. The fighters were introduced by randomly invented nicknames such as "Killer" and "Bearded Marvel."

The POWs also kept active by playing basketball and softball. The YMCA donated the equipment which included Louisville Sluggers and regulation size softballs. Augie gravitated to softball rather than pugilism, and since his ankle hadn't fully recovered from the injury he sustained after parachuting from his bomber, he couldn't play and was asked to umpire.

"Arguments kept popping up. And the games dragged on forever," Augie remembered. "The fellows were all young, and it seemed like it was impossible for them to distinguish between a fair and foul ball. They desperately needed someone to umpire. Since I knew the game so well, I was the choice. The games I umpired ran so smoothly that the men wanted me to umpire every single game."

This became Donatelli's first not so gentle foray into the world of umpiring. While the games were hardly professional caliber, they were competitive and did garner quite a bit of attention from the American POWs. In an ironic twist, perhaps the crowds at Stalag Luft VI may have rivaled the enthusiasm of some Major League crowds that were being drawn back in the United States. In April of 1944, Braves pitcher Jim "Abba Dabba" Tobin no-hit the Dodgers in front of a mere 1,984 fans in Boston. Although there was no official count, there might have been more captive eyeballs on hand in Prussia to watch the POWs compete, especially if you count the prison guards who watched the Americans to stave off shenanigans and prevent boredom. The ground rules forbid any POW to go near the barbed wire fences to retrieve an errant ball, and they relied on the guards, who carried machine guns and also served as well-armed ball boys. Softball wasn't nearly as popular as boxing, which captured the attention of all the entire camp, but the popularity of the ballgames amongst the prisoners prompted them to organize a league that involved competition between the different barracks, and Augie was called on to umpire those games.

"Umpiring those games in the prisoner camps was pretty rough, because they were so competitive in nature which was amazing considering the conditions we were under; but that was the way the boys wanted to play."

There was a heavily attended meeting among the members of barracks E to discuss how competitive the games were going to be.

"Do you guys want to win a championship, or do you want to play every guy in the barracks?" Donatelli asked. By this point Augie's ankle was well on its way to being healed and he wanted to compete in some of the games. The men voted that they wanted to play as competitively as possible for the Stalag championship. Some of the men complained vociferously when they were left off of the team roster. Augie claimed it started a verbal riot in the barracks. One of the POWs was especially upset.

"What the hell do you mean I'm not good enough?"

Some of the POWs were so upset that they weren't selected that they formed their own team. As the weeks passed, Augie's leg improved, and he put aside his umpiring and began to play, and the barracks E team that he played for eventually won the Stalag championship. Donatelli was the shortstop, and the first baseman was Cliff "Slim" Barker, who later went on to become an All-American basketball star at the University of Kentucky. Barker had left school after his freshman year to serve in the Air Force, and after the war, he returned to Kentucky and helped lead the Wildcats' "Fab Five" to two national championships. Barker ultimately went on to play for the Indianapolis Olympians of the NBA.

Behind the Barbed wire fences are prisoners of war playing softball with equipment donated by the YMCA. Photo courtesy of Donald Kremper

While Augie was playing ball in the POW camp, eventually articles emerged in local papers back home hailing Donatelli as a war hero. Augie's brothers, who were serving in the military, knew that he was missing in action. James eventually returned safely to the United States after serving in the South Pacific; Hugo was an Army private serving in Washington, D.C., and Steve was training with the Air Corps in Georgia. Augie's mother was informed that her son was missing by letter; they were notified on April 1st, 1944 that his bomber had been lost in battle. The notice came from Brigadier General Robert Dunlop, who reported that Donatelli was "missing in action."

Dear Mrs. Donatelli,

This letter is to confirm my recent telegram in which you were regretfully informed that your son, Staff Sergeant August J. Donatelli 13,047,431, Air Corps, has been reported missing in action over Germany since 6 March 1944. I know that added distress is caused by failure to receive more information or details. Therefore, I wish to assure you that at any time additional information is received it will be transmitted to you without delay, and, if in the meantime no additional information is received, I will again communicate with you at the expiration of three months. Also, it is the policy of the Commanding General of the Army Air Forces upon receipt of the "Missing Air Crew Report" to convey to you any details that might be contained in that report.

The term "missing in action" is used only to indicate that the whereabouts or status of an individual is not immediately known. It is not intended to convey the impression that the case is closed. I wish to emphasize that every effort is exerted continuously to clear up the status of our personnel. Under war conditions this is a difficult task as you must readily realize. Experience has shown that many persons reported missing in action are subsequently reported as being prisoners of war. However, since we are entirely dependent upon governments with which we are at war to forward this information, the War Department is helpless to expedite these reports.

In order to relieve financial worry on the part of the dependents of Military Personnel being carried in a missing status, Congress enacted (cont.) legislation which continues the pay, allowances and allotments of such persons until their status is definitely established.

Permit me to extend to you my heartfelt sympathy during this period of uncertainty.

Sincerely Yours,
ROBERT H. DUNLOP
Brigadier General

It took approximately two months for a letter to make its way from the POW camp to the United States, and Augie penned a letter as soon as he could. The letter most likely wouldn't have reached its destination until the middle of the summer when Augie's situation had already changed drastically. Information flowed into the prison camp much more readily. Some of the men befriended German guards, and bribed them with things that they had acquired through Red Cross packages. Cigarettes became a very popular tradable commodity. Remarkably, one of the POWs had gotten his hands on a radio which picked up BBC broadcasts from London. At midnight coded messages relayed other information such as the success of the Allied invasion during the summer of 1944. The Germans had announced over the camp loudspeakers that the invasion had been halted, but word among the POWs spread to the contrary thanks to the lone beacon of reliable information.

The Germans counted the prisoners twice a day at the prison camp. They assembled in the main courtyard and had suspicions that the radio existed, but were never able to locate it. According to Donatelli, Stalag Luft VI was filled with numerous relentless men who fearlessly put themselves in perilous situations to obtain information or attempt to escape. There were several escape attempts from the camp, and most of them ended miserably. One daring group attempted to dig a tunnel underneath the POW toilet facilty. The area was nothing more than a trench underneath a long line of wooden benches. In order to get to the tunnel, the men had to wade through human waste. Somehow, working in groups, the POWs broke through the wall of the trench and dug towards the fence. Using wood from the bed bunks as supports, they made tremendous progress. They cleverly distributed the dirt from the excavation project throughout the camp, including the surface of the POW makeshift basketball court. The project came to a miserable conclusion however when a Russian prisoner found himself sucked into the ground. The tunnel collapsed under his weight after a substantial rainfall the night before. The startled Russian didn't realize what he had fallen into, and began screaming at the top of his lungs as he frantically attempted to pull himself from the mud. The Germans came to his rescue and immediately began dismantling the underground escape route. Some theorized that the guards were aware that the POWs engaged in digging tunnels, but thought of them as more of a pastime than a legitimate way for prisoners to escape. That sentiment changed after 200 POWs executed a successful breakout through a series of tunnels at Luft 3. That story became popularized after the war in both book and motion picture called "The Great Escape." Most of the escapees died in the effort or were executed after recapture, and consequently the Germans clamped down on POW freedoms after the breakout.

Stalag Luft VI held thousands of men but the POW population often shifted as groups were transferred in and out of the camp for various reasons. Newly captured soldiers were added each week. During one such exchange, Donatelli was surprised to recognize one of the newly relocated men. He was the tail gunner on the same plane that Ed Dugan was on; the very same bomber that Augie watched spiral out of the sky.

"Brownie, glad as hell to see you," said Augie with his booming voice.

"Gladder to see you, Augie."

"What happened to the rest of the crew, what about Dugan," he asked?

"Dugan was in the bottom turret," said Brown, "when he got hit, we couldn't operate the turret mechanically to get him out. It was busted."

"Well, did ya get him out," Augie asked?

"Yeah," he answered, "but his eye was shot out, and half his nose was gone. He was in rough shape."

Hesitatingly, Donatelli asked, "did he make it?"

"I don't know, Augie," Brown replied, "all we could do was push him out of the plane; I saw his chute open, but that's it."

From Brown's bleak description, Donatelli was forced to assume that Dugan was more than likely dead. Several weeks later, the Germans brought in a new group of hospital prisoners. Donatelli walked to the gate as they were being carried in. He spotted another familiar face.

"Hey Dugan," Augie called out.

Ed recognized the voice, "where the hell are you, Augie? I can hear you, but I can't see you."

Dugan was blind.

"Hey Dugan," exclaimed a thrilled Augie, "I saw your plane go down and thought you were a goner."

"I don't know what happened, Augie," he said, "they must have thrown me out of the plane, because I'm still breathing."

Only two men survived from that plane; Brown, who was on his first flight, and Dugan. The rest of the crew was unable to escape. Despite the realization that their lives were in danger, the veteran crew opted to let the rookie and the injured Dugan bail out first.

"The men who died deserved some type of post-war recognition for their bravery, recalled Augie some forty years later, "but they never received it."

While the day-to-day life at the camp seemed to continue in an orderly fashion, the events that were storming on the horizon were anything but calm. The Russians were plowing through the German front in a major summer offensive. Their huge columns were headed directly for East Prussia. At the same time, not far from Stalag Luft VI, in Rastenberg, East Prussia, Hitler survived an assassination attempt at the hands of a senior officer, Colonel Claus Schenk von Stauffenberg. These major news events eventually filtered throughout the camp population, and though the Germans continued their charade of normalcy at the prison camp, the POWs knew that change was in the air.

FIVE

The March

It was the middle of July of 1944 when the men were summoned in groups for preparation of a sojourn outside the camp. None of the POWs knew what it was about, but they lined up dutifully at the far corner at the camp entrance. The airmen marched out of the camp and onto a dusty road. Locals watched and wondered what was going on as the men cascaded towards the train yard in Heydekrug, and were eventually packed aboard rail cars. The camp exodus wasn't conducted all at once, but rather in waves. Fifty men were jammed into each box car, and the train slowly advanced towards the port city of Memmel. To Augie's dismay the five hour train ride ended near a shipyard and the men were herded onto an old vessel.

The twilight of the early evening disappeared in an instant as the men were swallowed by the pitch-black darkness they encountered with each ladder rung as they descended below deck of an old barge. Although it was impossible to see anything, the low grumbling of voices gave the sense that there was a sea of men sitting below. As he neared the base of the ladder Augie's eyes finally adjusted to the darkness. He scanned the large open hull of the ship and was shocked to discover that there were hundreds of men packed onto the base of the ship like sardines. From a distance, a familiar voice shouted out.

"Hey Don, you've had it!"

The dark greeting came from Donatelli's friend, airman Jim Ballis.

"I'm not gonna say I'm happy to see you," said Augie as he grabbed the hand of his old friend from Portage, Pennsylvania.

"Seems like we've been down here a day already. They keep loading up," mumbled Ballis.

"Yeah, and there's at least 20 more men who are gonna be comin' down that ladder," said Augie.

This evacuation in July of 1944, which became known as the "Heydekrug Run," loaded more than 1,000 men into the bowels of two broken down Russian coal steamers named the "Isteburg" and the "Masuren." The ships were to cross the Baltic Sea, a voyage trip that would take three full days. The Belorussian offensive which had coincidentally forced the evacuation of Stalag Luft VI was codenamed Operation Bagration. Four Soviet army groups of 120 divisions composed of some 2.3 million troops plowed into the line, and overpowered the Germans who had less than half as many men. As a matter of necessity, the Germans had sent some units to France to counter the invasion of Normandy, and were outmatched by a ratio of nearly 10 to 1 in tanks and aircraft. By early July, the Germans had lost more than a half-million soliders.

As the minutes ticked by in slow motion, Augie felt that he had completely lost control over his destiny. He was hunkered down deep within the confines of a decrepit ship, in what seemed like deadly game of Russian roulette. If an Allied bomber decided that the ship was an appropriate target, it was entirely feasible that it would be sunk. The Russian Hammer and Cycle graced the side of the ship, but there was no guarantee that a night bomber crew would even discern or trust the emblem from the sky. It was in enemy waters, and therefore would be a legitimate target. There was also the additional substantial threat of mines, which were routinely dropped into the Baltic by British bomber crews with the intent of disturbing German shipping.

It was a gruesome possibility that crossed the mind of more than one man aboard the vessel. Deep within the ship, a sickly stench saturated the air. There were no toilet facilities except for several large barrels, and the smell was initially so debilitating that Donatelli found himself unable to urinate despite feeling the need to do so. As time went by, the air was so thick and suffocating that it became difficult to breath. The guards never ventured below because there was no room. Instead, they tied a long piece of rope to a bucket and lowered fresh water down. In an effort to get sleep, some tried to climb up to an iron casing that housed a metal rod for the ship's spinner. If a man managed to climb the nine feet up, then it was possible to stretch out along the long metal tube. The problem unfolded as the ship rocked back and forth, and men randomly slid off into the humanity below. Those who tried to fall asleep on the rod casing were awakened when they were sent sailing through the air. Elevating above the suffocating overcrowded deck made the fall seem worth the risk. Yet as the Baltic began producing large swells, it appeared as though ten or more men fell off in rapid succession. And with a bone-jarring thud, they crashed on top of the men who were situated below. To add to the nightmare was the loud sound of metal scraping against the hull of the ship. Men jumped from their comatose state to alarmed attention as the ghastly sound caused panic. The prisoners knew that the sound could have easily been that of a mine scraping the side of the ship.

Allied B-17s were known to drop bombs on a nearby German wharf. The planes, regardless of whether they were British or American, created a familiar drone to the airmen, followed by the sounds of bombs whistling through the air. There was nothing that might identify the two ships as transports for prisoners of war, a better assumption might be made that they were being used by the Nazis to transport supplies. The anticipation of one of those "friendly" bombs landing on the hull of the ship brought forth conjured images of the compartment flooding with water and a massive watery execution chamber. Donatelli could feel a shortness of breath with the realization of what might occur.

Very little conversation took place between the men, mostly because of the overwhelming sound of the engine, which clanked in the aft compartment. The second most prominent sound was an occasional loud cough. That changed rather abruptly when an array of distant explosions were heard outside the ship. Augie noticed through the darkness that the men sitting around him suddenly perked up with an unmistakable look of fear.

"Just relax," said Augie in a monotone voice, "there ain't no place to go."

"It's a good time to start prayin' to Mary mother of Jesus," a nearby voice chimed in."

Augie said that he imagined hearing a loud whistling sound, followed by distant explosions. Images flashed in Donatelli's mind of men struggling with their own friends to keep their heads above water.

Augie cursed his own bad fortune. How could he wind up in such a place? This was hell on earth. After all, he was a tail gunner – how could he die on a damned Russian coal barge? The feeling of helplessness was almost overwhelming. There was nothing to do except grind his teeth between prayers and maintain thoughts of his family. Surely if the boat sank his body would never be found and no one would know how he died. No one back home would ever even possibly imagine.

Hours later it was decided that the men were to be allowed to relieve themselves deckside, and so they ascended the ladder. It was no easy task. Wobbly legs strained as they ascended up each rung. Once on deck, the bright light blinded Augie for what seemed like at least a minute, but through his squinting glare he witnessed a shadow lurch forward and dive over the side of the ship. What followed was a collection of loud commands from the German guards. Apparently the POW had decided that this was an opportune time to escape, but Donatelli quickly surmised that it was not. From the comments that soon circulated amongst the airman, it was evident that the prisoner had lost his sanity. He had decided that he wanted to escape or end the torture.

Three guards converged to the side of the ship and without hesitation they opened fire into the water. When some of the men edged closer to see whether the man was hit, one of the guards threatened the POWs into backing away from the ship's railing. The escaping soldier might have had time for only a few strokes in the cold water. Augie wasn't able to get a look over the side, but he discerned the man's death from the reaction of the guards who seemed content to snuff out the young man's life as if it was all part of a day's work. Very little emotion was displayed when they hit their mark and surprisingly little additional anger was vented towards anyone else. Eventually the boat ride reached its conclusion without much ceremony, and the men were quickly herded off the boat, across a dock in the city of Swinemunde. The airmen were again shackled in chains and herded onto another train and transported southward. After a terribly crowded ride in the multiple box cars, the men arrived at the train yard and were not far from their next prison camp, Stalag Luft IV.

What ensued was a demonstration designed to break the men's fortitude and remaining spirit. The guards paired them off by two in what began is a brisk march. German shepherds flanked the POWs as they trudged forward. At first it was difficult to get one's legs attuned to movement after the confinement aboard the boat and then the cramped train ride. Some POWs were forced to jog the two plus miles. Others were given the privilege of walking with bayonets pointed at their backs. Some of the stragglers were even assaulted or attacked by the guard dogs. The guards urged the exhausted prisoners to pick up their pace, and with chains clanging and dogs barking, a collection of men lost their balance and fell to the ground. The punishment rained forth in the form of stabbings and additional beatings. The lunacy continued as contorted bodies piled up and those who simply gave up remained motionless in the dirt. Donatelli somehow managed to keep his feet moving and his group arrived near the entrance of the prison camp. Heaving for air, the survivors of the deadly gauntlet were escorted into a room, 12 men at a time, and forced to strip naked. There were six guards in the room – with one of them standing 6 foot 7 inches tall – he was later nicknamed "Big Stoop" by some POWs.

Here's how Donatelli described the ensuing events.

"The big guard raised hell with every prisoner, especially if the man happened to be wearing a religious bead. He hit one man in the small of his back with the base of his rifle. As the 12 of us stood there I was hopin' none of the younger guys made any foolish moves. After ordering us to strip, they commanded the prisoners to go through a range of movements in order to make certain that no one was concealing anything. They instructed us to raise our arms up, then we were asked to lean forward. The big German stood in front of the room demonstrating movements as he shouted out the corresponding German word for each motion. He demonstrated the bending motion and then shouted out ' Do it again!'"

"Es macht wieder!"

Donatelli misunderstood the order. He remained motionless. It appeared to be a signal of defiance. Without hesitation, the guard stormed toward him.

"What the hell do ya want from me?"

The guard lifted his heavy boot and smashed it down with great force on Augie's bare foot. The soldier behind followed with a jolt to the back of Augie's head. Donatelli dropped to the ground with blood streaming out of his left foot. He tried to stumble back to his feet but soon drifted into unconsciousness.

Prisoners of war marching into Stalag Luft IV. Allied POWs, Donatelli included, suffered a brutal introduction to this camp. Photo courtesy Donald Kremper.

The brutal introduction to Stalag Luft IV proved to set a tone. The camp eventually housed more than 9,000 men, and the conditions were clearly a drastic downgrade from the previous camp. The daily rations included boiled potatoes and a soup mixture made up of potato, turnip, carrot, sauerkraut, rutabaga, and horse meat. The concoction was distributed in a wooden bowl and accompanied with a daily ration of bread that was made up of rye, sugar beets, and tree flower. The Red Cross packages that filtered through were filled with items such as corned beef, vegetable stew, peanut butter, canned fish, chocolate and cigarettes. Oftentimes, the contents of the packages were traded to the German guards in return for favors, but many times the packages themselves were intercepted.

Stalag Luft IV, Lager A barracks 1, 2, and 3. The double barbed wire fences stood some thirty feed behind a low warning fence. Courtesy of Donald Kremper

There was no tolerance for any type of secret operation, and the Nazis who ran Stalag Luft IV attempted to be very diligent, especially after the various escape attempts at other camps. The camp itself wasn't well organized, however, since its construction was never fully completed because of a lack of construction material.

Part of the harsh treatment no doubt stemmed from the fact that the war was going badly for the Nazis. By contrast, the prison camps that housed German soldiers in the United States were completely opposite the conditions that Donatelli and his fellow POWs endured. There were more than 500 camps in the US, and by 1945 there were nearly half a million foreign prisoners. Some prisoners described their

POW experience as life in a golden cage, however there were recorded incidents of foreign prisoners who were killed during escape attempts.

Stalag Luft IV proved to be home for six months. It could only be described as a wretched existence. Armed guards patrolled the camp grounds 24 hours a day with dogs at their side, and they needed very little excuse to beat a prisoner if he seemed to arouse the slightest suspicion. The horrendously overcrowded conditions forced men to sleep on the ground in tents, and men became preoccupied with letters that sifted in from family back in the United States and discovery of how the war effort was going. The Nazis were careful to read each of the incoming letters and darken out portions of the letter that they deemed leaked any sort of war news that might spur the POWs to action. However, the Nazis couldn't control the steady stream of new prisoners, who were only too happy to share war news. There were also occasional distant explosions from the east that indicated the Red Army was continuing its advance.

As the winter months ebbed forward it became common knowledge among the POWs that the Germans had generated an offensive that became known as the Battle of the Bulge. With the Germans being pressed from both fronts, the supply line to the prison camps dwindled to a trickle. Combined with an extremely harsh winter, intolerable conditions turned even worse. Donatelli described meals composed of soup concoctions made of mashed potato and scant leftovers from the guard's dinners. All sorts of combinations were tossed into boiling water to generate bizarre hobo-like creations. With gallows humor intact, the men called one murky dish grass soup. The ingredients were deconstructed to be snails, grass, and other ghoulish ingredients unknown. When horses and dogs became casualties of war, the carcasses found their way to the prison camp and the men enjoyed soup made with horse meat. It got to the point where some men even set traps around the camp with the hope of catching birds or rats. With so little food to maintain their youthful vigor, the POWs spent an inordinate amount of time conserving energy. Many of the airmen began to succumb to a variety of terrible conditions including dysentery. Manic runs to the latrine were not uncommon, and since men stopped bathing and washing because of the extreme cold as the temperatures dipped to below zero, the hygiene was dreadful. To say that morale drifted to new lows might be an understatement, and the uncertainty of how they might be liberated proved yet another burden. In describing these scenarios so many decades after the fact, Augie used the phrase "holy hell" countless times. The previous prison camp, Stalag Luft VI, seemed like a distant fond memory. In retrospect, his newfound vocation of prison camp umpire was simply a whimsical diversion that he thought that he would never live to tell. At this point survival was the all important word; it was the dominant pastime.

With reports stewing that Hitler had contemplated using the prisoners of war as human shields and that the distinct but unspoken possibility remained that he might order a mass execution of all POWs. The holiday season offered a slight emotional reprieve as men gathered to pray and sing traditional Christmas songs. The guards paid close attention to these religious services because it was thought that they were simply rouses to plan an escape. Instead they were important emotional outlets that gave an inkling of hope. But it wasn't long before the brief respite changed course with the New Year. With January of 1945 came a resumed downward spiral in morale. The closed quarters of the draft laden barracks became a breeding ground for sickness. This was hell on earth, and it was difficult to imagine how the final outcome might be a good one. Perhaps the young airman who jumped shipside into the Baltic Sea had it right. He swam frantically towards the shoreline, as though it were a bright red exit sign in a dark movie house. Perhaps he saw it as an escape, a way to exit the play. Could it have been a calculated suicide that was not self-inflicted? He threw himself at the not so subtle mercy of the guards. But it was an end to the misery and suffering. His body had sunk to a watery grave, but was he better off than enduring the horrors that would undoubtedly ensue.

* * *

The Nazis gave little warning. The information came during the morning assembly — every single occupant of Stalag Luft IV was to be moved to another unnamed POW camp. The German commanding officer gave no reason for the move. So it was during the early morning hours of February 6, 1945 when there was a mass exodus of 10,000 men. They exited in groups that were a bit more manageable: 300 men at a time peacefully marched their way through more than a foot of snow, heading to locations unknown. They walked through a fenced in-corridor to begin a ponderous march through the frigid cold. For those prisoners who could not walk, because of sickness or injury, there was a wagon with the capacity to accommodate only 55 men. The guards left it up to the prisoners to decide which of the men were in bad enough shape to merit a ride. An unbiased count could have easily come up with more than 200 whose injuries made them unfit to walk for one mile much less walk for a month.

"I guarantee you a lot of these guys aren't gonna make it," said Augie muttering to himself in a low monotone voice.

Stanley Andrusek, who happened to be standing close enough to Donatelli to hear the dire prediction, answered back. "The more of us that drop the less prisoners they have to worry about."

The camp's commanding officer barked out instructions to the guards, who immediately began snapping the POW's into motion to begin the pilgrimage. German soldiers armed with both rifles and machine guns prepared to flank both sides of the line; their main task was to make certain no one attempted an escape. Everyone knew that the likelihood was quite high that there would probably be several escape attempts along the way. The guards expected it. The instructions were barked out for men to walk within an arm's length of each other. They had abandoned the idea of chaining the airmen together as they had in the past because there were simply too many men, and the process of chaining them would prove to be too ponderous. Packed together like an army of ants, the POWs cascaded out of the prisoner of war camp. There wasn't much talk among the men, just a quiet sense of relief to leave a prison camp that they would gladly never return to. There was a repeated warning given, making it clear that there would be no leniency for those who strayed off path. The price for disobeying that particular command would be very high. There was no mistaking the disdain that some of the guards held for the captured airmen. Allied bomber crews were referred to in German as *Luftgangsters* or *Terror Fliegers* (air gangsters or terror fliers). The Nazis felt the air raids often coldly targeted innocent citizens and factory workers. This was the sentiment of some of the prison guards. Literally, as the POWs marched, American and English bombers were shredding German cities. Innocent women and children were never targeted but were no doubt blameless victims;

the cruel nature of war was anything but impersonal. Donatelli had more than his share of exchanges with Nazi guards – and was no doubt destined for a few more.

During the long journey, items that were stockpiled from those care packages were all used. Since the men were told that the march would not last long, some decided to dispense with supplies, rather than carry them, an unfortunate error in judgment. No one could have possibly imagined that the entire trek would cover many hundreds of miles by foot in the dead of winter, and last nearly two full months.

Since the Germans were unable to transport any sort of food, the POWs were often left to their own wiles to make do with whatever rations they were able to carry themselves. The men were to walk for more than two months, and keep a pace of 20 to 25 miles per day.

"You speak Polish, don't you?" asked Donatelli of his walking partner Stanley Andrusek.

"Are you kidding… *Robi mowie jezyk Polski?* Why do you wanna know?"

"It'll come in handy," was Augie's only reply.

The morning sky was dark gray and wisps of fog emanated from the lips of all the airmen. Some were in reasonably good spirits to start, because they were leaving the camp that they despised. But none were naïve to the fact that this march would put everyone to the test each and every day, especially on days when the temperature remained below 30 degrees Fahrenheit. The prevailing hope was that the Nazis would order a mid-day respite if it got too cold, but that rarely happened. Initially, there was a certain amount of glee in escaping the sameness of life as a prisoner of war. After months of seeing the same bare buildings, tents, and barbed wire fences, the new surroundings brought a certain odd sense of excitement. The column of rag tag POWs trudged down the main road that wound its way through open farmland, but as the days went by and as the horrific bone chilling weather continued, the march became a battle for survival. As fate would have it, this was to be one of the coldest German winters ever recorded. There were times when the men trudged through knee-deep snow, and other times when the temperatures plunged to below zero. This extreme weather could easily sap the strength from healthy well-fed men. These were gaunt, tired, and sick POWs. The men often walked all day with no lunch, little rest, and very little clean water. The prisoners were wearing the same clothing they had worn for months prior to starting the march, now the cloths had become filthy from sleeping and resting in the dirt and snow. Once the Red Cross rations that filled their backpacks began to run low, it wasn't uncommon for the Germans to allow the prisoners to find their own food at the end of the day, and then allow them to build fires and cook the meals themselves. On occasion, the POWs scrounged up a stray chicken, but starving men were not above hunting down anything. They stumbled upon dead farm animals, perhaps killed during combat, or rodents often were turned into meals. Men also indulged in eating grain that was meant for livestock or just plain grass. When possible, they also begged and traded with passing civilians. The Germans provided bread on a few occasions, and also provided a watery vegetable soup. Some of the men had carried the contents of their Red Cross parcels in their backpacks, and rationed the supplies the best they could.

The mood had become very somber, because the reality of the predicament was a heavy burden. Not only was there trepidation over the sanity of this trek, but also the ultimate reason.

Why were we marching at all? Were the Russians already storming through Stalag Luft IV and gaining at our heels? Or were the Nazis simply marching the POW's to their death? Were they waiting for Hitler's final directive? Or would the men be used as some sort of bargaining chip?

It was late afternoon and little was being said among the men. All energy was being expended in keeping pace. Their occasional commands were like piercing daggers when shouted out. The words were also purposeful reminders that the guards remained alert.

"*Laufen sie schneller,*" Walk faster – came the order.

"Why are they moving us?" asked Donatelli to one of the guards whom he knew understood some English.

The guard responded with a shrug of the shoulder and a brief sarcastic response, "*Die Einrichtungen sind besser.*"

Augie burst out with a sarcastic laugh, catching some of the men around him by surprise. Heads turned to see what was so funny amidst this cold, dreary march. Donatelli translated the guard's claim.

"He said that the place we're going to has better facilities."

"Yeah," shouted another POW, "the facilities to do us in!"

Moments of dark levity were few and far between, and usually had a strong bent towards gallows humor or food. Donatelli commented on what he believed were his mother's best recipes, including palenta with sauce. This kind of talk eventually stopped because it proved best to not think of food. As the days wore on, the harsh conditions weakened even the hardiest of the airmen. Some, who weighed 150 pounds at the outset, had lost in excess of 20 pounds, and there was a horrid array of conditions that spread among the ranks including: typhoid, pneumonia, diphtheria, and tuberculosis. Even the sickest of the POWs had no other choice but to drink from ditches beside the road or eat snow, because those were the only sources of water. A doctor among the ranks helped as much as humanly possible considering the conditions and lack of sufficient medical supplies – all he could prescribe to help stave off dysentery were pieces of charcoal, which when sucked on would theoretically stave off the disease. Donatelli described dysentery as the most insidious of ailments, because of the involuntary and bloody bowel movements.

During some stretches of the march, the POWs found themselves walking side by side with German or Polish refugees, who were themselves escaping the advancing Russian troops. Some of these individuals and families were pulling carts filled with their life possessions. The tragedy and irony of war seemed apparent as average citizens and captured POWs suffered side by side on a long country road. The faces of those people made an impact on some of the prisoners, including Donatelli; there were young women with children and old men who could barely walk. No doubt that countless number of these innocent refugees were lost during the exodus. More than six decades after the war, mass graves were uncovered in Malbork, Poland that held the skeletal remains of 2,000 people; many with bullet wounds to the head. The bodies were discovered by accident as the land was being prepared for construction of apartment buildings. By some estimates more than two million died or were killed in the process of being uprooted from their homes and died from either exposure, lack of food, sickness, as they fled the massive Soviet counterattack.

It was a trying test when the total number of sick men among the POWs quadrupled and decisions were made as to who would ride in the wagon and who would walk.

When they were able to procure an extra wagon, some of the healthier POWs offered to help pull the wagon since there were no horses. This was no easy task because the road side was often covered with patches of snow or ice and these wagons could hold more than twenty men. Donatelli chimed in on who should walk and who would ride. His rank was Staff Sergeant – but he ranked higher simply by the force of his personality, his swagger, and the fact that at age 29, he was older than many of his fellow airmen. The toughness was something that came from his years in the Pennsylvania coal mines, digging for hours on end from his knees in dangerous candle-lit shafts. Augie had been through much since those days, and now the march had taken on a life of its own. It was something that seemed to have no conclusion or mercy. What was initially promised to be a three day stroll had turned into a long exodus – day after day, step after grueling step.

On some of the bitterly cold nights, the men occupied barns. They herded themselves in and packed into the wooden structure like sardines; when they slept in the open, the POWs huddled close together to generate some heat. No one cared that everyone was filthy, it was just a matter of survival.

Donatelli and Stanley continued to walk side by side. In front of them was a younger man who Augie referred to as the Italian. The men were leery of him because he spoke only Italian and no English. He had arrived at the camp two weeks prior to the march. The camp was composed of American, English, and Russian prisoners of war, but the men didn't often intermingle.

The Italian confided a small modicum of information to Donatelli, but only because Augie spoke a little Italian. He told Donatelli that he was from Boston and that his parents lived in Naples, Italy. When Donatelli asked about Boston, the Italian never responded with detail. He didn't know about the city's North End district, Fenway Park, or its fishing trade which he claimed to be a part of.

Some theorized that the Italian was a spy placed among them by the Nazis, but the Germans were much too cunning to use someone as ill equipped as the Italian to be an information gatherer. He couldn't understand English – or at least he pretended not to understand. It didn't add up. To break the boredom of the march, Donatelli decided to push the issue for all to hear.

"So che lie sono una spia Tedesca – I know you're a German spy," Augie accused in Italian.

The Italian responded with a startled look. *No, no, no- perche?*

"I'll tell you why," said Augie as his voice raised. "You say you are from Boston but you don't know anything about it. Who are the Red Sox?

The Italian responded with a poker face.

Donatelli threatened the frail looking younger man. If he didn't divulge his true identity that his life might be in jeopardy. The Italian seemed unflustered at the suggestion. Donatelli, losing his patience, hurled off-color remarks in Italian with the hope that it might make him lose his cool, but the mystery soldier remained emotionless.

Augie was always apt to react with his gut instinct. Sometimes during extreme circumstances his actions got him in trouble. He decided that the Italian wasn't worth the trouble, not in the middle of this long hellish walk.

By Christmas, Augie had sent one correspondence to his family, but hadn't received an answer prior to the start of the march. He often hoped that his mother would be spared receiving a second letter declaring her son's death, yet he knew for certain that she was better off not knowing that he was engaged in this long death march across enemy soil.

Details about the war's progress were hard to come by behind the enemy lines. It was only a matter of time before the allied flanks reached the Rhine on the western front, yet precious little information about the advancing forces came to the prisoners of war. Rumors had trickled in that the Allied campaign was going well, and the men had guessed that the entire reason for shifting the prison camp had to do with the allied forces breaking through the German fronts. Clearly, these were desperate times for the Nazis and the motivation for their actions were being quietly second-guessed even by those who were responsible for carrying the orders out. Guards who marched with the POWs even hinted from time to time that the war was near an end. The logic of moving the entire prison of war camp may have been a moot one. When Russian forces whisked past the camp en route to Berlin, they would not receive the satisfaction of liberating their comrades, but would instead find empty camps. Another reason was that by keeping the POW's in their control, the Nazis refused to admit defeat and sent a message that they would continue to fight. The Normandy invasion had already taken place. In December, the Germans had launched a counter-offensive that failed when American and British forces successfully withstood the infamous Battle of the Bulge. Many months of fighting still lay ahead but the sense that the war might soon reach its end became prevalent as the Allies punched their way towards the heart of Nazi Germany.

For the POWs, much uncertainly still remained - everything was up in the air - and nothing was taken for granted. There were too many unknown details, and some of the men decided to fill in the blanks with the thought that this was a trek towards death.

Forward progress was often curtailed because of weather, impassable roads, and the cumbersome progress of the large group. Patches of snow and an occasional collection of farmhouses and barns interrupted green rolling hills. In this leg of the journey there were no thick forests, just open farmland. The brief elation the men felt upon leaving the prison camp had long since dissipated and the conversations became less and less jovial as the days wore on.

When it came time to negotiate a slippery incline in the road, an airman who was suffering from pneumonia slipped and fell to the ground. It was not simply a case of exhaustion or him losing his footing. The fall had knocked him unconscious. The sick man was ordered to get to his feet. Two fellow POWs tried to drag him up the hill but a combination of poor footing and dead weight made the task impossible. Guards pushed the POWs forward and allowed the sick man to fall to the ground until the entire column marched over the hill. The guard patiently hovered above him as if to make certain that he was not perpetuating a ruse to escape. He was most likely put out of his misery.

When twilight came, the massive column stopped at a clearing surrounded by a heavy growth of pine trees and shrubs. On most nights the men slept in barns. They were packed into the wooden buildings so tightly that it was not possible for them to lie down; the overflow of men were forced to sleep outside. When there was enough room to lie down the men slept in the filthy straw or damp dirt. The smell of the dysenteric POWs who had slept there before still hung in the air, and coughing sounds of men with pneumonia continued through the night.

Donatelli saw to it that he sat alone with Stanley. They dug into their dinner, which was nothing more than a boiled potato. The men huddled in close proximity to generate some warmth and reveled in the fact that they were finally off their feet. The end of the day was something to look forward to. By now the walk had extended to three weeks in duration. Donatelli privately concluded that for him, the march had ended.

"Remember that question I asked you about how well you spoke Polish?" asked Donatelli. Stanley paid little attention to the question as he concentrated intently on eating every morsel of his potato dinner.

"Well, the reason I asked you was because you and I are gonna check out. We're gonna find ourselves some Polish farmers who are nice enough to put us up."

"You're crazy. Shut up and eat," Stanley mumbled in an annoyed tone of voice.

Donatelli leaned forward until he was nearly nose to nose with his partner. "That's right, I'm eating my grub and then when it gets a little darker you and I are going to get up and make a break for that brush. If we time it right it's easy. The guards are tired. They think we are too."

"Whaddaya mean think! I ain't movin," countered Stanley.

"You're coming. We're gonna find some Polish sympathizers. Got that? That's an order."

Stanley huffed in disbelief, but he knew it was futile to argue.

Just then, Augie caught the eye of the Italian who happened to be sitting alone some 10 feet away. Andrusek noticed him, too.

"That guy is gonna blow the whistle. Forget it."

Donatelli said nothing but then slowly brought his finger to his lips motioning for the Italian to keep quiet. There was no telling how he would react to an escape. If he was really a spy, he would no doubt alert the guards.

A low, thick layer of clouds that shielded the moon and stars gave Donatelli and Andrusek the benefit of darkness. The Nazi guards paced back and forth, crisscrossing the perimeter of the campsite.

The men determined the amount of time they would have when both guards were farthest away yet before they turned to pace back.

They calculated that there was at the most a scant seven second window of opportunity. The nearest cluster of bushes was approximately 100 feet away. They hoped that they could run the distance in a crouched position in 15 seconds, but at some point in the run it might be necessary to dive to the ground and crawl for cover.

"I'll call it out," whispered Donatelli.. "Get ready."

Donatelli glanced over at the Italian who appeared to be sleeping, and both guards' attentions were elsewhere. It was time.

"Now."

The men moved side by side in a low crouch, careful to make short, quick steps. The object was to move quickly and avoid anything that might make a substantial sound – branches, mud, ice, anything. Their eyes were glued as much to the ground as it was to the cover ahead. The brush was getting closer – still no sound from the guards. As they approached some pine trees, Augie decided to stay on his feet. Now, they were only seconds away from cover. Still silence.

"Holy hell," said Donatelli breathing hard, "they have no damn clue."

As they peered back toward the campsite, the silhouette of the nearest guard appeared to stop. Perhaps to light a cigarette – or perhaps he noticed something.

"Let's keep moving," whispered Stanley.

The men kept a brisk pace. For the first 15 minutes they ran as quickly as they could on the uneven terrain. Fear kept them in constant motion. Then in the ensuing hour, they ran and walked intermittently, moving as best they could through the trees and bushes, while negotiating through the darkness. There was no way of knowing whether they had been discovered, no way of knowing if the Nazis were in pursuit. The only thing that they could be certain of was that the more distance they put between themselves and the campsite, the better their chances would be. There were no visible stars and the trees and land features meant nothing. The only navigation available was the observation of moss at the base of certain trees. Moss grew predominantly to the north, so they continued their trek in a westerly direction. Finally, after one hour of this frantic pace they stopped to catch their breath.

"If we live through this," said Stanley as he heaved for air, "it'll be a miracle. Look what you got us into, Donatelli!"

"We're gonna be fine. I was right about getting the hell out of there. I was right about the Italian. I don't know who the hell he is, but he was no spy."

It wasn't until after the war that the Italian's story was revealed in headlines back in the United States. It turned out that he wasn't at all who he said he was, but no one imagined his true identity. The revelation unfolded in cruel fashion. Only months after victory had been declared in Europe, the family of the mysterious soldier received a telegram stating that he was in good health and coming home. They were ecstatic. Especially since their son had been reported missing in action for nearly a year. However, the anticipation of their loved one's arrival was met with a cruel twist of fate when they discovered that the man posing as their son was an imposter. In actuality he was a deserter of the Italian army who had stolen the dog tag and uniform from the body of a dead American soldier – the real American soldier had died in combat. When the Nazis captured him, the Italian knew he would be safer claiming to be a prisoner of war rather than a deserter. He continued the charade with the hope of making free safe passage to the United States, but upon his arrival in the U.S., he was confronted and finally extradited to Italy where he faced trial for desertion, impersonating an American enlisted man, and a host of other charges for which he spent considerable time in prison.

Augie, feeling a sudden sense of urgency, yanked Andrusek to his feet and the men stumbled forward. It was so dark that the best they could do was walk briskly, feeling their way across the hilly terrain to avoid stumbling into an embankment. There was an ever-present sense of fear mixed with a feeling of imminent danger. The only sounds they heard were the sounds of their own boots pounding into the snow, and a steady diet of branches to the face as they pushed through the woods. The combination of cold face and hands juxtaposed with the feeling of trickling sweat underneath the knee length coats became uncomfortable. After several hours of this, the exhausted men huddled behind a boulder. They could run no farther.

At daybreak, came a distant sound of planes. The noise cut into the silence, and brought Donatelli and Andrusek stumbling to their feet, as they came to a shocking discovery. It was an unmistakable drone; strikingly similar to the sound they were familiar with in air battle. It was a sound they hadn't heard in months. The two Americans had spent the night in the shadow of a German air base stocked with row upon row of Focke-Wulfs as far as the eye could see. They had stumbled into the lion's den, the last place on earth they wanted to be. Though they had walked through the night, a sudden burst of adrenalin brought the men to a complete state of alertness as they looked everywhere for any sign of guards patrolling the area. Then from the distance came an unmistakable escalating roar of an engine approaching from behind.

"For God's sake," Augie barked, "whatever you do – don't run!"

The Focke-Wulf buzzed overhead only a couple of hundred yards from the ground. He came in at an altitude in which the pilot had a clear view of the two escapees. As Donatelli and Andrusek turned, they immediately noticed the pilot was flapping his wings and was no doubt questioning their identity. If they gave the appearance of being startled there was a chance that the pilot would decide to fire a machine gun burst in their direction. Donatelli quickly raised his hand as if to send a friendly salute. The plane buzzed by overhead without firing. The men quickly realized that the pilot would most likely radio their position to the control tower, and that there was an imminent danger that guards might soon arrive on the scene. There was nothing that could be done to circumvent the airport, so the men walked in the general direction from which they came.

Fatigue and a lack of food and drink had already become an issue only 12 hours into the escape. They would have to survive on whatever the countryside would provide them; melted snow became the liquid of sustiance.

Avoiding all contact was the mission in the days ahead. Nights were spent sleeping tucked away in enbankments, caves, or inside an abandoned structure. The snowy forest provided little in the way of nourishment, meals were gathered by stealing them. On two separate occasions, dried salted ham and milk were cautiously taken from barns in the dead of the night, other times eggs were stolen. Progress was slow since they were forced to circumvent the main roads during the day, and in order to avoid all contact they decided to do the brunt of their travel through the forests. Their progress was not only curtailed by the weather and difficult terrain, but the nighttime also proved to be the best time to steal food.

There was only so much of the constant cold that the human body could endure, but there were few opportunities when the men could afford to chance the luxury of shelter. One night the temperature dropped well below freezing with cutting winds that made it difficult to breathe. The escaped POWs only option was to seek relief from the bitter cold or freeze to death. The decision was made to seek shelter in a hayloft. The plan was to remain submerged in a large pile of hay until several hours before the crack of dawn when they would make a hasty retreat into the forest. The presence of cows in the barn helped keep things quite a bit warmer. The newfound warmth lulled the men into a deep sleep. Not even the howling wind disturbed their slumber.

As dawn broke, they were awakened to the sound of children's voices. They were playing loudly in the barn. Donatelli peered through the hay and saw a young boy, no older then nine, racing toward him. He knew that there was no way he could injure the child to keep him quiet, but perhaps he could grab him and hold his mouth. No chance. The boy hurled himself directly into Donatelli, and then slithered out of his grasp and fell back to the ground. When the youngster came to the realization of his discovery he shouted at the top of his lungs.

"Ruskies! Ruskies! Ruskies!

The child apparently had been told of the Russian advances and came to the conclusion that the two American airmen were Russian soldiers. Both Donatelli and Stanley charged toward the door with the hope that they could somehow streak past whatever came their way. Instead, they ran directly into a man holding a double-barreled shotgun. He was a farmer in the midst of organizing the workers for that morning's chores. He pointed his gun directly at Andrusek, then to Donatelli, and then finally back to Andrusek. Both men stopped dead in their tracks – the Americans remained motionless with their opened hands raised in front of them.

Donatelli spoke in a calm but direct tone, *"Nein – don't shoot!"*

That was the end of it. The farmer said nothing as he lowered the long shotgun to his hip and herded the men behind a heavy wooden door and to the basement of a Baron's house. The only consolation that remained was that the cellar was warmer than the barn, and that Donatelli and Stanley finally had an opportunity for more sleep.

When they awoke it was almost as though a certain throbbing

numbness had overcome them both physically and emotionally. Perhaps it was because their future was as uncertain as ever. Punishment was the expected recourse for their escapade, either a beating or something far worse. The possibility of being locked up in solitary confinement was still very much a reality after their relocation to a new prison camp. As they were whisked away they came to the realization that if it wasn't for the misfortune of the sub-freezing weather, and the ill-timed gaffe of oversleeping, they might have actually found their way to freedom.

* * *

Prisoners of War line up for assembly at Stalag Luft IV. Roll Call was held when the German guards chose to check the barracks, which was done at random times during the day. Photo courtesy Donald Kremper

It was 1945, the war was still raging in Europe and in the Pacific, but the tide was clearly turning in favor of the Allied Forces. Information filtered through to the prisoners of war rather sparingly, but rumors were flying fast and furious. The Americans were plodding toward the heart of Germany from the west while the Russians were converging on Berlin from the East. The Red Army had pushed its forces toward the outskirts of Warsaw and had compiled a massive force for a final assault into Germany planned for April. Meanwhile, the Allied air offensive continued its strategic attacks into Germany by bombing key targets such as airfields, dams, and factories. The United States Air Force led by Lt. General Carl Spaatz, commander of the U.S. strategic Air Forces in Europe, favored pinpoint bombing of targets. The British RAF bombers specialized in saturation night bombing, which entailed dropping a large number of bombs in the general area of a target with the intent of doing as much damage as possible. The combined strategies brought the German infrastructure to a grinding halt.

Donatelli had ample time to lay awake nights pondering the cruelty of some of the atrocities he witnessed first hand. Battling the enemy at 20,000 feet with guns blazing was an expected danger of war. So was hurling himself out of a damaged B-17, and becoming a POW, but he could never have imagined some of the other things that he lived through. They were things that haunted him his entire life. After his recapture, he found himself at the mercy of slave labor guards in Brandenburg. Donatelli stated that he was forced to participate in the digging of mass graves designed for Russian soldiers. The Nazis used POWs to dump human carcasses into a long mass grave. Even some 40 years after the experience, Augie had difficulty describing the stomach-wrenching task. He grimaced as he tried. "I remember piles of bones." There were untold numbers of Russians buried near Brandenburg.

Whenever one of the Americans walked past a Russian prison barracks, he'd invariably hear, "Hey, Yankee!" That was the collective nickname for any American.

"The Russians always hoped that we would toss them some extra food. The care packages were nonexistent for Russian soldiers and the Germans seemed to treat them with lower regard than the rest of the prisoners. For the most part, the Stalag diet was composed of bread and a boiled potato. At dinnertime, Russian prisoners by the dozen came into the American barracks looking for handouts. One night Augie was given what seemed to be an unusually large potato, so he decided to give out a few pieces to one Russian. "Yankee, thanks" was his reply. No sooner did the phrase leave his lips than he was surrounded by other soldiers seeking another handout.

"Big mistake, Donatelli," said an American airman who happened to be standing nearby, "those guys will be hanging around you like a bunch of pigeons waiting for you to feed 'em from now on."

After that, Donatelli found it more prudent to limp out of the barracks and found a quiet spot to eat his food in peace. Normally it doesn't take too much food to keep a man alive, but when you combine a poor diet with physical labor, it wasn't uncommon for a man to lose 30 or 40 pounds off his body weight while a prisoner. There was a French prisoner by the name of Jule who had a unique work style that he used to combat the problem. A technique he was more than happy to share with Augie one day when the pair was asked to saw through a large fallen tree. With a circumference of at least six feet it would make for a substantial barricade. The two prisoners were given a long crosscut saw with large handles on each end. Augie was accustomed to digging for coal, but using a five foot long saw was another matter. Jule, however, was quite the expert. The men began tearing away at the wood but when the guard walked away, Jule decided it was time to take a break.

"A little bit work…A little bit eat"

The men stopped to eat some bread that the Frenchman had smuggled away in his coat. At the end of the day Jule picked up a piece of wood and slipped it underneath his coat. At night it got cold in the barracks and the Frenchman decided that the wood would come in handy. Unfortunately a guard spotted a piece of the wood jutting from the coat and ripped the front of the coat open. The guard wrestled the piece of wood from Jule and began beating him with it until the Frenchman collapsed to the ground. Donatelli helped Jule to his feet and led him back to the barracks. The next morning Jule's spirit seemed unaffected by the incident, in fact he approached Augie who happened to be standing within earshot of the guard who had beaten him up and brightly yelped, "Bon Jour, August!"

He then leaned in close to Augie and said, "Bien fine al guere." The war is almost over.

Word came of President Franklin Delano Roosevelt's death about a week after it actually occurred in April of 1945. The men couldn't help but feel a profound sense of sadness with the loss of such an inspirational leader and a great source of confidence and American pride. Only two months prior he had been at the Yalta conference in Russia with Churchill and Stalin mapping out details of the Allies' final assault on Germany. The very last speech Roosevelt delivered might have served as an inspiration to the prisoners. "The only limit to our realization of tomorrow," said Roosevelt "will be our doubts of today. Let us move forward with strong and active faith."

Exactly one month after Roosevelt's death, the Red Army was on the verge of liberating the prison camp. Over the months, the Nazi defenses had been dealt crippling blows from numerous Allied air strikes, yet overwhelming them was still a difficult task because of the fight till' death mind set of some of the ground troops. The camp was located at the top of a hill, making it difficult for the Russians to overtake, and the Germans also maintained a certain amount of air support, which effectively curtailed Russian advances.

After about a week's time, Allied bombers destroyed the Nazi airbase, which helped weaken their resolve immensely, and the Russians eventually stormed the hill. As Donatelli described it, the sight of Red Army soldiers cascading into that prison camp was surreal. It was midnight as the large tanks grinded up the hill and smashed their way through fences and anything else that stood against their advance. With the German resistance crushed the tanks overran an entire section of the compound in a matter of minutes, carving their way through wooden buildings as though they were made of cardboard. As far as the prisoners of war were concerned, the Nazis were officially finished. As the Red Army advanced, incredible jubilation shot through the camp, the freed Russian prisoners were especially celebrating wildly, quite happy to be reunited with their comrades. The screaming and hugging made it seem like a wild international New Year's Eve party.

"Freedom at last!" no matter what language, the sentiment was the same.

After about ten minutes or so of elation Donatelli came to the sudden realization that the Russians could care less about helping anyone. There was no offer of transportation, food, or any assistance whatsoever – they moved directly through the camp and continued their mad trek towards Berlin. All non–Russian personnel were left to fend for themselves. Donatelli and a group of other men decided to move in the same direction that the Russians were moving in with the hope that they would eventually run into some officials who could provide transportation to the American bases.

Augie's next real meal as a free man came some 12 hours later when he ran into a group of Italian prisoners of war. After the Italian Army capitulated with the Allies, some Italian soldiers were treated as enemies of Hitler's rapidly diminishing empire, and as a result some of them wound up in the same prison camps as the rest of the captured Allied forces. Approximately five Italian soldiers had discovered a rather large pig roaming the countryside. The animal was at least five feet in length. They somehow managed to guide the pig into a ditch. One of the men straddled himself above the pig's head and pulled its ears upward exposing its neck. Then another man slit its throat with a knife. The pig bucked around in the ditch for a while but it wasn't long before it bled to death. After some three hours of preparation and roasting over an open fire, Augie feasted on one of the biggest and finest meals he had enjoyed in nearly two years. Donatelli's weight had dropped from 160 pounds to 128, and by his description, "There was no finer tasting or satisfying meal on earth."

The next morning a search for any form of transportation culminated in the discovery of some bicycles and a ten-mile ride towards the west into another German town that was occupied by more Russian troops. That town became home for ten days until Augie boarded a train that led to an American base in eastern Germany. From there it was on to Nuremberg, the German city that became famous for the war trials. It was only a stop for Augie, but it would become the place where war atrocities were eventually revealed. The ensuing stop was Camp Lucky Strike. Named after a brand of cigarettes, it was an American military base on the Normandy coast near Le Havre, France. For purposes of secrecy, while the war was raging, staging-area camps were named after brands of American cigarettes. This way the camps could be referred to during radio transmissions without giving away any geographical information.

The meals returning prisoners of war were served consisted of steak and egg nog, a far cry from the potato a day diet the men had survived on in prisoner of war camp. It was at Camp Lucky Strike that a sense of normalcy finally returned to Augie's life and the realization of the war's conclusion was finally sinking in. Nearly four years of his life had passed serving his country. What next? A return to Bakerton, Pennsylvania was certainly in the near future. He was content to know he had survived his tour of duty and was headed back home.

SIX

Fast Lane

Donatelli returned to the United States by ship. His new found freedom catapulted him into a temporary state of euphoria. To add to the giddiness, he discovered that he was sharing his return voyage with actor Victor Mature. In the ruggedly handsome Mature, Donatelli saw a man with an incredibly bright future. So inevitably Augie began to contemplate his own path. Mature, who never regarded himself as a great actor – "I've got 67 films to prove it," he was widely quoted as saying. He went on to play Doc Holliday in John Ford's *My Darling Clementine*, and in 1949, he played Samson, opposite Hedy Lamarr in *Samson and Delilah*. What would Augie have to look forward to? Would he temper his expectations and return to the coal mines? His mood turned cloudy as he imagined himself swinging a pick and loading coal cars in a dangerous world of underground darkness. He pictured himself, soot covered, and eating his lunch underground. He imagined kicking the rats away from his lunch pail. The more he thought about it, the more he thought that he needed to try something different. He respected his friends and family who chose the miner's life, but Augie had other aspirations.

The ship landed in Boston in June of 1945 and Donatelli was soon back home in Bakerton. The reception included an Italian feast. The entire family gathered and celebrated with a bouquet of Italian delicacies, and war stories. Augie's return came with warm waves of greetings from family, friends, and coal miners; his loss of girth became a topic of conversation as did his war tales. Shortly after his return, he met a beautiful young lady who piqued his interest. She showed up at the front door one day with a birthday gift for his sister.

"Could you please give her this gift?" she asked.

"That's very nice of you," Augie replied.

Nothing else came to mind. In fact he couldn't think of another thing to say.

"I was totally speechless when I met her. My tongue must have been hanging out of my mouth. Later, I discovered that her name was Mary Louise Lamont, a girl I had known as the daughter of a foreman at the coal mine; but I remembered her as a little girl."

Augie was 32 years old at the time, and she was a decade younger. She was a brunette with beautiful features. The age difference didn't stop Donatelli from asking her out. They got along from the start, except for one not so insignificant item. Mary Louise, or ML as Augie would lovingly call her, wasn't particularly fond of baseball. In fact, she thought it was boring. Donatelli had joined a local semi-pro team called the City Fish, but she rarely stayed to watch him play. She much preferred the movies to the Fish.

Despite his desire to do something other than work in the mines, Augie found himself once again mining coal during the day and playing ball at night. But he was certain that mining was only a temporary occupation.

"It bought me time until something else came along."

Donatelli was somewhat naïve to the fact that at age 32, he was well past his prime as a professional prospect. Mary Louise's father was a mine foreman, and she had no objection to Augie trying to work his way into management. In an odd coincidence, Mary Louise's father was also the same man with whom Augie had his union related confrontation before the war. The same man who fired him years earlier, when he refused to work as part of a job action. Luckily for Augie, Mr. Lamont wasn't one to hold a grudge. He and Augie were back on good terms and he was more than welcome to work back in the mines. After the war, conditions had improved substantially, and the unions had become much more influential in protecting workers' rights.

Ironically, it was ML's father who helped point Augie in a different direction. That is, after Donatelli enjoyed the sudden epiphany that had blossomed from his experiences in a POW camp in East Prussia – umpiring. He thought the profession might be a way to get involved in something he liked and maybe make a living at it, too. After all, he seemed to have a talent, and the profession was clearly attaining more notoriety. A March 1947 article in *Life* magazine described the instruction at George Barr's umpire school, which had opened in 1935. A most uncomfortable photograph pictured Barr on the baseball diamond in long underwear. The attire was designed to absorb perspiration. The depiction indicated to even the most casual observer that the occupation was meant for men who could also absorb excessive punishment and didn't mind sweating profusely. In the expose, writer Noel F. Busch described the umpire's role as essential: "In baseball, the function of the umpire is not merely that of arbiter or judge, like that of the referee in other games. He represents authority. Dressed for this part in grim mask and dark suit that contrasts severely with the light uniforms of the players and the bright green turf, he roars and bellows, struts and frowns and issues the command, "Play Ball!"

The article described the umpire's role as that of an autocrat. For Augie, the symbolism might be more equated to staff sergeant than governing ruler. During the ballgames at the prison of war camps, the men respected Augie's umpiring judgment more times than not. And when they disagreed with a call, he was always able to back them down with the directness of a TEN-HUT!

When Augie discovered that Mary Louise's father knew Elmer Daily, the president of the Mid-Atlantic League, he didn't hesitate. Augie asked ML's father to set up a meeting to decide how he could proceed with his umpiring dream. He hoped for guidance on how to break into the profession, but instead Daily was less than optimistic about Augie's chances.

"Young man," he said, "you'll have a difficult time. Umpiring is a tough field with a lot of good men trying to break into it." Then Mr. Daily added, "I think you'd be better off going back to the coal mines."

Augie was somewhat discouraged. Yet despite the negative comments, Daily gave him information about a professional umpiring school in

Florida, headed by American League umpiring legend Bill McGowan. Donatelli immediately enrolled in the five-week course with his veteran benefits paying the $85 tuition. The training had a boot camp feel to it with the students doing some running, sit ups, and pushups, because as the reasoning went, an umpire had to be in good shape to be able to move around and be in position in time to make the correct call. There were 76 men enrolled in the course, and according to instructor and veteran major league umpire Al Sommers, most of the men were going to land paying jobs after the course was completed. This was a much more optimistic future than Daily had painted.

After getting into shape, the instructors went about the extensive process of teaching them how to make the calls both on the bases and behind the plate. They used both the three and four-umpire systems. At the time both were being deployed in the majors and minors. In a three-umpire system, which required a home plate umpire, a first base umpire, and a man at third; the first base umpire had to position himself between first and second base. With a runner on first, he might have to make the call at both first and second on a double-play ball. On a sacrifice fly, you had to line yourself with the fielder catching the fly and the base runner, so you could watch the catch and the base runner break off the base. At first, it sounded exceedingly complicated to Donatelli. There was even a time in those early days of umpiring school when Augie thought that he'd have a difficult time graduating.

The young umpires sat through numerous classroom sessions where they thought the various rules and the seemingly infinite situations that might arise during a game. The instructors mapped out the possibilities on the blackboard, and they sat through the endless scenarios with their attention focused on every word. They were taught when to bear down, when to relax, and when to take off their masks. Then the young men were graded on their judgment, hustle, ability, technique, and even their personal appearance.

At times the rule book was difficult to comprehend, especially for someone who was not an exceptional student.

"If you ever happen to read the baseball rule book, make sure you have a lawyer with you to interpret some of the material," joked Augie.

For instance, the rule on interference at one time, it had 30 different subheadings in different places in the book.

Rule 5.09: The ball becomes dead and runners advance one base, or return to their bases, without liability to be put out, when – (f) a fair ball touches a runner or an umpire on fair territory before it touches a runner or an umpire on fair territory before it touches an infielder including the pitcher, or touches an umpire before it has passed an infielder other than the pitcher.

The complications of the rulebook aside, Augie seemed to have an above average knack for hustle, judgment, and positioning.

"There are a few things I tell aspiring umpires when they ask me about the most important aspects of the profession. The first is outstanding judgment. This is something you either have or don't have. But perhaps the most important aspect of umpiring, assuming the trainee had good judgment, is positioning. If you're blocked out from having a clear view of a play, then your ability to judge a close play is useless. You must be at the right place at the right time."

Al Sommers was one of the first umpires to concentrate on positioning. An umpire had to know where to go and hustle to get there. For instance, if there was a play at third, where should the umpire stand on the foul line to see a play from the proper vantage point. If he stood behind the bag in foul ground, then there was a good chance that the fielder would obstruct the umpire's view. While umpiring first base, Augie felt he got a truer view of the base runner stepping on the bag from foul territory. While umpiring second, he wanted to be on the infield while making the call. American League umpires went to the back of the bag to make the call.

After a short period of time he absorbed the information, as he put it, "I took to all the procedures like a duck to water. It became common sense to me," said Augie, "and there was a simple but important phrase that we heard over and over again that I took to heart: always hustle, and keep your eye on the ball. Each day we were given group drills, where we lined up in rows like a group of soldiers might, and in unison all of us barked out the calls that the instructor requested. We'd bark out SAFE! and then we'd all give the safe sign at once. We had the same drill for the fair call, foul call, and the ball and strike signals. It was quite a sight to witness a group of 30 men give the same call all at once, and it's the same exact drill that young men go through today at umpire school."

One afternoon while umpiring at second base in slid a young man by the name of Jim Townsend from Covington, Tennessee. Donatelli hollered "ye're out!" Townsend stood to his feet and knocked the dirt off of his uniform. He then peered at the umpire. Donatelli realized that he knew the fellow, but it took a second or two to place him. When he did his jaw dropped open and he threw his arms around Townsend as if he was a long lost brother. The scene must have appeared surreal to casual observers, who probably thought it rather odd for an umpire to hug a man he had just called out. The last prevous time Donatelli had seen Townsend was in a German prison camp. They had played softball together there in many games, it was a happy reunion to say the least. The story was picked up by the Washington Evening Star on February 21st, 1947.

The students alternated between actually playing ball and being the umpires. During another one of those match games Augie was faced with making the call on a very close play at second base. He moved to within six feet of the bag as fast as he could, kneeling down, and then made a very decisive call: "YER OUT!" he yelled. The instructors ran over and pointed out that Augie had just rendered the best decision of the entire session, complimenting him on all of the things he did correctly.

"Where did you learn to call 'em like that, young man?" he was asked.

Augie answered, "Just thought that would be the best way to do it, sir."

That night during a meeting of the entire class, they gave Donatelli a great shock. The course was nearing its conclusion and Bill McGowan was making a scheduled speech to all 76 students. McGowan has been described by some as the Lou Gehrig of umpires. During his career he umpired eight World Series and was known for being a very confident man. While no official stat is recorded, he said to have worked in 2,541 consecutive games during a 16 year period. He had a colorful style that the National Baseball Hall of Fame described as "aggressive gestures that bordered on the pugnacious." Clearly, Augie and most of the student umpires looked at him as a legend. He garnered a reputation of getting the calls right and was thought of as one of baseball's top umpires for many years.

"If a manager or player has a legitimate protest, listen to the complaint for a brief period," Augie was told. "Tell him you called it the way you saw it, and then walk away. When he follows you, you might repeat that it was your judgment. Walk away with a warning finger. If he continues to protest, go through with your threat. Get somebody out of there."

During the tryout camp games, the student umpires where challenged in a variety of ways, including catcalls from fellow students as they observed from the stands. The young umpires were also treated to barbs such as, "Where's your seeing eye dog?"

During McGowan's presentation to the class of student umpires, he made a statement that caught Augie by surprise. McGowan began umpiring in the major leagues in 1925 and from the start was perceived as one of baseball's top umpires. His nickname was "Number 1." The Hall of Famer was also called the "Iron Man" of umpires.

"Men," said McGowan in a firm tone of voice as he puffed on a huge cigar as the young prospective umpires hung on his every word as if an epiphany was near at hand.

"I want to tell you that we have in our midst a man who will be a major league umpire in three years."

A loud rumbling sound filled the large room as the umpires wondered whom he was talking about. McGowan turned to Al Somers to ask him to identify where the star pupil was sitting.

Somers said, "He's the guy dressed in the white shirt over there." He nodded in Augie's general direction.

McGowan walked over, pointed, and said, "YOU!"

McGowan expressed the opinion with the confidence of George Patton. All of the students looked around because they were uncertain at whom he was pointing. Donatelli turned and looked at the fellow behind him, and McGowan shook his head and angrily pointed again, "no, no, no – I mean you!"

His finger was in Augie's face.

"You will make it to the majors in three years."

Everyone looked at Donatelli, and the classroom erupted with a loud applause.

McGowan said, "Stand up, son." Augie stood, and McGowan added, "Do you have anything to say?"

Donatelli reacted as if McGowan had made some sort of mistake. He repeated McGowan's statement in the form of a question, "In the majors in three years?"

McGowan replied confidently, "That's right. That's what I said, you'll be in the majors in three years."

Despite his outstanding marks at the school, Augie wasn't really sure how McGowan could make such a bold statement. Donatelli was known for being a confident individual, but the world of umpiring was something totally new. Yet if one of the greatest umpires in baseball history was willing to take a chance in forecasting Donatelli's future success, he'd have to work even harder not to disappoint the master. With each passing day his knowledge and confidence increased, and despite the self-doubts, the reality of being able to umpire at some level was very exciting. Of the 76 students in that class, 75 of them were placed in some type of professional league.

To show you how bad they needed umpires," Augie said, "Bill got jobs for all but one fellow. Don't tell the ballplayers what I said, but the one that didn't get a job wasn't even bright enough to be an umpire."

The demand for umpires at the minor league level was great, but the competition for major league jobs was even greater. At the time, there were approximately 500 minor league umpires, and the various leagues were growing in tandem with the post-war interest in baseball. However, there were only 27 major league umpires in the United States at the time. The numerical odds weren't very good for landing such a job. Yet after being singled out as McGowan's top prospect, Augie realized that this was an opportunity of a lifetime. He became more determined than ever.

Mary Louise Lamont, whom Augie would soon marry, was wary about the type of life they would lead. "She wasn't really certain what an umpire's job was. But it was only a matter of time before the baseball bug bit her, and she realized that I had a legitimate future in umpiring."

"I dragged Mary Louise to so many minor league games that she eventually became a fan of sorts. Sometimes it was hard for her to sit in the stands and listen to fans shower me with all sorts of verbal abuse, but she always told him that I appeared in control. She always felt confident in my ability to handle any type of situation."

After graduating from McGowan's school, he was given his first job as a professional umpire in the Class C league. It was referred to as the "Mad-Atlantic" League because it had the reputation for being rough-and-tumble. It was unusual for a rookie umpire to be placed in a Class C league, but McGowan convinced them that Augie was ready to jump over the Class D leagues. The ironic part of the assignment was that the president of the league was the very same gentleman who tried to convince Donatelli to stay out of umpiring – Mr. Elmer Daily.

"I was a good umpire for Mr. Daily," recalled Augie. "But at the time Class C ball didn't seem like much fun. I was trying to sharpen my skills, but the crowds had no mercy and seemed more interested in giving a rookie umpire the needle than watching the game."

Donatelli umpired in the Pioneer League, a rookie circuit which had teams in Idaho and Utah. Razzing the umpires became such an issue that a local paper ran the following story:

The *Desert News* in Salt Lake City, Utah printed the following commentary:

Umpire Donatelli was hit on the ankle by a foul tip in the second inning of last night's fray, and the fans actually applauded. Is this the sportsmanship that Salt Lake boasts about? Donatelli's work throughout the season has been beyond reproach, and the Pioneer League would sorely miss his service if he went elsewhere.

The sentiment was greatly appreciated but Donatelli had his eyes on the majors. The teams in the Pioneer League in 1946 included Ogden, Pocatello, Boise, Twin Falls, Idaho Falls, and Salt Lake City. There were only six teams, but some of the players made it to the majors, including Billy Martin, Solly Hemus, Dale Long, Harry Perkowski, and Bob Chesnes. That season, 1946, was a peak year for the minor leagues as never before in the history of the game had professional baseball branched out to so many cities. As a result, good umpires were in great demand. In 1947, Donatelli was promoted to the Class A ball in the South Atlantic League, better known as the Sally League. The teams in the Sally League in 1947 included Augusta, Savannah, Columbus,

Columbia, Greenville, Charleston, Jacksonville, and Macon. Donatelli signed a contract on February 20th that offered him $350 per month to be paid in semi-monthly installments. Augusta was the best team in the league that season. The one player that Augie remembered most from his stint in the Sally League was Don Mueller. Billy Gardner and Roy Hartsfield were also there, but Mueller, or "Mandrake" as he was called, seemed to always wind up in the same league with Donatelli. After only half a season in Class A, Donatelli was promoted to Triple A. The reason for the quick jump came as a result of a recommendation that came from one of baseball's most legendary front office names.

Brooklyn Dodgers General Manager Branch Rickey was famous for his ability to scout talent, and was responsible for bringing the great Jackie Robinson to the majors as well as many other talented ballplayers. One night in Macon, Georgia, in the Sally League, Donatelli happened to be working behind the plate. Rickey was in the stands scouting a young pitching prospect by the name of Dan Bankhead, who went on to become the first black pitcher in the majors. While observing Bankhead, Rickey was impressed with Donatelli. He didn't know the umpire's name, but when he returned to New York, he reported his discovery during a casual conversation with then National League president Ford Frick. He told Frick that the National League should consider signing him to a contract. It wasn't long after that, the National League asked the International League to buy his contract. Frick relayed the information from Rickey to the President of the International League, Frank Shaughnessy, who bought Augie's contract from the Sally League for $1,200, an unusually large amount of money at the time. As a result, Donatelli's stint in the Sally League lasted only a few months. He vividly recalled the subsequent conversation he had with Earl Blue, the President of the Sally League. Blue had summoned Donatelli to his office to inform him that his contract had been sold to the International League.

"I just sold your contract," said Blue matter of factly, "and I got $1,200."

"What do you mean," asked Donatelli?

"The International League gave me that amount, and you're going up to a higher league," replied Blue.

Augie was shocked.

"Hey," asked Donatelli naively, "I get some of that money, don't I?"

The fact that his contract was sold without even a consultation perturbed him. Once out of Blue's office, however, Augie's annoyance subsided when he realized that he was well on his way to the major leagues. His salary in the Sally League was $300 a month, but when he got the quick promotion to Triple A it went up to $325. In the coal mines his biggest pay check was for $107 every two weeks, so his decision to break into umpiring was paying modest dividends. However, he decided it would be wise to supplement his yearly salary by continuing to work in the mines during the off season. It wasn't until many months later that he discovered that it was in fact Branch Rickey who had given him a glowing recommendation; in a story that was later documented in the New York *Daily News* in 1950, legendary New York sports columnist Dick Young wrote the following in an article that was headlined: "Donatelli, New NL Ump, A Rickey 'Discovery.'"

There's a gay young guy here with the Dodgers, and he looks like a pretty good bet for "Rookie of the Year" at his trade in the NL. He is, in fact, pretty much of a cinch, because he's the only newcomer for 1950 – umpire Augie Donatelli whose phenomenal rise in the specialized profession is one of the warming success stories of the game. There was Branch Rickey in the stands at Macon. Rickey on that famous nationwide chase of his for a pitcher. The only thing that impressed Rickey that night, however, was the young umpire behind the plate.

When Augie moved up to Triple A, Mandrake Mueller moved up and when Augie finally got called up to the big leagues, he was there, too.

Mueller walked up to the plate and said, "Hey, Augie, are you following me around or something?"

In the International League, Donatelli saw glimpses of great talent. With each level of advancement through the minor leagues, he also sensed a marked difference in the quality of the facilities and the quality of play. They traveled by train, which at first seemed like a big improvement from the long bus and car rides of the lower leagues, but he found it almost impossible to sleep on those noisy trains. The repetitive clickity-clack sound of the train rattling along the track was almost too much to handle, but it was still better than the alternative of driving through the night. There were ample times when driving seemed the best way to travel, and Mary Louise often accompanied him during those early years. The games, for the most part, were played at night, so there was ample opportunity to find out what a town was like. He was always an early riser, and enjoyed going out for a walk and meal. According to him, it never seemed lonely because there was always someone who wanted to talk about baseball, but Donatelli made it clear that the life of a minor league umpire during the late 1940s was hardly a lavish one. Umpires' dressing rooms were many times nonexistent, which forced them to dress in a car or at the hotel.

Donatelli always made it a point to avoid what he termed as the ever present shady characters. The league warned umpires to maintain a standard and advised them to never associate in any way with gamblers. He was careful to abide by that policy. The gravity of that policy really hit home with Donatelli during a road trip through South Carolina while he was umpiring in the Sally League. A fellow umpire told Augie he wanted him to meet an old acquaintance. The two umpires pulled up to a house on East Wilburn Avenue in Greenville, and they got out of their car and approached a fellow sitting on the porch. "Augie, I'd like you to meet Joe Jackson." "Shoeless Joe," of course, was implicated in the 1919 World Series as having taken $5000 to throw the World Series. He hit .375 during the Fall Classic with a home run and 12 hits; a jury acquitted him but he remained banned from baseball for life. Until the day he died in 1951, Joe denied his involvement. Augie felt honored to meet the legendary player, but the harsh ramifications of Jackson's lifetime banishment from baseball saddened the young umpire. He was also struck by the legendary player's humble tone.

It was 1949 when Augie joined the International League and Triple A baseball. By then, he had already married his Bakerton sweetheart, and the decision had been made to move to Jersey City, New Jersey. There were twice as many opportunities for him to be at home because the league had teams in both Jersey City and Newark. His first daughter, Barbara, was born a few years earlier, and he was more determined than ever to make a success of umpiring. But at this point, the self-heralded occupation was still nothing more than a glorified summer job. The family headed back to Pennsylvania during the winter months as Augie continued to work at the Barnes & Tucker coal operation. Maintaining an off-season occupation was not uncommon for the umpiring set. According to Shag Crawford, "I did everything in the off-season to make ends meet except rob a bank, and I was on the verge of that a few times. It was difficult to get a job because nobody wanted to hire me on a part-time basis."

Donatelli was informed over the telephone by Ford Frick himself that his contract was going to be purchased by the National League for the 1949 season. It was a conversation he recalled vividly.

"We've decided to bring Lon Warneke up this season," Frick told Augie, "but we'd like to sign you to a major league contract and bring you up next year."

Donatelli's confidence soared to new heights. He had rocketed from a hot-shot top ranked umpiring prospect to a direct flight to the majors in only four years. He was to replace umpire George Barr whose career spanned 17 seasons. Barr was most remembered for an incident that occurred in 1943, when after calling a balk on pitcher Johnny Allen, he was attacked and nearly choked to death with his own tie. The horrific incident made baseball brass do away with the tie as a regular part of an umpire's garb.

With the major leagues tauntingly within his reach, Augie remained sharp as a tack throughout the 1949 season, hustling on every play, making crisp sharp decisions. Then he was selected to be part of the umpiring crew for the Junior World Series in 1949 between the Indianapolis Indians and the Montreal Royals. In Game 5 of the Series, Donatelli was the home plate umpire. The Royals had a 2 – 0 lead in the fourth inning. Chuck Connors homered for the Royals. This was the same Chuck Connors who later gained fame as the actor who starred in the television series, *The Rifleman*. Pitcher Dan Bankhead wasn't able to protect the lead. He walked men in the fourth and fifth innings, and both times the runners scored to tie the game at two. The game went into extra innings with the score deadlocked at 4. The climax of the game occurred in the bottom of the tenth when there was a close play at the plate after Indianapolis' Nanny Fernandez walked and attempted to score on a double by Roy Weatherly. Fernandez was an infielder who had spent time in the major leagues with the Boston

Braves. Toby Atwell, the Montreal catcher, blocked Fernandez off of home plate before he received the ball. Donatelli audaciously called it an illegal obstruction and he decided to allow the runner to score for Indianapolis. The Indianapolis crowd of 8,704 went wild and they won the series the next day. The Montreal players went berserk over Augie's call.

"You can't make a call like that. You didn't make the call on a play like that all year!"

"For a second," recalled Donatelli, "I thought they were going to cream me. The Montreal team swooped down on me. Luckily for me, the senior umpire of the crew was a big husky fellow by the name of Pat Padden, who was able to clear a path for me into the umpires' locker room."

The call was a gutsy one to make, because obstruction was rarely, if ever, made during that entire season, and Donatelli was making it during a Triple A championship game.

Donatelli was convinced that he had made the correct call, but there were some who sought retribution. After the game, the losing players walked past the umpires' locker room, yelling obscenities and hurling empty glass soda bottles over the door. The room was located right next to the Montreal clubhouse, so the umpires were able to hear every single foul word, so the umpires wasted precious little time evacuating the room.

Crew chief Padden stood firmly behind Donatelli's decision, and spoke to reporters. He said, "Donatelli is the greatest young umpire I've ever seen." He continued. "He has – how you put it? – the courage of his convictions."

He made the statement despite the fact that Donatelli had overruled him on a balk call the night before. "He put me on the spot," Padden said, "but I went along with him because I have so much confidence in him."

Soon after making the obstruction call, league president Shaughnessy called Donatelli to his office to question the decision. The Montreal club screamed bloody murder in the local papers, claiming that the obstruction call had been completely ignored by every umpire all season long. He sat with Shaughnessy with a ready answer to the criticism.

"Why, Mr. Shaughnessy," he said, "it was you who told me to call that very play just a few weeks ago." Shaughnessy had in fact told the umpires to follow the rule book on such decisions.

"Look kid," replied Shaughnessy, "it's okay to be technical with your calls, but not too technical."

More than a half-century after that call, both the casual fan and the ardent student of the game might wonder how Donatelli had the gumption to make such a decision under the biggest spotlight of his career to that point. An error in judgment might have been enough to derail his meteoric rise to the major leagues, but such self doubts were buried deep within the umpire's psyche. At age 35, and only five years removed from his very first umpiring assignment in a prison of war camp in Nazi, Germany, Donatelli was streaking towards the plum assignment of a lifetime. In 1950, there were less than 40 men in the entire country who held jobs as big league umpires. Now that he had been awarded a major league job, he was determined to convince everyone that the National League had made the correct choice. Sending an umpire to the big leagues after only four years of seasoning was an unusual tact, but Donatelli's ability simply jumped off the field and demanded the attention of experienced baseball men. The National League had passed over dozens of minor league umpires who had been toiling for years to give Donatelli his big shot. McGowan's prize student was on his way. Umpire Ed Vargo was once quoted as stating that umpiring is a profession in which you are expected to be perfect on the first day on the job, and then continue to improve every day thereafter. If a young umpire made a few mistakes his reputation could be easily sullied.

To add to the pressure, Augie's very first major league game was scheduled to be in New York City. The date was April 18, 1950. The headlines featured Wisconsin's Senator Joe McCarthy, who accused individuals of having socialist and communist ties. The sports pages, however, focused on the home opener at the Polo Grounds, a game between the Boston Braves and the New York Giants. It was a clear, crisp day, and the air was charged with energy. There were 32,000 spectators in the stands, and also a few celebrities: legendary boxer Joe Louis, Mrs. Lou Gehrig, and Augie's boss, National League President Ford Frick. At the time, league presidents were responsible for hiring and firing of umpires, and Frick would have a close up look at his prize umpire. Some months after this first game, Frick said that Donatelli had the promise of becoming one of the great umpires of all time – unusual praise indeed. Umpires were rarely given such positive attention, especially so early in their career. In some ways the high praise made Augie a target of managers, who hoped to garner any edge they could with their constant chatter. It was very obvious right from the start that Augie would draw attention and even challenges from managers, who expected nothing less than perfection from an umpire who was projected to become an all time great. That first ballgame at the Polo Grounds was also the very first regular-season major league contest that Augie's wife, Mary Louise had ever attended. Donatelli was glad that she was at the ballpark, but he was also on edge about the potential problems. The game was in New York City, a place where fans were not shy about hurling their unfiltered comments at players and umpires alike. Mary Louise had never seen a game played in front of this type of raucous crowd, and certainly a rookie umpire could potentially be a prime target of hurtful barbs. Augie was as battle tested as an iron clad B-17, but his beautiful wife was potentially as defenseless as a sparrow.

Augie told her, "When you go to the park, don't tell anybody who you are, or who I am. Sit there and no matter what you hear, don't turn around, and never answer back, no matter what anybody calls me. If you can't take it, just leave the park and go home."

Mary Louise became indoctrinated to the lifestyle and became supportive of her husband. "The umpire's wives used to say that we were the wind beneath our husband's wings. We were." The fans weren't apt to hold their opinions to themselves, but ML bravely weathered the callus observations that flew from the stands. Augie had learned to ignore the remarks, but she was occasionally sensitive to them. As time went by she always took resolve in the fact that her husband could handle himself.

The crew for that opening day in 1950 consisted of only three umpires. Lee Ballanfant was behind the plate, and Al Barlick and Donatelli were assigned the basepaths. Three-man crews were standard for regular season games from the mid 1930s until 1952. At this point in his career, Ballanfant was 60 years old and quite slow afoot. In fact, there were reports that Warren Giles, who became National League President in 1951 wanted to release the veteran umpire, but fellow umpire Barlick stood up for Ballanfant and convinced Giles that he was still solid. Ballanfant was not known for being fleet-afoot even earlier in his career. During the 1940 National League pennant race, in the first inning of a pressure packed game between the Dodgers and Cardinals, he got in the way of a ball thrown to first base during a double play attempt. The ball remained in play and the Dodgers went wild. But even quick footed umpires run into problems, and it didn't take long for Augie to taste his first disputed call.

When the opener got underway, the Braves started an offensive barrage against Giants' starter Larry Jansen, who had lost two previous opening day starts. Boston's Bob Elliott hit a two-run homer off Jansen, and the Braves were off to a quick start. Sal "The Barber" Maglie came into the game, but the Braves went on to score 11 runs on 12 hits. Augie was involved in his first official major league dispute when Warren Spahn led off the sixth inning with a base hit. Donatelli ruled that Alvin Dark had trapped the ball while attempting to make a sliding catch.

Manager Leo Durocher emerged from the dugout and took a direct rout towards the rookie umpire. The intimidating, raspy-voiced, sharp witted manager had joined the Giants in 1948 after nine years with the Brooklyn Dodgers. It would be the first of many encounters between Durocher and Donatelli.

"I know you've got the jitters, Augie, but you've got to keep your eye on a ball like that," complained Durocher.

"Leo, he trapped the ball," was Donatelli's answer.

It was a mild-mannered complaint from Durocher, who decided to take it easy on the young umpire. The biggest dispute of the game occurred the inning before when New York's Whitey Lockman belted a ball that traveled out of the park for a home run. Al Barlick gave the home run sign but Braves' skipper Billy Southworth thought that a fan had deflected the ball, and that it would have otherwise bounced off the wall. This was an era before every close play was scrutinized on video, and umpires never received the benefit of the doubt unless the call benefited the home team. The first rudimentary use of instant replay didn't occur until the mid-1950s. That innovative piece of television history was credited to the Canadian Broadcasting Corporation's presentation of *Hockey Night in Canada*. The crew used a method that instantly developed kinescope footage, but videotaped instant replays didn't become a regular feature of sports broadcasts until the 1960s.

The issue of umpires using videotape in their decisions didn't come to fruition until 2009. Prior to that landmark decision, any use of videotape was deemed inappropriate.

"Use of the video replay is not an acceptable practice," NL President Len Coleman stated in 1999. "Part of the beauty of baseball is that it is imperfect. Players make errors. Managers are constantly second-guessed. But the game is played and determined by two teams between the white lines."

That April opener in 1950 also carried added historic significance, because it was the debut of Sam Jethroe, who became the first black player to wear a Boston Braves uniform. Jethroe had spent seven years in the Negro Leagues, and hit .340 for the Cleveland Buckeyes. He didn't disappoint in his debut, as he smashed two hits, including a home run. Jethroe was more than a novelty in Boston, because the Red Sox didn't have a black player on its roster until 1959, when Pumpsie Green called Fenway Park home.

Boston won the opener by a lop-sided final score of 11–4. It was a wild game, but afterwards Augie was convinced that he had done a good job. Both Barlick and Ballanfant complimented him on his work, and he subsequently received multiple Western Union Telegrams, including one from the Sterling Coal Company office, congratulating him. It read:

A.J. DONATELI = NATL LEAGUE EMPIRE *(sp)* CARE POLO GROUNDS=HEARTIEST CONGRATULATIONS AND BEST WISHES FOR MANY SUCCESSFUL SEASON=STERLING COAL CO OFFICE PERSONNEL=

Mary Louise had never stepped foot inside a major league park until her husband's very first big league game at the Polo Grounds in 1950. The lifestyle of a major league umpire was anything but typical. Mary Louise couldn't conceal the fact that she hated the fights, callous language, and the way umpires were treated. She enjoyed her husband's success and enjoyed her semi-celebrity status back home in Ebensburg, but having her husband away from home for so many months was more than a challenge, especially with their second child, Carol, on the way.

As American League umpire Ernie Stewart once said, "The worst thing about umpiring is the loneliness. It's a killer. Every city is a strange city. You don't have a home. Ballplayers are home fifty percent of the time, umpires are not."

In sharp contrast with today's umpires who enjoy weeks of vacation time during the season, the umpire of 1950 was at the mercy of an unyielding schedule and also the slower travel between eight cities. "Back then, an umpire worked on a 10-day schedule," Augie recalled. "They give you a schedule and it's up to you to be at the games named."

Many years later Augie described his wife's trepidation about his career, "My wife was convinced that I'd be better off looking for a more conventional job that kept me closer to home, but there was no way I was going to walk away from baseball. I loved the game, and now that I had a taste of major league baseball, it would take wild horses to drag me away. After some time, my wife just accepted the fact that I was destined to be an umpire." And M.L. became very supportive of his career.

The emotional strains that an umpire faced combined with the intense public pressure made the occupation impalpable. Every move was potentially open to public scrutiny; every good call was completely ignored. To a fan, cheering for the umpire made as little sense as cheering on a judge, traffic cop, or corporate manager. Despite her trepidation, Mary Louise continued to clip and save articles about her husband's success. She clipped a cartoon out of *American Legion* magazine that especially struck a painfully familiar chord. It featured an umpire barring his front door as angry fans attempted to barge into his living room. His curvaceous cartoon wife calmly stood by his side and asked, "How did things go today at the ball park, dear?"

Then came the 1950 feature film release of *Kill the Umpire*. It was a slapstick comedy featuring William Bendix and William Frawley. Bendix played a baseball fanatic who managed to become an umpire who earned the nickname Bill "Two Call" Johnson. In the film, gamblers attempted to bribe "Two Call," and one of his decisions ignited a riot. The movie was an off-the-cuff comedy, but it clearly didn't portray umpires in a proud light.

"Hi honey, what's for dinner," asks the umpire?

His wife angrily replies, "Boiled catcher's mitt."

The fact that the film was released during Augie's rookie year couldn't have helped Mary Louise's feelings about the profession.

Donatelli's second game was also at the Polo Grounds, and once again the Braves prevailed over the Giants in a rather uneventful contest. Donatelli was then assigned to work behind the plate at Ebbets Field in Brooklyn for the Dodgers' home opener. Their opponents that day were their hated archrivals, the Giants. It was a chilly, cloudy day in Brooklyn but a good crowd was on hand. The Giants were hungry after losing their first two games, but Brooklyn's Preacher Roe held New York in check. Roy Campanella belted a 400-foot grand slam to left field that put the game out of reach. The Dodgers won handily, and Leo Durocher was steaming mad after his club started the season 0–3.

Perhaps the most memorable aspect of Donatelli's first season came in the final weekend of 1950. By season's end, the Phillies and Dodgers had emerged as neck and neck combatants, and were scheduled to play each other in the last series. Donatelli silently marveled at finding himself on the field in the heat of the pennant race. He was on the same perfect green grass as great Dodgers legends such as Jackie Robinson, Gil Hodges, Roy Campanella, Duke Snider, Carl Furillo, and Pee Wee Reese. The Philadelphia Phillies, known as "The Whiz Kids," were spearheaded by Dick Sisler, Del Ennis, Richie Ashburn, and Eddie Waitkus. The first-place Phillies had squandered a seven-game lead in nine days, including two consecutive losses to the Dodgers a week before in addition to the loss a day prior. The Phils found themselves desperately trying to preserve a one game lead. It was October 1st, the final regular season game, but if the Dodgers defeated the Phillies, both clubs would have ended the season in a tie, thus forcing a three-game playoff. This was the pre-divisional era, and first place meant a pennant and a trip to the World Series.

There were 35,000 screaming Dodger fans on hand at Ebbets Field to witness a game that started out as a duel between Brooklyn's 6' 4" Don Newcombe and Robin Roberts of the Phils. In the sixth inning, Dodger shortstop Pee Wee Reese lofted a fly ball to right-field. The ball landed on top of the wall and got lodged in a fence. Reese thought the ball was still in play and continued running full speed around the bases until Augie circled his arm, signaling that it was a homer. Reese's blast tied the score at 1 – 1.

"The ground rule was clear on that play; if the ball stayed on the screen it was a homer," said Augie. In the ninth, the Dodgers threatened to pull off a last-inning victory, and with rookie Cal Abrams on second and Pee Wee on first, Duke Snider delivered a line drive to center that Richie Ashburn fielded. Abrams raced home as third base coach Milt Stock gave him the green light. But Ashburn, who was known for a weak arm, threw a bullet to catcher Stan Lopata who slapped the tag on Abrams. At the time, Augie later felt that Stock made a mistake in sending Abrams home because the ball got to Ashburn so quickly, and because there were no men out. It was a play that took some heart out of the Dodgers, because it looked like they had won it. The Phillies bounced back in the tenth when Dick Sisler smashed a three run home run into the left-field stands. Augie watched the ball sail right over his head, and listened to the normally rabid confines of Ebbets Field turn as silent as a mortuary. Roberts finished the game, a 10 inning complete game for his 20th victory of the season. The Phils hadn't won the National League pennant in 35 years, and were a losing club only a few years before. Now the Whiz Kids were on their way to the World Series to face the Yankees, who would eventually emerge as spoilers to the Phillies' World Championship dreams. Donatelli's season ended with the Phillies' celebration at Ebbets Field.

"That was a hell of a way for my first season as a major league umpire to end," recounted Augie. You appreciate that kind of stuff when you think back on it, because while it was going on, I was worried about doing my job. But it was one of the greatest pennant races ever."

He also recalled his first umpiring crew with great respect, especially Barlick. Al was a 10-year veteran by 1950, having been called up to the majors at age 25. He was elected to the Hall of Fame in 1989, and was always known for his booming voice. To the umpires, he was known as a no-nonsense arbiter. To Donatelli he was a man that commanded respect.

"He was a guy who would fight for you, if he liked you. Just like he fought for Ballanfant before the season started. Al was also good at giving young umpires advice and guidance."

According to Donatelli, Barlick often advised, "Never look for trouble, there's no need to, because the problems will come to you."

During the 1946 World Series, Barlick was behind the plate when Enos Slaughter made his mad dash for home, a play the umpire called one of his most memorable in 28 years as a big league umpire. Umpire

Doug Harvey recalled an occasion in which Barlick straightened him out during his rookie season of 1962.

"Drysdale was pitching to Mays," recounted Harvey, who was elected to the Hall of Fame in 2009. "Mays smashed one down the line foul and Don took Mays's buttons off on the next pitch and knocked him down. Willie fell back, spun around on one knee, and got right back up. Then Mays said, "No, ump, he's not throwin' at me." I knew Drysdale was throwing at him, but I listened to Willie. On the next pitch, Mays cracked a double. After the game, Barlick blew his stack. He said, 'Don't ever let a ballplayer tell you what just happened. Decide what you're going to do and do it.'

Barlick was a mentor to many umpires, including Donatelli. But Augie also felt a special attachment with another Hall of Famer, Jocko Conlan, with whom Augie developed a great friendship.

"Jocko was what we called in those days, a real stand up guy," recalled Augie.

Conlan's first opportunity to umpire in the majors came while he was still an active player with the Chicago White Sox. In 1935 during an extra inning game in St. Louis, with the temperature on the field at 118 degrees, home plate umpire Red Ormsby suffered a sunstroke. As Jocko told the story, "Rogers Hornsby was managing St. Louis, and Jimmie Dykes the White Sox. Hornsby came over to Dykes and said, "We have to get an umpire to replace Red." Just off the cuff, I said, I'll umpire. I wasn't playing because my thumb was hurt. Rogers Hornsby said, "I like him – he'll call 'em as he sees 'em, I'm sure. As the game progressed, Luke Appling hit a potential three-base hit. I was faster than Luke at the time, and anyway I didn't have to run the bases. I called Appling out. My manager started screaming, "What a decision! You're on our team!" Then Appling said to Dykes, "He just had me, Jim."

While Conlan was asked to umpire a game involving his own team, Donatelli had the destinction of being asked to assist a player. In 1952, George "Catfish" Metkovich, a member of the Pittsburgh Pirates, was having a difficult day in the field against the Brooklyn Dodgers. After Duke Snider smashed a ball that ricocheted off of Metkovich's leg, the first baseman turned to Donatelli and screamed, "Augie, don't just stand there. Get a glove and give me a hand!"

Augie declined the request.

Anecdotes aside, Donatelli admired Conlan greatly. In some ways the two men were mirror images of each other. They were the same size – both stood 5' 9" tall. They were both relatively small men who were capable of standing their ground against some very rugged players. And neither men thought of their lack of height as a disadvantage.

"It was our good judgment and strong presence that commanded respect. Some players thought that I had a chip on my shoulder," recalled Augie, "but honestly I never thought I needed to prove that I was tough. Most of the players had no idea about what I went through during the war. They could care less. But after living through the experiences in the coal mines and in the service, I knew what I was made of."

It was that toughness that helped Donatelli advance to the major leagues as quickly as he did. During spring training the young umpire stood his ground on a disputed call that raised the ire of legendary Yankees manager Casey Stengel. Nothing intimidated this coal mining kid from Bakerton. Perhaps part of that confidence came from the realization that if he didn't command respect, the game would eat him alive.

"Hell, I didn't have a chip on my shoulder," recalled Augie. I was as firm as I had to be to get the job done. That's the way things were in the coal mines, that's the way it was in the military, and that's the way I had to do things as a major league umpire."

By 1955, only five years into his major league career, baseball writers voted him the National League's best umpire, but it wasn't an honor that went without baggage. Umpires were tested every single time they took the field, and in some ways being honored and singled out by the writers made Donatelli more of a target.

Baseball Hall of Fame umpire Jacko Conlan helps Augie cool off with a squeeze from a wet sponge. Photo courtesy The Donatelli Collection.

Standing from left to right are umpires Tom Gorman, Artie Gore, Augie Donatelli; and seated is Jocko Conlan. Photo courtesy of the Donatelli Collection.

Donatelli returned to umpire's school as an instructor, where the class enjoyed a visit from New York Yankees legend Joe DiMaggio who tried on umpire equipment. At the center of photo is Hall of Fame Umpire Bill McGowen at far right Donatelli. Photo courtesy The Donatelli Collection.

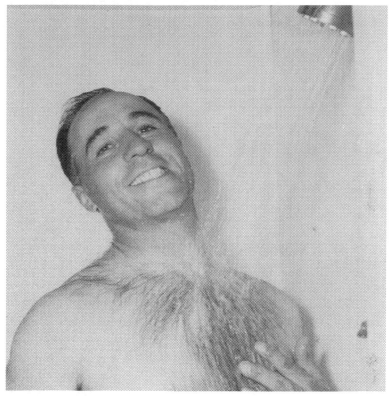

Donatelli often used the phrase "to the showers!" when ejecting players and managers from a ballgame. Photo courtesy The Donatelli Collection.

SEVEN

To the Showers!

During Augie's second major league season, some of the realities of the lifestyle had already become second nature. The constant travel became a grind, but Augie adapted. Transportation by air was commonplace since baseball had phased out rail travel. His mantra was that he had seen life's tough side during the war and in the coal mines, and umpiring in the Majors was "a breeze" by comparison. He often reminded himself of that very thing, even when he was alone on the road instead of at home with his wife and children. He gladly endured life as a minor league umpire, which included long car rides, tiny motel rooms and low pay, so the accommodations as a big league umpire seemed luxurious.

As for the work itself, the baseball was brilliant, but managers, players, and fans were unforgiving. Donatelli always felt an unstated pressure. If he couldn't do the job – or if a league boss thought he wasn't up to snuff – there were 30 guys ready to take his place. There was a common belief among veteran umpires that it took a newcomer at least five years to prove himself. It took a blink of an eye to get saddled with a bad reputation. Another big challenge for a major league umpire in the 1950s was handling the colossal personalities that patrolled the dugouts.

There were only eight National League clubs and the familiarity between the teams and umpires often generated contempt. Larger than life characters like Leo Durocher and Jackie Robinson were interested in winning baseball games, and badgering the umpires was part of their toolbox. The chatter was constant. The banter with umpires often included disguised insults, and from time to time outright rhubarbs.

Donatelli wasn't normally one to be trifled with, but that didn't deter ballplayers and managers from doing what they do best. Most respected Augie's abilities, which included his quickness afoot, or what was often termed "hustle."

"He always hustled," admitted one ballplayer, who wasn't particularly fond of Augie's style.

He had a certain flair in the way he made a call, which wasn't necessarily something players appreciated. His sharp, dynamic actions caught people's attention and left nothing to doubt regarding his opinion on the play. It was one of the things that caught Branch Rickey's eye when he scouted him in the minor leagues. Ballplayers, on the other hand, were always looking for things to chide umpires over. They could be non-relenting in their banter, most of which was unflattering. Some players weren't shy about chastising the occupation in public.

Hall of Famer Johnny Evers was quoted as saying, "My favorite umpire is a dead one." Christy Mathewson, who was called the "Christian Gentleman," made the following observation: "Many baseball fans look upon an umpire as sort of a necessary evil to the luxury of baseball, like the odor that follows an automobile."

Donatelli gained a reputation for having a quick hook for those who second-guessed his decisions, and he developed a patented direct military-like order for those who challenged his calls. "To the showers!" he would scream when he decided to eject them from the game. But Donatelli also quickly gained a reputation for getting the calls right, especially when it came to balls and strikes.

"Augie was a legend," said Ron Luciano, a flamboyant American League umpire from 1968 to 1980. When I was first starting out and in the minors, Augie's name always came up. Whenever his name was mentioned everyone would bow their heads and say – wow." Luciano extended the syllables of the word "woooooowwww" to punctuate the conviction of his sentiment. "I remember going to the El Cap, his brother's restaurant in St. Petersburg. All the minor league umpires would go there, and when Augie first walked in, I remember being amazed at how small he was. He was a big legend with lots of pep and energy, but he was a small man."

Augie checking his gear in his Pennsylvania home in the 1950s. Photo courtesy The Donatelli Collection.

He only stood 5'9", but Augie had always been a better than average athlete, and remained very quick on his feet. That ability became an important asset. Augie stated that he was once clocked at 10.5 seconds for the 100 yard dash, which was much faster than most of his colleagues He quickly gained the reputation of having an uncanny knack for anticipating where a play would go. There were times when he got so close to a play on the bases that he seemed to be part of the action. He felt that his quickness allowed him to get into position so that he could get the best line of sight. During an era in which his colleagues made rather mechanical signals, Augie got down low on one knee and made crisp motions. And as his minor league umpiring cohort Pat Paden so accurately stated, he also had the courage of his convictions. Once he made up his mind, it was usually made up for good even if a play involved one of his colleagues.

During a contest in the 1950s, fellow umpire Tom Gorman was behind the plate in a 7-0 game in Pittsburgh, with Donatelli umpiring at third base. There were two outs in the ninth, and the bases were loaded with Pete Castiglione batting. The pitch whisked in. It was tight. Castiglione hit the ground and the ball bounced in front of home plate. The pitcher quickly fielded the ball and fired to first base where an out call was made. Gorman made no signal. All the players ran off the field as though the game was over, and the other umpires did the same except for Donatelli, who approached Castiglione as he sat on the ground and in obvious pain. Augie, still a young umpire at the time, couldn't get over the fact that Gorman walked away so nonchalantly without making any kind of call. True the score was lopsided, but to Donatelli that wasn't the point. Augie walked off the field and headed for the umpire's locker room where he found Gorman lighting up a cigar.

"Tom," said Augie, "that ball hit Castiglione."

The room suddenly went silent.

Gorman then fired back with an annoyed tone of voice, "What the hell, that ball bounced off the bat, it never touched him."

"What are you talking about, Tom? The guy is hurt. I'm telling you it hit him."

Gorman didn't buy it, and told Augie to forget about the play and the game. Back at the hotel, Donatelli's phone rang at 2 A.M.

"Hello, Augie I'm looking for Tom Gorman. I know you don't want to hear this but I need a quote from Gorman. It's about Castiglione, his hand is broken."

"Well, Gorman left town," said Donatelli as he slammed the phone back on its cradle.

Donatelli was angry with himself. He regretted his inaction the moment he saw the batter get hit. 'I should have run in there and stopped the play,' he thought. It was the type of call that could only be viewed as a screw up. It was also a play that people might talk about. The play generated some uproar, but more importantly, it served as a valuable lesson for Donatelli.

Umpires rarely admit to mistakes. Babe Pinelli was one of the few umpires who openly admitted missing a call. When a manager argued a decision that Pinelli knew he had muffed, the umpire allowed him more time to argue.

"Go ahead, go ahead," Pinelli would mumble under his breath. After hearing the manager out, he'd say, "That's enough. Go back to the dugout. I admit I kicked the call."

That wasn't Augie's style. He went by the same philosophy as his umpiring predecessor, Bill Klem, who was long considered the prototypical national league umpire. Klem said that he "never missed one in his heart." Donatelli felt the same way. The blown play in Pittsburgh was an exception because he knew that he had made a mistake of non-action and vowed never to make another one like it.

For decades the number one rabble-rouser and chief agitator of most umpire's was Leo Durocher. "The Lip" was his moniker, because he gave EVERYONE a piece of his. Leo was a natural when it came to raising people's ire, including his teammates. And the prospect of locking horns with big name stars didn't daunt him. As a member of the Yankees in the early twenties, he was not well liked by teammate Babe Ruth, who snidely referred to him as the "All-American Out." Leo was a firebrand with an evocative way about him that elevated simple conversations into heated debates. He once joined forces with a stadium security guard to pummel a loud-mouthed fan under the stands. He is perhaps best known for uttering a callous phrase that made its way into everyday language, "Nice guys finish last." The quote took on a life of its own, and in later years he backpedaled on his landmark comment. "I didn't mean to say you couldn't be a nice guy and win."

Yet regardless of the nuances, there was no denying the connotation of the statement. Durocher cherished a good fight. He managed in 3,739 major league games and accumulated 2,008 victories, ranking him in the top 10 on the all-time list. His baseball fame and bigger-than-life personality brought him into contact with many celebrities; he was close friends with actor George Raft, with whom he shared a Los Angeles home. Raft often portrayed gangsters in motion pictures such as the 1932 film Scarface. Durocher embraced the glare of publicity and made appearances on numerous television programs, including *The Munsters*, *Mr. Ed*, *The Beverly Hillbillies*, and *What's My Line*. He also eventually became a color commentator on NBC's Game of the Week.

Some of his alleged associations carried unsavory undertones, including a casual friendship with gangster Bugsy Siegel. Leo also had a well-publicized marriage to divorced actress Laraine Day, which became the subject of much gossip. Leo managed the Dodgers the year Jackie Robinson broke the color barrier, and in spring training he was quoted as telling his squad that he would not put up with players who disagreed with Robinson joining the club. "I don't care if the guy is yellow or black or if he has stripes like a zebra. I'm the manager of this team and I say he plays."

He received credit for nurturing a young Willie Mays to stardom, and Leo was skipper of the New York Giants when they shocked the Brooklyn Dodgers in the famed playoff game in which Bobby Thomson smashed the so called shot heard round the world, a walk-off home run hit off of Ralph Branca at the Polo Grounds in New York. Durocher was a shrewd Hall of Fame manager who looked for every edge possible, and challenging the judgment of umpires was one of his favorite pastimes. He was ejected a remarkable total of 95 times, many of those exits were credited to Donatelli.

In 1951, Durocher paid a rare public compliment to an umpire. After being notified that Augie was going to work the remainder of the New York Giants' spring training games instead of veteran umpire Lon Warneke, Durocher exclaimed, "That's fine, Donatelli is a good man. Will someone remind me to send Ford Frick a gift as a token of my appreciation? Warneke is alright, but Donatelli is one of the best."

Augie bristled upon reading the comment in the newspaper. The thought of getting praise from Durocher at the expense of Warneke didn't sit well. The respected Warnake held the distinction of being the only man ever to play and umpire in both a World Series and an All-Star game. In fact, he played in five All-Star Games. He was also a former teammate of Durocher's in St. Louis, and nearly came to blows with him the year before when the two argued over a call. Augie was certain that he'd have ample opportunity to change Durocher's rose-colored outlook.

The next year, Durocher's Giants were playing the Braves in a doubleheader at the Polo Grounds. Donatelli was umpiring second base during the first game of that doubleheader when Walker Cooper, the Braves' catcher, started rubbing dirt on every single new ball that came into play. Leo the expert provocateur was being provoked by the catcher's machinations. The umpires decided to let it go.

As the innings wore on, Cooper, who knew he was driving Durocher crazy, continued the psychological ploy and put each and every ball through the "Cooper treatment." Leo reached a boiling point from the bench.

"How can you let him get away with that?" bellowed Durocher with his loud, raspy voice. "He's scuffing up the ball for the pitcher!"

After the Giants failed to score that inning, Leo walked out to the mound and asked to take a look at the baseball. Augie tossed it to him. Durocher inspected it briefly and then in a fit of rage, fired it into the ground and began covering it with dirt from the mound. Sensing an ejection at hand, the crowd went wild.

"I'll show them what a dirty ball really is," he screamed as he continued his tantrum, flailing his arms wildly as he covered the ball with even more dirt.

"There... see that! THAT's a dirty baseball!"

"You think I'm gonna let you get away with that?" growled Donatelli.

Durocher fumed out of control. He fired a barrage of profanities at Augie as he flung dirt everywhere.

"Go get cleaned up, you're through!" Augie responded.

With that, he signaled Durocher's ejection by making a sweeping motion. Durocher, who had turned beet red, hollered at the top of his lungs, "You ought to take a shower Donatelli, cause YOU STINK!"

Leo charged at Augie bringing back his fist with the intent of delivering a knockout punch, but several Giants players intervened at the last moment. They escorted Durocher off the field and back into the clubhouse. Donatelli had clearly joined the ranks of his fellow umpires on Leo's most-wanted list. Generally, the rule of thumb for ejecting someone pertained to physical contact, profanity, or showing the umpire up. Durocher's confrontation with Augie that day struck the bell on all three counts, and commissioner Ford Frick punished him with a five game suspension.

"You never denied a player his beef. If he wants to tell you he thinks you're wrong, that's his privilege. But if he uses bad language or insults you personally, he gets the run, and fast. Otherwise an umpire would lose control of a game in a hurry," said Augie. There's also the case of the man who prolongs his protests. You walk away from him and warn him that if he follows you, he's out. Then it's up to him."

For eight seasons Donatelli partnered with Jocko Conlan, an eventual Hall of Famer and a man Augie looked upon as his mentor. Conlan was known for a quick grin and a good sense of humor. He was a gentleman who wore polka-dotted ties, but when it came to Leo Durocher the gentlemanly umpire turned dark and surly. He had more than his share of disputes with Leo. None worse than the time the two men literally went toe to toe in Pittsburgh. The ugly confrontation happened after Pirate catcher Hal Smith misjudged a popup. When the ball dropped, it hit in fair ground and bounced foul.

Jocko quickly called it foul. Durocher charged out from the dugout and claimed that the ball had bounced off of Smith's glove before rolling into foul ground.

Conlan explained, "The ball didn't come within three feet of his glove."

"The hell it didn't," countered Durocher.

After a long profanity filled tirade, Durocher kicked Conlan in the shin guards. Jocko lost his composure. He kicked Durocher right back with his steel plated shoe. First he kicked Leo in the right leg and then the left. Both were solid shots.

Donatelli charged in from third base and bellowed, "Drop 'em" as if to tell the combatants to drop their feet back to the ground. Conlan's vicious kicks dug deep into Durocher's leg. Jocko responded by ripping the mask off his head and tossing it aside. He then pulled off his chest protector and raised his fists. For some reason Durocher, who rarely walked away from any sort of fight, turned around and went back into the dugout. He had been ejected, of course, but the fans seemed disappointed that Leo and Conlan didn't square off.

To say that the umpires reviled Durocher might be an understatement. During an actual physical altercation between Leo, who was managing the Giants, and Brooklyn outfielder Carl Furillo, umpire Babe Pinelli screamed out, "Kill him, Carl, kill him!" Furillo lost his cool after discovering that Durocher had ordered his pitcher to bean him. Furillo stood on first base for a few moments and then charged towards the Giants' dugout. He knocked Durocher to the ground and got him in a vicious head-lock. The outfielder's grip was only loosened when one of the Giants' players stomped on the outfielder's hand with such violence that it broke a bone.

This was the type of confrontation that symbolized the era, but it was certainly nothing that hadn't transpired years before. Young Augie had heard the stories of terrible free-for-alls from retired umpires and even Conlan himself.

In the early days of the profession, umpires were often spat upon, spiked, kicked, and verbally abused without much recourse. Fans hurled all sorts of objects at umpires. There were also physical attacks. One of the worst recorded incidents involving an umpire occurred in 1907, when Billy Evans, who held the distinction of being the youngest umpire in major league history at age 22, was hit by a thrown bottle during a ballgame in St. Louis. He nearly died from a fractured skull.

On another occasion Evans got into a fight with Ty Cobb. As the scrap began, he called upon the Georgia Peach to fight by the Marquis of Queensbury rules. Cobb ignored the plea, and by all accounts pummeled the umpire. Little was done to discourage the rowdiness. Owners and team officials understood how hatred of umpires helped generate interest and lured fans to games. Through the decades "Kill the umpire!" was a phrase that remained in baseball's vernacular, and the formation of its meaning was much more literal than most think. There was also high turnover in the occupation since few men were willing to put up with the dangers of the job or the lifestyle. In 1939, umpire George Magerkurth became involved in an embarrassing altercation during a Reds - Giants game. Cincinnati's Harry Craft hit a ball that went into the upper-left field stands down the line. Magerkurth called it a fair ball. Giants' shortstop Billy Jurges and Magerkurth began screaming at each other with so much emotion that the umpire unintentionally showered the player with a spray of saliva.

"Don't you spit at me!" Jurges yelled at the umpire. It was only a few seconds later that the men were intentionally spitting at each other. Jurges drew a massive fine and both men also drew 10 game suspensions.

The profession slowly gained in prestige and by the time Donatelli entered the scene in 1950, as a highly regarded young umpire, the job had earned a slightly greater degree of respect. Those who abused umpires were fined and suspended. The abuse abated, but never really stopped. In July of 1959 in a game between Los Angeles and St. Louis, a fan actually left his box seat and charged after umpire Bill Jackowski. The Cardinals claimed that catcher Johnny Roseboro had dropped a called third strike. The fan and umpire actually exchanged a barrage of punches before the fan was wrestled the to ground.

Sportswriter and editor Art Rosenbaum of the *San Francisco Chronicle* wrote in 1965, "An umpire is a loner. The restraints of his trade impose problems not normally endured by players, coaches, management, press and others connected with organized baseball. He is a friend to none. More often he is considered an enemy by all around him – including the fans in the stands who threaten his life."

Players and umpires often engaged in their own private little war of words that the fans were never privy to. Catcher Clyde McCullough of the Pirates would often make a habit of talking to himself while indirectly making a point to the umpire.

"I wish I had a bat in my hand," he'd mumble. "I'd have knocked that cripple over the fence. It's too bad there isn't anybody around here who can see those strikes."

During the entire one way conversation, McCullough would never turn his head towards the umpire. Subtle insults were also a tact artfully employed by Pee Wee Reese. According to Augie, the Dodgers shortstop was always a bit gun-shy when it came to the inside strike. With Donatelli behind the plate, Reese usually recoiled on an inside strike and voiced a complaint.

One time a pitch was a bit tighter than usual. Augie called it a strike. Pee Wee backed off the plate and gave Donatelli a funny look. He tapped his spikes with his bat and said, "Hey Augie, you're the second best umpire in the league." Donatelli ignored the comment. As the game progressed, Reese's words began ringing in his mind. 'The second best umpire?' What did he mean by that? If it was Reese's attempt to brown nose the umpire, it hardly seemed to be appropriate to call him second best and it wasn't a stinging enough comment to be a putdown. Why not just fire some sort of an insult. The next time Reese came to bat, Donatelli asked for a clarification.

"Pee Wee, what did you mean when you said that I was the second best umpire in the league? Who is the best?"

Reese shot back, "Everyone else is tied for first, Augie."

The answer came back so matter-of-factly that Donatelli just grimaced.

During a game between the Brooklyn Dodgers and Chicago Cubs third baseman Randy Jackson smashed a long fly ball with the bases loaded. Duke Snider raced back to the ivy wall, went up to make the catch when a fan leaned over and deflected the ball and it bounced back onto the field. Snider scooped it up and fired it to Reese. Donatelli signaled for a home run. Snider claimed that the fan had changed the trajectory of the ball. He was convinced that the play should have been deemed a ground rule double. Not having the modern day convenience of video replay, it was clearly a judgment play but Pee Wee then began arguing that Donatelli had not gone far enough into the outfield to get a good look. Augie decided to throw both Snider and Pee Wee out of the game. The shortstop then charged to the spot that he thought the umpire was when he made the call and hollered, "you made that call right here!" He was pointing to the outfield grass behind third base.

Donatelli was so miffed that the shortstop was accusing him of being out of position that he gestured to throw Pee Wee out of the game yet again.

"You've already thrown me out once!"

Reese then fired the baseball into the grass to mark the spot that he thought the umpire was standing when he made the call.

Insults and compliments seemed to come in waves, which some might perceive to indicate that the umpire was doing an even-handed job. Solly Hemus said of Donatelli: "He was the best ball-and-strike umpire there was. He was very sure of himself and you never saw him out of position."

In August of 1952 the Cardinals and Giants were battling it out in a key game in St. Louis. New York hitters were being shut down by Cards left-handed pitcher Alpha Brazle. With the score 3 to 1 in the top of the seventh, Bob Elliott came to bat with one out and Bobby Thomson on first following a single. Elliott complained about a called second strike and kicked the dirt hard. Donatelli felt Elliott had gone too far and ejected him. A heated argument followed. Coaches Freddy Fitzsimmons and Herman Franks were managing the Giants while Leo Durocher was serving a five-day suspension. The rhubarb involved a combination of coaches and umpires, including Al Barlick, Tom Gorman, and Lee Ballanfant, who restrained Elliott. After a long, heated exchange, the game resumed with the count no balls and two strikes to Bobby Hofman, who was sent to the plate to finish the at-bat. When the next pitch was called a strike, Hofman also kicked the dirt hard and created a dust cloud. Donatelli did not hesitate. He gave Hofman the heave-ho and more ugliness ensued. The umpire had thrown out two players in the same at bat! St. Louis won the game and the Giants were knocked into third place. The following day the *New York Times* story sub-headline read: *Another Dispute with Umpire Donatelli Marks Setback of Polo Grounders*

In an opening game of a series between the Giants and Dodgers at the Polo Grounds, Eddie Stanky, nicknamed The Brat, got into a confrontation with Donatelli over a check swing. Stanky lost his temper and began a verbal assault. Not wanting to lose his fiery second baseman, Durocher ran out and made peace. He stepped between Stanky and Donatelli, picked up the player's bat, stood it on end, and calmly told him to finish his business. The infuriated Stanky mumbled to himself and then hit a home run. When he got back to the dugout the Dodgers began giving "The Brat" the business.

"Hey, Eddie, screamed out Carl Furillo, "since when have you been part of the act of that Hollywood man – I mean ham."

"Here's your bat, Eddie, dear," mimicked Pee Wee Reese. "Don't get thrown out of the game, sweetie."

Eddie only grinned.

Branch Rickey once said of Eddie, "He can't hit and can't field …

all he can do is beat you." He was a no-holds barred scrapper in the mold of Durocher himself.

Stanky's antics began a wild fight in a game against Philadelphia when he began a distracting waving motion with his arms perfectly timed to his pitcher's delivery. He thought of the idea a few games before when Boston's Bob Elliott complained that umpire Al Barlick was in his line of vision during his at bat.

When the umpires, including Donatelli, tried to stop Stanky from performing his waving motion in Philadelphia, Durocher charged to Stanky's defense.

"What's wrong with trying to fool the batter, anyway?" asked Leo. "Everyone tries to do that in one way or another."

Stanky was subsequently fined and ordered to stop. It was all about trying to gain an edge, and the umpires determining a line which could not be crossed. Augie recalled an incident in Philadelphia in the seventies when Phillie shortstop Larry Bowa took a throw from his second baseman for an attempted forceout at second base. Umpire Bob Engel made the out call. Engel, however, missed the fact that Bowa had dropped the baseball.

"I saw that Bowa had dropped the ball, but since Engel refused to ask for help, I said nothing. It was Bob's call, and he was convinced that the runner was out so I kept quiet even though I saw Bowa fumble the ball. It was a mistake on my part, I should have gone in right away and made the correction, but I respected Engel and also knew he could be quite stubborn at the time, so I said nothing. An argument ensued, and it persisted until eventually they convinced Engel to ask me for help. I told everyone that Bowa had dropped the ball and that the runner was safe. I think both Bob and I were at fault on that particular play."

Donatelli also recalled a play that occurred in San Francisco when Orlando Cepeda hit a line drive toward the foul pole and landed foul by 30 feet. The umpire whom Augie was working with and whose name he refused to reveal, called it a fair ball.

"I couldn't believe my eyes. How the hell could a major league umpire make that bad a call unless he lost sight of the ball completely? It lasted at least a total of 15 minutes with every profanity you could imagine being tossed around. Finally, the umpire came over and asked me for help on the call, and I screamed out, "FOUL BALL!" That started another argument, but at least I was certain that I had made the correct call. Some umpires wanted help," continued Donatelli, "others don't, guys don't want to be shown up. I never particularly liked to have a call changed, but then again I don't ever recall having one changed on me in nearly 30 years of professional umpiring."

During a doubleheader at Connie Mack Stadium in Philadelphia, Donatelli ran into another situation that might have warranted an overturned call. It involved a tricky ground rule. At that time, the ballpark had light poles located up against the outfield wall, and the base of the poles were encased in wire cages that extended to the top of the wall. The ground rule stated that if a ball landed on top of the cage it was a home run. During the game, a ball hit off the top of the cage, and was ruled a ground-rule double. After he made the call, he told Donatelli that if the ball had hit the top of the cage it would have dropped through because there was no wire mesh on top of the cage.

"I knew he was wrong, but he refused to listen to me."

"There's no hole on top of that cage. The wire runs up against the pole. That's the way it's been for years," Augie argued.

"You're wrong, Augie," the other umpire insisted.

The umpire who made the call turned to the dressing-room attendant, who was always quiet as a dormouse, and asked him.

"Yes sir, there's a hole out there," he said.

Donatelli persisted, "Look, you've got 10 minutes before the next game starts. Go out there and check."

When he returned the umpire said, "Augie, you're right. There's no hole in that cage."

Overruling a fellow umpire, especially one for which there is mutual respect for was not a matter to take lightly. Umpires were taught to quickly forget mistakes or human misjudgments, because they might cloud a decision on an ensuing play. But it wasn't an easy thing to do. It was natural to stew about an argument well after it was over. If it was a play that led to an ejection, players were often fond of keeping the beef alive. Umpires were the gatekeepers to the game's integrity. They had the power akin to a judge – many offered their objections but their power was absolute. They were the guardians that kept it balanced. Whether the player was a star or a scrub, if he usurped an umpire's authority Augie felt he needed to be exiled to the showers. By the nature of the game, it was a decision that was often made in a matter of seconds. One thing for certain, Augie wasn't shy when it came to pulling the trigger.

Early in his career Augie had a wild confrontation with Brooklyn pitcher Russ Meyer, nicknamed "Mad Monk" or called "Rowdy" by some. The pitcher had a history of engaging in altercations with players and even a photographer. Coaches were somewhat fearful of removing him from ballgames. They were careful to keep their hand out of their pockets, so that they could defend themselves should he go berserk. The Phillies had grown so tired of his antics that they traded him to the Brooklyn Dodgers. In May of 1953 Meyer was pitching against his former teammates in a nationally televised ballgame. With the score tied in the seventh inning, Meyer vehemently disagreed with Donatelli's interpretation of the zone. After calling the 11th straight ball that forced in the go ahead run for the Phillies, Meyer stormed towards home plate. Catcher Roy Campanella jumped in between the umpire and the irate pitcher.

"You're a homer, Donatelli," screamed Meyer, a Pennsylvania native. Augie deemed the comment ludicrous because he grew up as a fan of the Pirates and not the Phillies.

"What did you say?" asked Augie in a disturbed tone.

"You're a damned homer."

"You're out of here!" Augie quickly retorted.

The eccentric pitcher then flung the rosin bag he had been clutching into the air. It flew skyward some thirty feet and when it returned to earth the bag hit the pitcher directly on the top of the head. In Augie's eyes the throwing of any kind of equipment was even more grounds for ejection. Not only was Meyer embarrassed by the fact that he had been plunked by the bag, but he was out of the game. On his way off the field, the pitcher fired an obscene gesture in Augie's direction. The sentiment was caught on television and generated immediate public outrage. Threats were made to arrest the pitcher, and a subsequent decision was made to prohibit cameras in all major league dugouts – a ban that lasted a decade.

Public outbursts such as Meyer's gave fuel to private speculation in which Donatelli doubted the maturity of grown men who played baseball for a living. In retrospect the stories seemed humorous, but as these incidents piled up, their cumulative toll weighed heavily. Was the task of an umpire to be judge and jury to a great national pastime, or was he a bouncer at a nightclub filled with men imbibed on a kid's game? They cared little about the difficulty of making split-second judgments, they cared nothing about him or his family; they were only interested in seeing that the call go in their favor. One moment in particular made him question the good sense of his major league brethren.

During the heat of the National League pennant race in 1969, Durocher managed the eventual runner-up Cubs. It was the initial season of divisional play, and the Cubs had a commanding nine-and-a-half game lead by mid-August. By early September the Amazin' Mets had pulled to within striking distance of first place. At the time, Chicago hadn't made a trip to the World Series since 1945. Leo got into a heated battle with Donatelli during a Saturday afternoon contest, and Augie tossed him out of the game.

On Sunday morning both men attended Mass in downtown Chicago. Durocher was sitting in his pew, and when Augie walked in he noticed that the spot next to Leo was open for the taking. In an effort to extend an olive branch, the umpire boldly decided to sit beside the man he had thrown out of the previous day's game. One could only imagine the thoughts that crossed Durocher's brow during the service; then came a point in the Mass when the Priest asked for everyone to share a sign of peace. Traditionally members of Catholic congregation shake hands with those seated in their vicinity. Donatelli turned to Durocher, reached out his hand and calmly said with a smile pursing his lips, "Peace, Leo, peace."

Durocher, with a sullen look on his face, grabbed Augie's hand as firmly as he could, leaned in towards the umpire and whispered, "WAR, AUGIE, WAR!."

EIGHT

Pitching Zeroes

The year was 1968, and the legendary Don Drysdale was zeroing in on Walter Johnson's seemingly insurmountable consecutive innings scoreless streak of 55 2/3 straight innings set in 1913. The smooth-talking handsome Drysdale was front and center in the national consciousness of baseball fans. Every fourth day, fans mindfully followed Drysdale's exploits in the box scores. By this time, Sandy Koufax had retired and the Los Angeles Dodgers were a middle-of-the-pack ballclub that struggled mightily to score runs, but the pitcher's remarkable dominance during this stretch made big headlines.

Donatelli was no stranger to Don Drysdale. He umpired behind the plate for many of the "Big D's" games, including some of his very first spring training games with Brooklyn, prior to the team's move to LA. Augie recalled a game in 1956 in which a 19-year-old Drysdale battled to make the monumental jump to the big league roster. The hard throwing sidearmer was a massive presence on the mound, who had command well past his years. It was late in spring training when manager Walter Alston gave the young pitcher a start against Milwaukee, a powerful hitting club that featured Hank Aaron and Eddie Mathews. Drysdale left the game after six impressive innings.

"Drysdale probably could have gone nine," Alston told reporters.

"Somebody else thought so, too," a reporter said. "A neutral party."

"Yeah, who was that?" Alston asked.

"Augie Donatelli."

"Well he should know. He umpired the game."

"Donatelli said the kid was the best pitcher he'd seen all spring," the reporter added.

"He may be at that," Alston said, smiling.

Weeks later, the Dodgers offered the teenager a major league contract.

Said Alston, "If Drysdale can pitch the way I think he can pitch, for all I care he can be 15."

Drysdale soon honed a reputation of being a fierce pitcher, who threw aggressively to the inside of the plate. He knocked batters down with regularity and had no misgivings about doing so. Donatelli recalled a particular game that Drysdale pitched. As the scenario unfolded, the Cincinnati Reds had two runners on base and Gene Freese was the batter. Freese was a good pull hitter, and Drysdale threw him a high curveball that he belted over the fence for a home run. The next time up, Freese walked up to the plate very slowly, knowing that Drysdale was going to seek retribution. He fully expected to be decked by a fastball. This was an era in baseball in which it was common for a pitcher to aggressively back a hitter off the plate. It was thought of as proper pitching strategy.

Drysdale prowled around the mound rubbing the baseball, making sure not to look directly at Freese. This wasn't personal, just business. Just as a boxer might fight a man he had a good relationship outside the ring. Freese was a journeyman, who had played for the Pirates, Cardinals, Phillies, and White Sox, but in 1961 he was a key member of the National League champion Reds. The third baseman played in 152 games and hit 26 home runs.

Freese hovered outside of the batter's box, as if he were a condemned man trying to stall for time. Everyone, including Donatelli, knew what was coming. Augie then whistled out to Drysdale to get his attention.

"We're ready, stop wasting time!"

Drysdale wound up and threw a fastball right at Gene's head. The ball ricocheted away and Freese went down in a heap. It was apparent that the baseball had hit either Freese's bat or his helmet. Freese had raised his bat around his face as he backed away from the pitch, and it was impossible for Donatelli to see whether the ball had hit his helmet or the bat. Augie suspected, from the sound of it, that the ball had ticked the bat. He looked at Freese who was lying on the ground with his eyes wide open. Augie concluded that the reaction didn't seem right for a man who had just been hit in the head.

"The ball didn't hit you," Augie said with an air of certainty, although he was anything but.

To his credit Freese honestly replied, "No."

Gene's uncomplaining tone probably came from the fact that he wanted a chance to swing at Drysdale's next pitch, so that he could get another shot at taking Drysdale deep. Donatelli turned toward the stands and screamed, "Foul ball!"

As a chorus of loud boos cascaded down, Reds manager Fred Hutchinson bolted out of the dugout and barked, "What the hell is going on here?"

Freese admitted to the manager that the ball hadn't hit him and Hutchinson backed down. The incident pointed to the fact that Drysdale was emblematic for his era. He was a brassy competitor who saw nothing wrong with owning the inside portion of the plate.

On May 31, 1968, with his consecutive innings scoreless streak still intact, the Dodgers led the Giants 3 to 0, when Drysdale found himself in an impossible predicament. In the bottom of the ninth, he walked Willie McCovey, then Jim Ray Hart singled to right, and Dave Marshall also walked to load the bases with nobody out. With both the streak and the game on the line, the big crowd at Dodger Stadium was standing. The fourth batter of the inning was 26-year-old Dick Dietz, a good-hitting Giants' catcher, who worked the count to two balls and two strikes. Catcher Jeff Torborg flashed the sign for a slider. Drysdale delivered a pitch that plunked Dietz on the left elbow. Dietz began trotting towards first base, and for an instant it seemed as though Drysdale's streak had come to an end. Plate umpire Harry Wendelstedt, who at the time was only in his third year in the major leagues, made a call that shocked everyone. Wendelstedt deemed that Dietz had not attempted to get out of the way of a pitch. He was not awarded a base, and the pitch was called a ball. The crowd roared with approval, and a 25 minute argument soon followed.

Drysdale watched as Dietz, Giants manager Herman Franks, and third base coach Peanuts Lowrey were bellowing loud complaints in the direction of home plate umpire Wendelstedt. It was a rarely made call, and in such a key situation it was almost unheard of. The call came within the context of a season in which Ron Hunt made a regular habit of being plunked by pitches, and reached base 25 times by doing so. In 1971, he was hit 50 times. Ironically, on this day, Hunt who played for the Giants was not at the heart of the controversy.

After the long delay, Dietz stepped back in the batter's box with the count three balls and two strikes. He fouled the next pitch off, and then ended the stalemate with a fly ball to shallow left. The bases were still loaded with one out when Drysdale faced pinch hitter Ty Cline. Cline ripped a hot shot to first baseman Wes Parker, who threw home for a force play. Then pinch-hitter Jack Hiatt popped out to end the ballgame. Drysdale had completed his fifth straight shutout, and Dodger Stadium was in a complete uproar over the accomplishment.

After the game, Franks said, "It was the worst call I've ever seen."

Donatelli wasn't part of the crew, but he quietly thought the exact opposite, and described it as a gutsy call.

Only a few weeks later, Donatelli found himself squarely at the center of the tempest. Drysdale was on the verge of breaking the record, and Donatelli was the home plate umpire. As he watched Drysdale fire his warm up pitches on June 8, Donatelli felt the electricity. A capacity crowd of 50,000 was on hand in Los Angeles on a Saturday night to see the 31-year-old pitcher make history. Drysdale was determined not to disappoint the hometown crowd. He held the Phillies scoreless in the first two innings. Augie recalled that the noise at Dodger Stadium was deafening.

The plot twist came when Philadelphia skipper Gene Mauch, widely regarded as one of baseball's sharpest young managers, requested that Augie check Drysdale's cap and hair for what Augie later termed as "excess moisture."

"In other words," recalled Augie, "Mauch was trying to convince me that Don was loading the ball up with a foreign substance. That was a whale of an accusation to make about a fellow who was about to break one of the greatest pitching records in baseball history."

Augie deliberated the accusation in his mind. It wasn't the first time that an opposing manager had made the observation. Weeks earlier, in the midst of Drysdale's fourth straight shutout, Al Barlick had inspected Drysdale's cap and glove after Houston manager Grady Hatton had made a similar complaint. Augie was mindful of the potential problem and examined the ball closely from time to time. There was no definitive proof, yet as the game moved along, Donatelli felt that there was an "outside chance" that Drysdale was doing something to the ball. It was also very possible that Mauch was trying to use Augie to break Drysdale's rhythm. Other than checking the ball, Donatelli decided not to interrupt the flow of the game.

"Oftentimes if an umpire went to the mound and searched a pitcher for a substance, he'd just delay the game and not accomplish anything. The moment was a big one for Drysdale, and I didn't want to put unfair pressure on him because of Mauch's badgering. I needed a real reason."

Hall of Famer Don Drysdale is in pursuit of a record scoreless innings streak, Donatelli behind the plate, infielder Roberto Pena batting for the Phillies, and the catcher is Tom Haller. Photo: The National Baseball Hall of Fame Library, Cooperstown, New York.

Augie proved to be very much the pragmatist, "Some pitchers use the spitball and I believe it should be legalized. It is impossible to catch a pitcher using the (wet) one because he is allowed to wet his fingers as long as he wipes them off." Despite the comment Donatelli realized that he had to enforce the rules as they stood, and his suspicions about Drysdale that day involved another foreign substance.

In the third inning, after Ken Boyer made a nice play on a hard-hit ball by Roberto Pena, Drysdale broke Walter Johnson's all-time record. The big crowd gave Drysdale a tremendous standing ovation. The record that had stood for 55 years had fallen. The record was in the books, but there was more side-drama set to unfold. In the fifth inning, the streak ended when Tony Taylor scored on a sacrifice fly hit by Howie Bedell; Drysdale's new mark stood at 58 and 2/3 innings. Oddly enough, it was the only run that Bedell drove in during the 1968 season. He batted nine times and only had one hit.

As Drysdale walked off the mound at the end of the fifth, Augie intercepted him at the third base line. He quickly grabbed the hat off the pitcher's head.

"What the hell are you doing?" an astonished Drysdale asked.

"Just checking you out," Donatelli answered. "Just making sure everything is okay."

Then Donatelli ran his fingers through the pitcher's hair.

"What the hell is this all about?" he asked. "Get away from me."

"Don't you talk like that to me," replied Augie.

"I'll tell you whatever I want to tell you. Usually when someone runs their fingers through my hair, she gives me a kiss, too."

"Don, you're throwing the greaseball," Augie yelled.

"No, Augie," Drysdale replied, "you know I don't throw that stuff."

Donatelli later admitted that he felt ill at ease approaching Drysdale after such a historic moment, but he also felt that he had finally noticed something that obligated him to do so. Augie was standing only three feet from the pitcher, and thought that he had detected the scent of Vaseline, or some type of grease. Drysdale stood 6' 6" tall and towered over Donatelli.

"Okay, okay, Augie," he said, "What do you want me to do?"

"Don't go any higher than your shoulders," Donatelli answered, "and don't rub your hand on your face or your neck."

"Drysdale answered, "Okay."

"Get out of here," Donatelli added. "Go back to the dugout. You're okay. There's nothing wrong with you. Get out of here."

Augie was far from certain that Drysdale never did anything to the ball, and prior to the warning Donatelli said, "His ball was moving like crazy and sinking out of this world." The very next inning after the warning, he was knocked out of the ballgame. Drysdale never admitted to using a foreign substance on the ball, but he never minded that opponents thought he did.

"What they say and what I did are two different things," said Drysdale, "I just went about my business. If they thought I threw a spitter, then I threw a spitter. If they started to think about the spitter, I'd throw them something else. That's part of the game; that's the game plan. There's always a psychological war going on between the pitcher and the hitter."

Donatelli thought that Drysdale was always looking to gain a certain mental advantage over his opponent; whether that meant throwing at a batter or throwing him a greaseball every so often – just to get the batter thinking. Pitchers did whatever was necessary to survive. Preacher Roe enjoyed tremendous years with the Brooklyn Dodgers using the spitball as part of his arsenal. Roger Kahn's *The Boys of Summer*, described an incident involving Roe, who earned the nickname 'Preacher" because he uttered the word as a three-year-old, in deference to a minister who took him rides on a horse drawn wagon. Roe studied the umpires, as a prisoner might study turnkeys, wrote Kahn. He was always on his guard. His closest call came when he had wet the ball, and suddenly Larry Goetz charged from his blind side. Goetz had been umpiring at second. "The ball, the ball, Preacher," Goetz roared.

Roe tossed the ball just beyond the umpire's reach and it rolled on the grass. Reese snatched the ball, rubbed it, and tossed it to Robinson, who performed the same maneuver before tossing it to Gil Hodges at first. Hodges threw it over to third to Billy Cox. Cox looked at the ball and gave it to the umpire along with a few choice words. Umpiring was not a profession for the meek. Controlling a group of baseball warriors like the Brooklyn Dodgers was almost as improbable as detecting a spitball. Before 1920 there was no rule stopping pitchers from using the spitter. Back then, pitchers used petroleum jelly, tobacco juice, and pine tar to increase the effectiveness of their pitches. But one of the masters didn't emerge until the 1960s when Gaylord Perry admittedly used everything from Vaseline to Preparation H.

Augie umpired many compelling pitching performances in front of loud raucous crowds, but one of the best efforts seemed as though it was played in front of a private audience at Wrigley Field. The official attendance figure was 2,918. A 29-year-old right-hander by the nickname Sam "Toothpick" Jones took the mound on May 12, 1955. Jones, a rookie, stood 6' 4" yet he earned the moniker "Toothpick" not because of his slim build, but because he chewed toothpicks while pitching. The Cubs had acquired the soft-spoken pitcher from the Cleveland Indians organization in an off-season deal that sent Ralph Kiner from the Cubs to the Indians. Jones, who had pitched for years in the Negro Leagues, was labeled a disappointment with the Indians, but his curveball was anything but. Donatelli called it, "The best I had ever seen." Augie wasn't alone in that opinion, Hobie Landrith, who later caught Jones with the Giants said, "You've never seen a curveball until you've seen Sam's curveball. If you were a right-handed hitter that ball was a good four feet behind you. It took a little courage to stay in there because he was wild and he could throw a fastball very hard."

Donatelli was the first base umpire that day, with Hal Dixon at second, Jocko Conlan at third, and Artie Gore behind the plate. It was a briskly played game. The closest thing to a base hit came in the seventh inning when Pittsburgh's Dick Groat hit a bouncer up the middle that Jones was somehow able to get his glove on and deflect toward second baseman Gene Baker, who made a slick play to nail Groat at first. It was clear that Jones was making a bid at a no-hitter, and was on the verge of being the first black pitcher to fire a no-hitter. It had been nearly four decades since Cubs' fans had witnessed a no-hitter at Wrigley; Hippo Vaughn had fired one back in 1917. In the ninth inning Jones walked the first three batters he faced: Gene Freese, pinch-hitter Preston Ward, and Tom Saffell. The bases were loaded and Cubs manager Stan Hack was on the verge of pulling Jones with one more walk.

Hack walked out to the mound and snapped at Jones, "Get that ball over, that's all!"

The potential tying run stepped to the plate in the form of shortstop Dick Groat with nobody out. Toothpick dug in, and using his great curveball, struck out in succession Groat and rookie Roberto Clemente, a future Hall of Famer. Then Frank Thomas stepped to the plate with two outs. Thomas, who stood 6' 3" tall and hit 286 homers in his career, was a feared slugger. On the first pitch to Thomas, Jones broke off an incredible curve that Thomas swung through. His second pitch was out of the strike zone. Then Thomas swung through a hanging curve for strike two. With the meager crowd making all the noise they could muster, Jones threw yet another curveball that home plate umpire Artie Gore called a third strike. Jones's' teammates swarmed him, and remarkably he later admitted that he had no idea that he had pitched a no-hitter until he was mobbed by his teammates.

"I was just out there throwing fast balls and curves," said Jones, who credited his catcher Clyde McCullough with the no-hitter. "Clyde deserves all the credit. I just kept throwing what he told me." Jones had made history by becoming the first black pitcher to throw a no-hitter.

The on field banter between players, managers, and umpires was always compelling stuff, and in a game with such colorful personalities, occasionally there would be surprise twists. Picher Jim Brosnan, who played for the Cubs, Cardinals, Reds, and Chicago White Sox recalled a time when Donatelli actually give him a word of encouragement. Brosnan was pitching in the Los Angeles Coliseum against the Dodgers: "I had a two - two pitch for a third strike. Charley Neal was the hitter. I had him K'd and I moaned and stared out toward center field. Augie was working second base, and he said: 'Don't let it bother you. Throw another strike.' It was a confession that the umpire had missed the pitch. Donatelli was encouraging me, telling me 'You've got to do it over again.'" Neal struck out swinging on the next pitch.

Augie rarely tossed words of encouragement to any player but he admitted that the human element of the game was sometimes too compelling to resist, and the comment seemed like a natural one for Donatelli. Augie wan't quite as supportive during two other memorable pitching performances from Brooklyn Dodgers hurlers in 1956, but sometimes surprising words of encouragement came from players to him.

On May 12, Carl Erskine faced the New York Giants at Ebbets Field. He walked two, struck out three and completed the second no-hitter of his career. "Oisk," as he was nicknamed, was suffering through arm problems. He had a sore left elbow, and on the day of the game he was suffering from muscle spasms in the back of his shoulder. Erskine was given a cortisone injection the day before, but when he arrived at the park he was so sore that he nearly asked Dodger skipper Walter Alston for the day off. It was always Alston's custom, when he stepped out of his office before a game, to hand the starting pitcher a new ball to warm up with.

As Erskine later recalled, "I had never asked out of the lineup before, so I hesitated. When Alston came out of the office and brought out a brand new ball. I wanted to hand it back to him. But for some reason, I didn't."

Donatelli commented, "Since I was working behind the plate for this one, I could see that Carl had fairly decent stuff despite his arm problems. Erskine's fastball wasn't overpowering, but his control was very good and he used his changeup pitch very well."

His opponent that day, Al Worthington, was also throwing well.

As usual, the Dodgers were fired up and ready to play against their hated cross-town rivals, but this time the Dodgers had an added incentive. There was an inflammatory article in a New York paper that morning in which the Giants chief scout, Tom Sheehan, was critical of Brooklyn's entire club. He intimated that catcher Roy Campanella and second baseman Jackie Robinson were past their prime, and that Erskine was no longer capable of winning with the "garbage" he'd been throwing.

According to Erskine, "Robinson read every issue of every New York paper." Carl added, "He cut the article and saved it and put in his pocket. The article might have motivated Jackie, but to be honest, it didn't help my confidence any."

It didn't seem to Donatelli that Erskine had any trouble with his confidence, or his arm. "He was outstanding, and it was a pleasure to work behind the plate, because he rarely complained about any ball or strike calls."

The umpires called Erskine the "great surveyor," because after throwing a good pitch that was close to the strike zone but called a ball, Erskine would raise his head sharply as if to ask, 'Where was that one?' He never cursed or complained; he just shifted the position of his head as a surveyor might while measuring a piece of real estate. In this case, the real estate was the strike zone.

The Brooklyn Dodgers bench was much less subtle. The home plate umpire was the main target of their wrath. The complaints flowed freely, but on this occasion they might be interpreted as words of encouragement.

"Bear down, Augie!" they'd scream.

"C'mon Augie," cried a voice after he'd call an Erskine pitch a ball. "You're better than that!"

Brooklyn fans were similar to the players – they were loud. Erskine was pitching a no-hitter and as it progressed into the later innings, a leather-lunged Dodger fan kept reminding Carl that he was on the verge of a no-hitter.

"That's it, Oisk," screamed a heavily accented voice from the stands, "no-hit da bums!"

From Donatelli's perspective the game progressed smoothly. There were no disputed plays, and the Dodgers made some exceptional defensive plays to preserve Erskine's no-hit bid. In the fourth inning, Willie Mays smashed a low liner towards the hole between third and short, and Jackie Robinson, who was playing third base made a wonderful diving grab. Two batters later, second baseman Daryl Spencer hit a ball to deep right-center field. Carl Furillo made a spectacular over-the-head grab near the fence.

"Furillo got a great jump on the ball," recalled Augie, "If he hadn't, it was a certain double."

Late in the game, the webbing in Erskine's glove broke and Carl was forced to borrow the glove of teammate Don Bessent. Erskine wasn't particularly superstitious, but he was uncomfortable with Bessent's glove.

Donatelli set himself up behind Dodger catcher Roy Campanella. Erskine finally stopped fidgeting with his glove. The score was 3 – 0 in favor of Brooklyn. The first batter in the ninth inning, pinch-hitter George Wilson, fouled out. The next hitter was leadoff man Whitey Lockman, who smashed a long fly ball to right that looked like a sure home run. But at the last instant, the ball hooked foul by a matter of inches. Then on an 0 – 2 pitch, Lockman pounded a very hard bouncer up the middle that Erskine somehow managed to knock down and throw to first base in time for the second out of the inning.

"Whew," recalled Donatelli, "that was a close one. Not that I was rooting for him, but holy hell, an umpire is as human as anyone else. If a fellow gets that close to a no-hitter, you don't mind seeing him get it."

The last batter was shortstop Alvin Dark, and Erskine got ahead in the count quickly, no balls and two strikes. This was it. The Giants were down to their last strike. Dark dug in, and Erskine peered in for the sign from Campanella. Donatelli adjusted his mask and positioned himself behind the catcher. Dark swung and tapped an easy hopper to Erskine, who fielded it with Bessent's glove. At that point, the crowd-noise swelled in anticipation, and the no-hitter became official as Erskine took careful aim at first baseman Gil Hodges and threw in time for out number three.

Brooklyn fans cheered wildly as the Dodger players celebrated on the mound with Erskine. Jackie Robinson, however, decided he had one last piece of business to attend to. He circled over to the Giants' box, where scout Tom Sheehan was seated. Jackie pulled the folded article out of his pocket, the same article in which Sheehan had called Erskine's stuff garbage, handed it to the somewhat embarrassed scout and said, "How do you like that garbage?"

Said Donatelli, "Robinson wasn't afraid to let people know how he felt; he was a great competitor to say the least."

Donatelli subsequently had a run-in with Jackie in June of 1956 that resulted in a $50 fine being levied against Robinson by National League president Warren Giles. In a game against the Cincinnati Redlegs, the 37-year-old Robinson, who was playing in his final season, grounded out in the eighth inning, but complained that the ball hit his toe in foul ground before it rolled back into fair territory. Augie called it a fair ball and threw Robinson out of the game when he fired his helmet away.

"When Donatelli told me I was out of the game, I barked back 'I don't give a damn.' For that I get fined?" complained Robinson. "Why? I didn't curse, except for saying that one word (damn) and it's a word practically every ball player in baseball uses at one time or another and gets away with it. If Donatelli said I cursed, he's a liar, but I don't think he did and I'm going to do everything possible to make Giles tell me why I was fined."

In *Jackie Robinson*, a biography by Arnold Rampersad the incident is depicted as something more malevolent. Rampersad wrote: "Unquestionably, racism played a role in such incidents; no supporter of racial integration or black players, Giles and many baseball administrators quietly detested a defiant Negro like Jack and sought ways to squash him. Jack was often a visible target for whites venting their anger against blacks as the nation underwent changes that had been unthinkable only a few years before."

As for Donatelli's part in it, he was widely known for not taking guff from any player of any race, religion, or creed, and would undoubtedly have thrown any player out of the game for disputing such a call in a similar way. In fact, he ejected a white ballplayer, Bob Elliott, in 1952 for kicking the dirt violently after a called strike. Giles, a former infantry officer during World War I, was a hard-nosed executive. During his long service as National League president, the league grew from eight teams to twelve and helped expand the game to the West Coast by promulgating the moves of the Dodgers and Giants. It might be difficult to find three more steadfast men than Giles, Robinson, and Donatelli. If one could imagine that the three were locked in a room to debate the issue, chances were quite good that many unabashed opinions were exchanged. To my knowledge such a meeting never took place but the three men butted heads on more than one occasion. Donatelli clashed directly with Giles on many umpire-labor issues. Robinson fumed at Giles for many of his umpire-related proclamations over the years. Clearly, no baseball executive could change Robinson's aggressive nature. Jackie was known for talking up a storm during ballgames, carrying out endless one-way conversations with umpires, while shouting encouragement to his pitcher.

The following was some of Jackie's banter as depicted in Roger Kahn's *Boys of Summer*: "(Ball one) Oh, no Ball shit. Don't worry. Bear down, Ralph. Where was it? Where was the pitch? Goddamnit, ump, do the best you can. Don't let him bother you, Ralph. Bear down. (ball two) Good pitch. Goddamn good pitch. Where you looking ump? Stay in the game. Bear down, Ralph. Don't mind him. Hey, ump, what the bleep are you trying to do?"

Giles issued a memo that asked "all Dodgers and especially Jackie Robinson to strive for courtesy in their address to umpires."

Robinson was irate that he had been singled out in the memorandum, and made no bones about it to Giles himself. He also wasn't shy about not sugarcoating the topic to the public.

"Anything I do, they'll give me the worst of breaks. I know what I am up against. I'm not blind. I think I know what's going on. Certain umpires are out to get me."

Years later, however, Jackie admitted to having a very short fuse when it came to umpires.

"I know it's wrong for me to lose my temper," Robinson said. "It doesn't do me any good and I really make an effort not to. The wife is after me about it all the time, too. But when an umpire makes an obvious mistake it seems I automatically blow up. I just can't help myself."

The Sporting News publicly criticized Jackie because of his "umpire-baiting," and his run-ins with Frank Dascoli, which turned the race issue inside-out, when the umpire accused Jackie of baiting him with ethnic slurs like "wop," and "dago" – charges that Robinson vehemently denied.

It wasn't only Robinson who battled with the umpires. The Dodgers were filled with masters of inventing convoluted names and semi-disguised insults. They created their own slang vocabulary. They used curious invented words like, "mawdicker" and called Dascoli "adaigo dancer."

In September of 1956, Donatelli got into a heated shouting match with Solly Hemus, who was playing for the Phillies. The fiery infielder had a reputation for battling both players and umpires. Sal "The Barber" Maglie, a one-time Giant mainstay took the mound for the Dodgers against Philadelphia. At this point in his career, Maglie was also considered past his prime, but his record was 11 and 4 and the Dodgers were in the thick of a pennant race battle with the Braves and the Reds. Maglie, working on only three days rest, retired the first eight batters he faced. The Ebbets Field crowd was in a frenzy as the 39-year-old Maglie held the Phillies hitless through seven innings. The Dodgers had a 5 to 0 lead after Roy Campanella, who was in the midst of a batting slump, hit a two-run homer to left-field to break out of it. The eighth inning brought a sudden burst of controversy that involved Donatelli. Augie was umpiring at first base. Willie Jones earned a lead-off walk, and after Elmer Valo popped out, Solly Hemus hit a hard grounder to first base that Gil Hodges pounced on and fired to Pee Wee Reese at second to start a perfectly executed 3-6-3 double play. Donatelli called Hemus's grounder a fair ball and the double play complete when Hodges took the throw from second. Hemus went berserk after Augie called him out at first. The fiery Hemus drop-kicked his helmet, and went nose-to-nose with Donatelli and even bumped into him. Donatelli ejected him.

Maglie took advantage of the Dodgers' solid defense and used only 110 pitches that night to become the oldest man to complete a no-hitter since 41-year-old Cy Young recorded the final no-hitter of his career in 1908.

"The main thing is that we won the game," said Maglie.

The Dodgers edged out the Milwaukee Braves by a single game and the Cincinnati Redlegs by two games to win the 1956 National League title as Maglie, Newcombe, and Clem Labine led the way. Newcombe won the MVP Award and the very first Cy Young award, and the Dodgers seemed primed to repeat their heroics of 1955; but the Dodgers lost a seven game World Series to the Yankees.

Donatelli was involved in yet another no-hit bid five years later in 1961. This time it was a pitchers' duel between Sam "Toothpick" Jones of the Giants and Warren Spahn of the Braves; and it was the 40-year-old Spahn and not Jones who was gunning for the no-hitter. The lefty hurler compiled 21 victories that season, and went on to pitch until the age of 44. During his brilliant career Spahn pitched 5,244 innings, recorded 2,583 strikeouts, and 363 victories as the winningest lefthander of all time. He compiled 13 twenty-win seasons. Spahn had pitched a no-hitter at the end of the 1960 season against the Phillies, and on April 28, 1961, he was vying for the second no-hitter of his career after not pitching a single no-hitter in his first 15 seasons.

Spahn had just turned 40 and he was pitching against a ferocious San Francisco lineup that featured Harvey Kuenn, Willie Mays, Willie McCovey, Orlando Cepeda, Felipe Alou, and Ed Bailey. Donatelli was behind the plate. The Braves scored in the first inning when they tallied an unearned run off Jones. Jones struck out ten batters, seven in the first three innings. Spahn had masterful control that day. He only gave up two bases on balls and both of those baserunners were erased on double plays started by Spahn himself. The game was played on a cold Friday evening at Milwaukee's County Stadium with a rather sparse crowd of 8,518. Spahn didn't have an overpowering fastball, but his pinpoint control kept the hard-hitting Giants lineup off balance. The closest thing to a base hit came in the ninth inning when pinch hitter Matty Alou dragged a bunt down the first base line. Spahn raced to the ball, scooped it with his bare hand and made a backhand flip to first baseman Joe Adcock, just in time to get the fast-running Alou. Then, pinch hitter Joey Amalfitano grounded to shortstop Roy McMillan who bobbled the ball, then fired to first to clinch the no hitter. Spahn had faced the minimum 27 batters to earn a 1 to 0 victory.

Willie Mays said of Spahn's performance, "He was all pitcher, with amazing control. He kept the hitters off balance with his changing speeds, and he never put the ball where you could get much bat on it."

"How do you figure it?" Spahn asked. "All those years of coming so close and now two of them. Sure. I was trying for a no-hitter, but I figured one in a lifetime was enough, so I was just out there trying to protect that one-run lead. It's just a crazy wonderful game."

Spahn became the second oldest pitcher to throw a no-hitter; Cy Young pitched his third and last no-hitter at the age of 41 in 1908.

Years later, after Spahn and Donatelli had both retired, they ran into each other at old-timers games. Warren enjoyed ribbing Donatelli.

"Hey, Augie," Spahn would say, "the only reason you worked on one knee was because that's the way coal miners worked when they're shoveling."

"He never forgot those days in the coal mine," recalled veteran umpire Ed Vargo, "Every time we had a big rhubarb, after it was over, Augie would go back to his position and pretend he was shoveling coal. That was his way of saying, 'Being out here is better than working in a coal mine.'"

Donatelli would often get down on one knee when he called a game behind the plate. He felt the low angle gave him a better view of the strike zone and a better opinion of the low strike.

Spahn also jokingly accused Donatelli of being more nervous than the veteran pitcher was during the no-hitter.

"Warren," answered Donatelli, "you hit the corner and I called it."

Spahn replied, "You're right, Augie. With you back there, a pitcher only got what he earned; no more, no less."

According to Spahn, "Donatelli always gave you a very good opinion of the strike zone," he said. "Whenever Augie Donatelli was behind the plate, I was very comfortable that I was going to get a good called ballgame."

Three years after Spahn's no-hitter, on April 23, 1964, Augie was the home plate umpire when Ken Johnson of the Houston Colts battled Joe Nuxhall of the Reds in a terrific pitchers' duel. Johnson was a thirty-year-old 6' 4" knuckleballer who was coming off an 11-17 season. The Colts had a weak-hitting lineup that didn't score many runs. Johnson's fortunes changed at the end of the 1963 season when he won five straight games. Then in 1964 he won his first two starts and was in the midst of a seven game winning streak when he took the mound against Nuxhall. There were only 5,426 fans in Houston's Colt Stadium to witness this pitching duel. Both pitchers were practically untouchable through eight innings. Nuxhall had held Houston to only five hits and struck out six.

In the top of the ninth, with one out, Pete Rose put down a bunt and Johnson threw the ball wildly to first. Rose was safe and ran down to second base on the error. The next batter was Chico Ruiz, who hit a grounder that bounced off of Johnson's leg towards third baseman Bob Aspromonte, who fielded the ball and threw Ruiz out as Rose advanced to third. With only one out to go to complete the no-hitter, Vada Pinson hit a hard grounder to second baseman Nellie Fox, who fumbled the ball, and allowed Pinson to reach first and Rose scored the only run of the game. Johnson then retired Frank Robinson on a fly ball. A run had scored, but he still hadn't allowed a single hit. Johnson was on the verge of becoming the first pitcher in history to complete a no-hitter and still lose.

In the bottom of the ninth with two outs, Pete Runnels grounded a ball to Deron Johnson at first. Johnson fielded the ball and tossed it to Joe Nuxhall ,who was covering. First base umpire Stan Landes called Runnels out to end the game – or so they thought. Augie noticed that Nuxhall didn't have complete control of the ball. All of the Reds players were running off the field when Donatelli reversed the decision and called Runnels safe at first.

"That's when all hell broke loose," recalled Augie.

"What are you talking about?" Nuxhall screamed. "The first-base umpire said the man was out, he was on top of the play!"

"It was clear as hell to me that you booted the ball," replied Augie, "the runner is safe."

Reds manager Fred Hutchinson went into a tirade, but Donatelli stuck to his guns. After the commotion died down, Cincinnati decided to play the game under protest, but the very next batter, Johnny Weekly took a called third strike to end the game. Johnson had officially become the first pitcher to allow no hits and no earned runs and still lose.

Fox was described as being near tears after the game. He approached Johnson in the Houston dressing room and said: "Ken, I'm sorry I had to mess it up."

"Don't feel bad about it, Nellie," Johnson replied. "I put the guy on myself."

The snake-bit pitcher was referring to the throwing error Johnson made on Rose's bunt.

No-hitters seemed to follow Donatelli almost as frequently as manager's tirades. In June, 1965, Jim Maloney of the Reds struck out 18 Mets. Donatelli was the second-base umpire. Maloney, whose career was cut short because of a damaged achilles tendon and a shoulder injury, was a dominant pitcher in his prime. In 1963, he was 23-7 and in 1965 he was 20- 9. Maloney also once struck out eight consecutive batters, including Hank Aaron and Eddie Matthews.

Maloney was so dominant in that game against the Mets that after facing him, players would turn around and go to the bench, shaking their heads. Center fielder Billy Cowan, said after striking out on three pitches against Maloney in the first inning, he walked back to the dugout and told his teammates, "Just forget it!"

Remarkably, Maloney gave up no hits through eleven innings, when rookie Johnny Lewis, a .250 hitter, smashed a home run to centerfield to end the no-hitter and win a stunning 1 – 0 game for the Mets.

Just two months later, Augie was also umpiring second when Maloney fired another dominant game. The venue was Wrigley Field in Chicago. Said Maloney, "I had the best stuff I ever had that day. I really felt that I was unhittable."

This was the first game of an afternoon doubleheader and Maloney cut through the Cubs lineup with 12 strikeouts, using his quick fastball and sharp curve. Although Maloney may have "felt" unhittable, his control was clearly off. He issued a mind-boggling 10 walks.

When Maloney came to bat in the seventh inning, opposing catcher Ed Bailey predicted that the pitcher would falter.

"You look pretty good, but we've got someone hiding in the weeds who will knock it out of the park on you."

"You might be right," Maloney answered, "it wouldn't surprise me at all after what has happened before."

Maloney stood 6' 2" tall and weighted over 200 pounds but his personality wasn't nearly as fierce as his fastball. Bailey, who caught Maloney earlier in his career, knew him well.

"He was a fun-loving guy," said Bailey. "If you were playing with him you'd have fun agitating him, and if you were playing against him you'd have fun agitating him, and if you were playing against him, you'd try to agitate him. He was a big strong boy, who was going to always give you his best all the time, no matter what anyone said or did. And if his best wasn't good enough, forget it. It wouldn't bother him."

The game remained scoreless until the top of the tenth. With one out, Reds shortstop Leo Cardenas hit a fly ball to left field that hit the flag pole. It was a home run off of Cubs' starter Larry Jackson to finally break the deadlock and give Maloney a 1 to 0 lead. Jackson had pitched a remarkable game himself.

Maloney took the mound in the bottom of the tenth looking to complete the no-hitter. The Cubs had a very solid lineup featuring Billy Williams, Ernie Banks, and Ron Santo. But to Maloney the names mattered little. He had an unusual psychological approach to pitching. After each out, he'd count how many more men he needed to get out to finish the game. After retiring the first man he faced, he'd say to himself, 'Only 26 guys to go.' Maloney counted backwards like that throughout the entire ballgame. He looked at hitters as though they were just another repetition in a workout – only three more pushups to go. But now only three outs remained for a no-hitter.

The home plate umpire, Mel Steiner, bore down as the intensity elevated to a new level.

"I don't think an umpire really gets hung up in the tension," Bailey later commented, "They're not gonna do anyone any favors."

Maloney walked the first batter he faced in the bottom of the tenth. He then ran the count to three balls and one strike to Billy Williams; Williams, however, flied out. The next batter was Ernie Banks. Maloney recalled, "I figured Banks would go for a homer – that's only common sense. So I pitched him low and away. He tried to pull the ball, but he hit to Cardenas for a double play and that was the ballgame."

Only two balls were hit out of the infield the entire game off of Maloney, who had thrown a staggering 187 pitches and had a full count 15 times. He had pitched a one-hitter in April, a no-hitter loss to the Mets in June, and then his second no-hitter of the year. After the game it was announced that the 25-year-old Maloney had earned his second $1,000 raise of the season. Bill DeWitt, president-general manager of the Reds, said he gave Maloney the raise since baseball, at the time, didn't allow bonuses for performance.

The Cubs were the focal point of another pitching performance that Donatelli recalled quite vivedly. On August 19, 1969, Ken Holtzman fired a no-hitter at Wrigley Field in front of over 37,000 fans while the Cubs were in first place.

"An umpire felt more pressure in front of a big crowd," recalled Augie. You couldn't help but notice the commotion. Of course, you blocked it out, but sometimes it was tough."

Dick Stello worked the plate for this game and Augie was the first base umpire.

Ron Santo hit a three-run homer in the first inning to give Holtzman a lead he never relinquished. Holzman threw extremely hard, but was aided by several spectacular plays. Second baseman Glenn Beckert made two terrific plays at the expense of Felipe Alou. On one of Alou's grounders, Beckert made an off-balance throw from behind the first base bag. It was a close play at first, but Donatelli called him out.

Then there was a long fly ball off the bat of Hank Aaron in the seventh.

Said Holtzman, "I said (to myself) that takes care of the no-hitter and the shutout. Then I looked up and Billy was climbing the wall for the ball."

Williams backed against the left field wall and grabbed Aaron's long fly to help preserve Holtzman's no hitter.

In the ninth inning, Alou hit a ball into short center. Shortstop Don Kessinger and centerfielder Don Young nearly crashed into each other, but Kessinger came up with a fine catch to save the no-hitter yet again. The Cubs won 3 to 0 and managed to maintain an eight game lead in the Eastern Division over the New York Mets.

"You saw another Koufax out there today," bellowed Durocher. "Years ago I said he could be another Koufax and maybe this is the beginning."

The 23 year-old Holtzman was of Jewish faith and a lefty just as Koufax was.

He had pitched the fifth no-hitter of the 1969 season, but it wasn't the last. On September 20th, Donatelli was behind the plate when Bob Moose fired a no-hitter against the Mets in front of 58,874 fans at Shea Stadium. This game was in the heat of the pennant race as the Mets were trying to hold off the Chicago Cubs and move closer to clinching the division title. The key play of the game came in the sixth inning when Wayne Garrett smashed a liner to right field. Roberto Clemente made a leaping one handed catch at the fence to steal a home run.

"That was one of the finest catches I had ever seen," recalled Augie.

Moose seemed to gain strength after the play, because in the eighth inning he struck out the side – Ron Swoboda, J.C. Martin, and Bud Harrelson.

The last no-hitter Donatelli participated in occurred on September 2nd, 1972. He was the first base umpire in a game that was nearly perfect. It was only a mere strike away from perfection. With 13,000 fans present at Wrigley Field, Chicago's Milt Pappas gave the San Diego Padres fits for nine innings. Bruce Froemming, who was only in his second season, was behind the plate. Pappas took his perfect game into the ninth inning with only a few close calls. In the fifth inning, Don Kessinger made an outstanding play on a sharply hit grounder by Nate Colbert to deep short. It was an easy call for Donatelli because the throw beat Colbert by a half a step. But in the eighth inning there was a close play when fleet-footed Derrel Thomas hit a shot off of Pappas's glove that rolled in back of the mound. Pappas fielded it and fired to first base. Thomas flew down the line but the throw beat him by a whisker. In the ninth, center fielder Bill North fell down chasing John Jeter's leadoff fly ball, but Billy Williams made a running catch.

The perfect game remained intact with two outs in the ninth inning. Pinch hitter Larry Stahl stepped to the plate. Stahl was quickly in the hole with a one-ball and two-strike count. Pappas threw three sliders that missed the strike zone, and Stahl laid off all three pitches. The perfect game went up in smoke. Three pitches later Pappas got Gary Jestadt to pop out and end the game and capture the no-hitter

After the game Pappas said to reporters, "Those pitches to Stahl weren't that far off and I was hoping he (umpire Froemming) would sympathize with me and give me the call. But they were balls, no question about it."

Decades later in an interview with writer Joe Lemire for SI.com, Pappas offered a completely different opinion.

" I just felt that the last three pitches — because I had one ball and two strikes on the last hitter — were there on the outside corner, but he called them all balls. If you look at Don Larsen's perfect game in the World Series, the last pitch thrown to [Dale] Mitchell went under his chin, for God's sake. The umpire knew what was going on, that there was a perfect game going on, and he called him out. Dale Mitchell never said a word. Yet you've got Bruce Froemming saying years later that he didn't know I had a perfect game. How dumb can that be? The umpire didn't even know what was going on in the course of a ballgame, which was ludicrous. I just don't understand why he called those pitches balls when there was a perfect game on the line. He's a very arrogant man… Mine didn't sink in really until I got home that night, when the phone started ringing and I was watching it on TV and realizing exactly what happened — that I should have had a perfect game."

According to Donatelli, "Froemming did a good job in calling those pitches balls, he kept the perfect game out of his mind and called the pitches the way he saw them, the way you're supposed to."

In 24 big league seasons, Donatelli was involved in 9 no-hit games. He worked four of those behind the plate. Other umpires who were fortunate enough to call multiple no-hitters include former American League Umpire Frank O'Loughlin, who called balls and strikes from 1902 to 1918 and called six no-hitters behind the plate. Harry Wendelstedt, Bill Dineen, and Bill Klem called five no-hitters behind the plate; eight umpires called four.

Great individual pitching performances are unforgettable days for an umpire. There were many times when an umpire became the focus of attention during situations that turned ugly. Those were the moments that umpires would like to forget.

NINE

Bums and Heroes

For an umpire, the needling was ever-present. The better arbiters numbed themselves from the constant cacophony that cascaded down from the stands. They often pretended not to hear it, but it was impossible to ignore, since catcalls from the stands happened before, during, and after many games. Problems with the fans were one thing, but a direct assault from a player was something that had to be thwarted at all costs. There was one incident early in Augie's career that reminded him more of a barroom brawl than anything that belonged on the baseball diamond. It occurred during Augie's second season as a major league umpire and it confirmed the fact his newly found career not only oftentimes made him a lonely target of derision but sometimes put him in the way of physical harm.

On August 11, 1951 the Brooklyn Dodgers led the New York Giants by 13 1/2 games. New York then went on a sixteen game winning streak that cut the Dodgers lead in half. Brooklyn felt the pressure as their lead continued to slip away like an uncontrollable rising tide. And as the troubled waters of the pennant race rose, the loose camaraderie the Dodgers enjoyed earlier in the year seemed to dissipate. Tempers were short.

By September 27, Brooklyn's lead was just a game as they played the finale of a four-game series in Boston. The Dodgers had lost two out of the first three games of the series to a fourth place Braves club.

It was the eighth inning, Donatelli was the third base umpire, and Frank Dascoli was behind the plate. With the score tied at three and nobody out with runners on first and third, Earl Torgeson stepped to the plate. Preacher Roe, a 22-game winner, was on the mound. Campanella signaled for the infield to move closer in order to cut off the run at the plate. Roe threw a curveball that the left-handed hitting Torgeson grounded slowly to Jackie Robinson, who fired the ball to Campanella in an attempt to cut down the runner, Bob Addis, who was charging home. Campanella adroitly blocked the plate, but the call from home plate umpire Frank Dascoli was safe. Stunned by the call, Campy quickly bounced to his feet and went directly at Dascoli, barking at the top of his lungs over the roar of the crowd.

"No, no, Frank, he's out!" screamed the catcher.

Dascoli turned his back on Campanella, which enraged the big catcher even more.

"I had him! I had him!" he shouted. "It wasn't even close. Man, I had him, I tell you!"

"He was safe!" Dascoli yelled back, again he turned his back on the catcher and began dusting off the plate.

Campanella went berserk and went toe to toe with the umpire as he fired his mitt into the dirt. Much of the Brooklyn team crowded around the wild scene at home plate.

"You're out of the game!" Dascoli shouted. Coach Cookie Lavagetto tore into Dascoli and was also ejected by the besieged home plate umpire. Donatelli and the other umpires tried to keep things from spiraling out of control by running interference.

"I didn't call him anything," Campanella later said, "I never called an umpire names in my life. I just said 'no, no, no, no, I had him! I asked him how he could call Addis safe when I had the plate completely blocked – and he threw me out of the game."

When play finally resumed, the Dodger bench continued to needle Dascoli.

It so enraged the umpire that he turned and ordered the bench cleared. Umpire Jocko Conlan marched into the dugout and led the players out and into the locker room. The players fired more insults as they were led away. A total of 15 Dodgers left the field, including pitcher Ralph Branca.

"What made it even worse," recalled Campanella, "was that I was due to hit in the next inning, with men on first and third and only one out. And a left-hander, Chet Nichols, was pitching, too. Instead, they put in Wayne Terwilliger and he hit into a double play. We lost the game by one run. I'll always believe I could have gotten that run in from third."

Dodgers manager Charlie Dressen said, "Campanella didn't touch or cuss Dascoli, Roy had a perfect right to protest such a lousy decision and so did Cookie Lavagetto. Why that's the first time Cookie has been kicked out of a game in 20 years."

After the game, tempers continued to flare, as visiting Dodger fans gave the umpiring crew a horrific time on their way to the dressing room, showering them with profanity and garbage. Donatelli was right in the middle of the onslaught. Then, as the four umpires made their way to the locker room, the ejected Campanella was waiting in street clothes to resume his argument with Dascoli. The umpire engaged the catcher briefly before escaping into the umpire's locker room. They quickly turned the lock on the wooden door in what they hoped was a safe haven. It wasn't long before the Dodger players began milling around, loudly cursing at Dascoli through the closed door. The players began banging loudly on the door, and finally attempted to kick it in. A team of six policemen promptly rushed to the scene to guard the door of the umpires' dressing room.

Later newspaper accounts indicated that it was Jackie Robinson who did the most damage to the door.

"I was really worried whether we were going to get out of that situation in one piece," Augie later admitted.

Reporters approached the four umpires after that game, and at first none of the four would talk. Finally, Dascoli made a statement: "Campanella threw his glove on the ground. That calls for an automatic ejection."

The players later countered that Dascoli should have given Campanella more slack considering the significance of the game. Manager Charlie Dressen lambasted Dascoli to the press some 20 minutes later, "Addis never touched the plate, Campanella blocked him perfectly, but you can't talk to that Dascoli. We've had trouble with him all season."

Braves manager Tommy Holmes had a different opinion. "I had a perfect view of the play from the third base coaching box. Addis slid without being tagged."

The controversy even turned into racial overtones when Robinson was blamed for kicking in the door panel.

"No," shouted Robinson. "Anybody who says I did it is a damned liar. Whenever I'm in a crowd and something happens," said Robinson, "right away it's me."

Donatelli later said that he believed that it had been Preacher Roe who actually broke a panel on the door. Roe was not accustomed to losing in 1951. The setback was only his third loss of the year. Many of the Dodger players assaulted the door, either kicking it or pounding at it on their way to their dressing room, so it was only a matter of time before it would give way. Robinson and Campanella were fined $100 apiece and Roe was fined $50. These were rather substantial penalties during an era in which players received salaries well under $20,000 per year.

After this devastating setback, the Dodgers went to Philadelphia to finish out their final three games of the regular season, while the Giants played the Braves in Boston. New York swept its final two games against the Braves. In total, they had won their final eight games to keep the pressure squarely on the Dodgers. On Sunday, September 30, 1951, the Dodgers and Giants were tied in the standings; Donatelli was in Boston to umpire the Giants' final series of the year. There are a series of time elapsed photos of Donatelli calling a 20-year-old Willie Mays safe at second after stealing a base against the Braves.

Meanwhile in Philadelphia, the Phillies were leading the Dodgers 8 to 5 in the fifth. The scoreboard at Shibe Park flashed that the Giants had won its game 3 to 2, and Brooklyn desperately needed to mount a comeback; a loss would hand the National League pennant to Leo Durocher and their hated rivals, the Giants. To that point, Jackie Robinson was having a bad game. In the first, he hit into a double play. In the second, he mishandled a ground ball. It was a mistake that cost the Dodgers two runs. Then he made an error in the fourth. Robinson ended the '51 season with a .992 fielding percentage and only seven errors, but he seemed to struggle in the most important game of the year, until the very last play of the game. The Dodgers rallied to send the game into extra innings. Then in the 12th, Philadelphia loaded the bases with two outs, and Eddie Watkins of the Phils hit a ball that appeared to be the game-winning hit over second. Robinson made an incredible diving catch to save the game. As Campanella later described it, "It was a flying belly-whop catch the likes of which I never saw before or since."

The Western Union operators were so certain that Waitkus's ball had dropped for a hit that a mistaken headline was flashed across the country:

"Phillies win! Dodgers Lose Pennant!"

Red Smith wrote of the catch that Robinson, "stretched at full length in the insubstantial twilight, the unconquerable doing the impossible."

In the 14th inning with two outs, Robinson hit a Robin Roberts pitch into the upper left field stands for a home run. After the final three outs were recorded, the 1951 pennant race had ended in a tie. Of course, that set the stage for the historic three-game playoff that ended with Bobby Thomson's ninth inning homer that became known as the "Shot heard around the world."

New York baseball was an indelible part of Donatelli's early career. His participation in the drama of 1951, in only his second season as an umpire, was only the tip of the iceberg. The very first Fall Classic he umpired was the 1955 World Series. The matchup featured the New York Yankees against the Brooklyn Dodgers.

"It's impossible to have more excitement in one town over a sports event than a subway series, and the Yankees against the Dodgers was a great battle. Mary Louise came to New York City from Pennsylvania by train."

Donatelli was comfortable knowing that she was nearby, and it was the first World Series she had ever attended. At the time umpires weren't provided with good tickets, so she wasn't sitting in a prime location.

"I never got nervous going to the games," recalled ML. "I knew he was in control. And he always was. He got along fine. I remember one time his sisters came to the game. Two of us went to get something to eat. The other sister stayed behind to watch the game and sure enough Augie got into an argument on the field. The other sister came running out into the corridor where we were waiting on line. She was so upset. I said, don't worry he'll be all right. I never worried about him umpiring. One of the things that attracted me to Augie was that I was quiet and he was always revved up to do something. That was excitement."

Donatelli was comfortable knowing that she was nearby, and it was the first World Series she had ever attended, but she certainly had seen her share of minor league parks.

"One of the things we always did well was travel together. I was great at helping him pack, and we often had to drive long distances during the early days when Augie umpired in the Sally League. We would drive all night. We never had money to stay in air-conditioned rooms. Our car wasn't even air conditioned."

In the fifties umpires weren't provided with good tickets, so ML wasn't sitting in a prime location, but the electricity and energy that emanated from New York City was inescapable. Walk down any street of any borough and one easily found a radio blaring play-by-play of the ballgame. In '55, the Dodgers had clinched the National League pennant by 13½ games and were in first place for 166 of the season's 168 days. Brooklyn fans were exhausted by the claims of "Wait til next year." This was the sixth World Series meeting between the rivals, and the Dodgers had yet to find a weakness in the mighty Bronx Bombers.

Donatelli moved around New York without being recognized, at least for the most part. Mary Louise often lamented that when her husband was recognized he would be engaged in endless baseball banter.

"There were times I had wished I brought a novel with me," she said.

There were also times when Donatelli was stopped and asked for an autograph, and most times he complied.

"Umpires are happy not to be recognized," said Augie. "You didn't want to be attacked by some nut. I know Jocko Conlan received threatening letters at times throughout the course of his career and was even accosted on the street. Luckily, Jocko knew how to take care of himself. Harry Wendelstedt and Bruce Froemming's lives were threatened prior to a playoff game in Philadelphia. The FBI even became involved. Nothing actually happened, but those are not the type of circumstances that an umpire should not have to work under."

During the '55 Series, the umpires stayed at the Sheraton Hotel, which was located in midtown.

"When it was time to go to the park, a few of us would take the subway and never felt like we were in danger. On our way to the game we almost never talked about baseball. We talked about restaurants, our families, the weather, anything under the sun, but we rarely talked baseball. If we did, it was always about situations that might come up during the game. We never talked about how well guys were doing or the type of things fans might discuss."

In 1955, Augie recalled arriving at both Yankee Stadium and Ebbets Field and often randomly greeted players when he arrived.

"I'd always try to greet the players of Italian descent in a way they'd appreciate. Whenever I ran into Carl Furillo – they called him Skoonj which came from the Italian word for snail, scungilli – I'd ask, Come sta?" An Italian phrase for how are you. Furillo was born in Stony Creek Mills, Pennsylvania, and was known for his cannon throwing arm, and his knack for fielding balls hit off the right-field wall at Ebbets Field. Furillo batted .314 and collected 95 RBIs with a career high 26 homers.

He had a similar greetings for Yogi Berra and Phil Rizzuto.

"Yogi was a nice guy, a very pleasant type. As for Phil, it was unusual for me to get Rizzuto into much of a conversation because he moved too fast. You'd say hello, and before you knew it, he'd scoot off somewhere."

The umpiring crew for the 1955 World Series included: Donatelli, Bill Summers, Lee Ballanfant, Jim Honochick, Red Flaherty, and Frank Dascoli. By this point, the wild incident involving Dascoli and the Dodgers from '51 was water under the bridge but it wasn't forgotten. In May of 1952 when Dodger players were reported as taunting Dascoli, league president Warren Giles sent a letter to manager Charles Dressen denouncing ethnic slurs from players that were directed towards umpires. Giles singled out Robinson. Robinson confronted Giles in person after another exchange of formal letters between O'Malley and Giles.

"I am satisfied that the matter is ended," O'Malley announced, "and that Jackie Robinson did not address anyone in uncomplimentary terms."

On May 13, Giles visited Brooklyn to present Roy Campanella with the 1951 MVP trophy, stating: "The National League is also proud of Jackie Robinson."

Game 1 of the Series was Donatelli's very first glimpse at "the House that Ruth Built." He had been there prior as a visitor, but it was his first look from the field as an umpire, and with slightly less than 64,000 fans on hand, he termed it, "A sight to behold."

Donatelli on the field at Yankee Stadium, where he served as umpire during the 1955 and '57 World Series. Photo Courtesy of the Donatelli Collection.

The first controversial call of the Series occurred in the eighth inning of the Series opener. With Whitey Ford pitching, Jackie Robinson stole home. Bill Summers made the safe call, but Berra thought he made the tag before Robinson hit the bag with his shoe. Yogi went nose to nose with the umpire. Even decades later Berra autographed a photo of that play with an editorial comment, the catcher wrote above his own signature, "He's still out!" Despite Robinson's daring steal and despite the fact that the Yankees were hobbled by injuries to Mickey Mantle and Hank Bauer, New York won the first two games. Some of the Dodgers were filled with self-doubt, including first game loser Don Newcombe, who said, "We were seriously worried whether we would ever beat the Yankees."

It wasn't until Game 2 that Donatelli found himself in the heat of the battle. Brooklyn's starter for that game was Billy Loes, who set the tone after the second pitch to leadoff hitter Hank Bauer. After home plate umpire Lee Ballanfant called it a ball, Loes glared harshly at the umpire. From that point on, he gave Ballanfant a collection of obviously hard stares. Augie took it all in from his position as the right field umpire.

Donatelli recalled the first World Series play that went in his direction.

"I was the right-field umpire, and Duke Snider belted a ball down the line that bounced near the stands in my direction. Fans were reaching out for the ball, and I was careful to keep a sharp lookout for the possibility of fan interference, Elston Howard glided over to field the ball and made a perfect throw to second base to nail Snider. It was a nice play by Howard, and I felt relieved that I had made my first World Series call, even though it was a non-call." There was no dispute or argument over the play when it occurred, but there was enough discussion and complaining after the game to merit a story the next day. One headline read: "Irate Dodgers Blame Umpire for Poor Call."

(UP) The Dodgers were roaring mad after yesterday's game at right-field umpire Augie Donatelli. They blamed him for killing a possible big inning that might have made them winners…they insisted that Donatelli blew the call because he was elaborately gesturing that the hit was fair, waving his arm toward centerfield with his back to the grandstand.

Donatelli knew that he had made the correct call and wondered why Walt Alston didn't bother to complain about the decision until after the game. The Dodger skipper said, "I thought that a fan touched the ball because it dropped dead on the ground and Elston Howard was able to grab it right up and make the throw that got Duke at second."

In Howard's view, "I was closer to it than anybody and I ought to know, the ball hit the red cinder path and bounced up and hit the top of the wire gate. It bounced right back on the ground and I picked it up."

Augie and his wife traveled back and forth from Yankee Stadium as though they were regular commuters. They left the Sheraton Hotel, located on 69th Street and headed for the ballpark on the subway. Umpiring at Ebbets field was always an experience. As the saying went, "Anything could happen in Brooklyn and usually did." The fans were always extremely vocal.

"Hey Donatelli, go back to the mines," was an occasional refrain during the series.

There was also a steady stream of off-color comments. Brooklyn starter Johnny Podres wasn't greeted with much enthusiasm when he walked out to the mound for Game Three. The youngster was celebrating his 23rd birthday on that day and Alston gave him the surprise start on a hunch.

"My impression of Podres was that he always was a tough customer," recalled Augie. "I never had any trouble with him, but he was known for being a guy who was good at raising cain. Johnny was a tough competitor."

Podres fired a seven-hitter to win Game 3 for Brooklyn. They also won games 4 and 5 at home. The Yankees won Game 6 by a score of 5 to 1 after starter Karl Spooner was reached for five runs in the first inning. The Dodgers not only lost the game, they also lost Duke Snider to a knee injury. Snider, who hit four home runs in the series, wrenched his knee while chasing a fly ball hit by Moose Skowron. He stepped in what was termed a "depression" in the field. It wasn't only Snider, 36-year-old Jackie Robinson was hobbled during Game Six when he aggravated a tendon in his foot. The Yankees were playing without Mickey Mantle, who pulled a muscle at the tail end of the regular season and was only available to pinch hit, and Hank Bauer who had pulled a muscle in the second game of the series.

It was a pair of lefthanders for Game 7, Tommy Byrne of the Yankees against Podres.

Said Podres before the game, "I'm the fair-haired boy. I'll do it up right for us."

Donatelli was the right-field umpire and had a good view of one of the most exciting plays in World Series history. The Dodgers jumped out to a 2 to 0 lead. In the top of the sixth, Pee Wee Reese singled to center past Rizzuto's outstretched glove. Snider, who was doubtful to even play, laid down a bunt and made it to first base safely after an error by Skowron. Roy Campanella also put down a sacrifice bunt. Reese advanced to third and Snider to second. Furillo was intentionally walked to load the bases. Stengel replaced Byrne with Bob Grim. Gil Hodges drove a ball to deep right center, scoring Reese with the Dodgers' second run of the game. Hodges also drove in the Dodgers' first run in the fourth inning with an RBI single that scored Campanella. Then with the bases loaded and two outs, Alston sent George Shuba to pinch hit for second baseman Don Zimmer in a critical at bat. Shuba grounded out to first baseman Moose Skowron, who tossed the ball to pitcher Bob Grim covering first base to retire the side. Since Zimmer was out of the game, the Dodgers brought Junior Gilliam in from left field to replace him at second, and then sent the speedy Sandy Amoros into left field. In the bottom of the sixth, Podres faced Yogi Berra with no outs and the tying runs on first and second. The big crowd at Yankee Stadium hoped that their clutch catcher might come through with another big hit. Berra, the AL MVP that season, sliced an opposite field fly ball down the line in left. Amoros made a running catch and fired a perfect throw to Reese, who relayed to first to double Gil McDougald. It's widely regarded as one of the greatest clutch catches in World Series history. Many later pondered what might have happened had Gilliam remained in the game in left field. Most concurred that Gilliam might never been able to catch Berra's shot and perhaps the entire outcome of the Series might have been altered.

Said the happy Cuban, "I run and run and run."

The *New York Daily News* headline blared: "Who's a Bum?"

Augie realized how fortunate the Dodgers were that Berra's ball didn't drop, and later expressed how lucky he was to be on the field to experience a World Series as a major league umpire.

After the game agents swarmed around Podres's locker, trying to get him to sign contracts for TV appearances and endorsements.

Not now, fellows," Podres said. I'm dead tired and too confused to think. There's nothing I'd like more now than to go to sleep then tomorrow go fishing."

Since beginning play in Brooklyn in 1890, it was the Dodgers first and only World Series title. And it came against their cross-town rivals, the team that had humiliated them in five previous World Series meetings. Podres found himself in the midst of a wild Brooklyn celebration. The team held a victory dinner at the Bossert Hotel in Brooklyn Heights, and despite police barriers established two blocks around the hotel, Podres was barely able to reach the party because of the overwhelming crowds that flowed onto the street.

Donatelli's first game behind the plate in a World Series occurred in Game 4 of the 1957 Fall Classic between the Milwaukee Braves and New York Yankees. The city of Milwaukee was thrilled to a small-town Mardi Gras-like fervor as they faced off against baseball's corporate giant from the big city. The Yankees and their fans looked down their noses at Braves fans and even proclaimed their enthusiasm as bush league. Milwaukee fans sported cowbells and whenever Casey Stengel marched out to the mound to talk with his pitcher, the fans counted his steps from the dugout to the mound and back. At one point Casey, upon his return to the dugout, threw a tauntingly elaborate kiss of appreciation to the fans at County Stadium. It was in the middle of this carnival atmosphere that Donatelli umpired his first World Series game behind the plate. Warren Spahn was on the mound for Milwaukee and Tommy Byrne for the Yankees.

The Braves were threatening to tie the Series at two games apiece. Milwaukee had a 4 – 1 lead going into the ninth inning with Spahn still on the mound. Yogi Berra and Gil McDougald guaranteed to make the ninth-inning interesting when both ripped two-out singles. Then with the count three balls and two strikes, Elston Howard hit a long homer to left that tied the score at four and sent the game into extra innings. The Yankees took the lead in the top of the tenth, and the first batter in the bottom of the tenth was pinch hitter "Nippy" Jones, who was batting for Spahn. Byrne threw an inside pitch to the pinch-hitter. The batter pulled back.

"I was expecting Byrne to come right at him and ram a fast ball right down the middle of the plate," said Donatelli. "Jones wasn't a big threat, and he was cold off the bench. Instead, Byrne threw a screwball that landed at Nippy's feet and skipped past Berra. The pitch nearly landed behind Jones, so I figured it could have hit him, but I didn't see the ball hit him, because I was screened out."

Augie looked at the pinch-hitter and shouted, "That's a ball!"

As the ball rolled towards the backstop Jones was complaining to Augie that the ball hit him, and when the ballboy retrieved the ball, Jones was quick to ask to see it. The ball boy, Chad Blossfield, who years later was to become an FBI agent, received a prime example of fine detective work. It was Blossfield who had shined the player's shoes prior to the game as part of his daily routine.

"Give ME the ball!" barked Augie.

"Yogi Berra started to holler that there was no mark on the ball but Donatelli grabbed it quickly and there it was" recalled Jones.

"Yup," said Augie many years later, "it was as plain as day, a big black mark on the ball from the shine off Nippy's shoe. I pointed for Jones to take his base and showed the ball to Berra. He said, 'Gee, that lucky son of a gun.'"

That ended any arguments that the Yankees might have had. Stengel chose not to argue, but instead decided to make some moves. Casey sent Byrne to the showers and in came reliever Bob Grim. Stengel also decided to pull Mantle from the game because of his bad leg, and shifted Tony Kubek from left field to center, and inserted Enos Slaughter into the game to play left. Milwaukee manager Fred Haney sent Felix Mantilla in as a pinch-runner. Then Red Schoendienst put down a perfect sacrifice bunt that sent Mantilla to second. Johnny Logan delivered a double off Grim, and Mantilla raced home with the tying run.

"Logan might have had a triple on the play," recalled Augie. "The Braves third-base coach was screaming, 'C'mon, c'mon' but Johnny put the brakes on at second."

Up stepped Eddie Mathews with the potential winning run on second. Donatelli remembered that Yogi turned to the Yankee bench; he wanted to walk Mathews intentionally.

"No, don't walk him. Pitch to him," declared Casey.

The on-deck batter was Hank Aaron, a right-handed hitter, and Grim was also a righty. Stengel, however, decided to have Grim pitch to the left-handed Mathews. Hank had belted 44 homers that season and had driven in 132 runs, and Mathews had hit 32 homers but he too was a future Hall of Famer and was widely regarded as one of the greatest third baseman to ever play the game. Between 1954 and '66, Mathews and Aaron combined to hit 863 home runs to move ahead of Babe Ruth and Lou Gehrig as the all-time home run hitting combo. For Stengel, it was pick your poison. With the count two balls and two strikes, Mathews converted Grim's fastball into a towering blast to right field that tied the Series at two games apiece and sent Milwaukee into a wild frenzy.

"I had the best feeling of my life when it left my bat," said Mathews.

As the ball sailed out, Donatelli was standing next to Berra and heard Yogi's comment over the din of the crowd. "I knew we should have walked him," said Berra.

Donatelli thought very highly of Mathews who he considered "a super tough competitor and was certainly the type of guy you wanted in your corner." Augie will forever be linked with Mathews since both appeared on the very first cover of *Sports Illustrated* which was published in 1954. Donatelli is perched behind Mathews as he uncoiled his powerful swing. At the time, Augie didn't think a great deal of the cover. "Covers come and go" he said, but as the years went by he appreciated it greatly. When the magazine celebrated its 35th anniversary with a party in New York, Donatelli attended alongside fellow cover boys Larry Doby, Kareem Abdul-Jabbar, Frank Gifford, Tom Seaver, Rafer Johnson, and Otto Graham.

In the aftermath of that come from behind Braves win in '57, Casey Stengel was caught up in a crowd of fans. One cigar smoking Braves' enthusiast walked right up to the veteran manager and asked him, "How would you like to manage Kansas City or Pittsburgh?" Some teenagers shouted, "You're a busher, you're a busher!" in retaliation to comments from Yankee supporters that intimated that Milwaukee was a bush league town.

Stengel also had a run in with Donatelli in Game 7 of the Series. In the third inning, with one out and a man on first, Johnny Logan bounced a grounder to Tony Kubek. It appeared to be a double play ball, but Kubek's high throw to second pulled Jerry Coleman off the bag, and the relay to first was too late to get Logan. Stengel argued the call with Donatelli, who was umpiring at first. It was a key play because instead of being out of the inning, Yankee starter Don Larsen had to pitch to Mathews with two men on. The clutch slugger ripped a double into the right-field corner that scored two runs. Then Hank Aaron delivered an RBI single to score Mathews and the Braves led 3 to 0. It was more than Braves' starter Lew Burdette needed. He pitched a 5 – 0 seven-hitter to become the first pitcher in 52 years to fire two shutouts in a World Series. The previous man to accomplish the feat was Christy Mathewson.

There were times during the Series when Stengel and the Yankees accused Burdette, who had compiled 24 consecutive scoreless innings, of throwing a spitball.

"As far as the umpires were concerned, Lew was innocent," commented Augie. "It's true that no matter how sure you were that a guy wasn't cheating, there was always the outside chance that he was throwing the spitter only in certain situations."

But Stengel was much less accusatory once the Braves took the seven-game Series, and Burdette had accumulated three complete game victories. "He is the best pitcher I have seen in three games against us this year. How many runs did we make against him? Two, that's all there is to it."

Donatelli's next World Series was in 1961, when the Yankees faced the Cincinnati Reds. That was the season in which the combination of Mickey Mantle, Roger Maris, and Moose Skowron decimated the American League with their home run power and the Yankees collected 109 wins. The year will always be remembered for Maris's accomplishments. The son of Croatian immigrants surpassed Babe Ruth's vaunted single-season home run mark of 60. Maris figured prominently in Game 3 of the Series. Hitless in 10 at-bats until the ninth inning of that game, he hit a home run that put New York ahead to stay. The win gave the Yankees a two games to one lead in the Series.

Donatelli was behind the plate during Game 4 of the Series. On the mound for the Yankees was Whitey Ford. That day, Ford broke Babe Ruth's World Series record of 29 2/3rd consecutive scoreless innings, and extended his consecutive scoreless-innings streak to 32, which was eventually surpassed by Mariano Rivera during the 2000 World Series.

Ford broke Ruth's mark before leaving the game in the sixth inning because of an ankle injury.

"It was an easy game to work behind the plate," said Donatelli of Ford's performance in '61. The Yankees won 7 – 0 and went on to win the Series in five games.

Augie reminisced about another game as being much more difficult from his perspective because of an injury he sustained.

"In the '67 Series between the Cardinals and Red Sox (Game 4), Bob Gibson's first pitch of the game was fouled off by Boston's Jerry Adair, and the ball hit me on the hand. It hurt like hell. I continued to umpire, and luckily the game turned out to be one-sided."

The final score was 6 to 0 as Gibson struck out six batters.

"I also remember staying up the entire night with my hand in a bucket of ice to keep the swelling down, just talking to my wife and some friends of the family. 'How are you going to hold on to the indicator tomorrow, Augie?' someone asked. I remember saying, hell, I haven't used one of those things in years!"

Game 7 of the 1967 World Series was in Boston, and again it was Bob Gibson who pitched like a master.

"Whenever I think back to that '67 season, Bob Gibson is the man who stands above the rest. He was injured during the regular season when the Pirates' Roberto Clemente hit a line drive off his leg that fractured a bone. But Gibson came back and was MVP of the Series against Boston. He won three games, allowed only three runs, and even won the seventh game."

His opponent was Jim Lonborg, who pitched as well as Gibson in the Series. He had won two games and had even allowed fewer hits than Gibson, but in Game 7, Lonborg was pitching on only two days rest while Gibson had three. The difference was very apparent in the final score as the Cardinals tallied seven runs off Lonborg in six innings. Gibson smashed a home run in the fifth inning, and Cardinal second baseman Julian Javier hit a three-run home run. The Cards won Game 7 easily by a score of 7 to 2. After the final out was recorded, the Cardinals surrounded Gibson on the mound.

As the Cardinals celebrated, a thought flashed through Augie's mind. He considered himself a family man and by this point he had four children: Carol, Barbara, David, and Patrick. He thought of his two sons.

"Dave and Pat were always used to the idea that I was an umpire, but they just looked at it as another day at the office. They were much more impressed by the players than they were by pop, but I was sure proud of my sons and all of my children for that matter. It was a great source of comfort and pride for me just to have them around and introduce them to people. I think it was only in later years that they began to appreciate and understand some of my accomplishments and some of the experiences I went through during my lifetime."

Without skipping a beat, Donatelli raced into the pile of St. Louis players and zeroed in on the caps of Dal Maxvill and Julian Javier. As they celebrated, he plucked the caps off of their heads – neither of them noticed. If you zero in closely on the historical film of that World Series celebration, there recorded for posterity is Donatelli streaking across the screen and grabbing the caps and running out of frame. The players had no idea what had transpired, nor did they care. The umpire's only intent was to grab a pair of souvenirs for his two sons. Mission accomplished.

TEN

Pride of the Umpires

Donatelli always introduced himself the same way.

"Hello. Augie Donatelli, National League Umpire."

Representing the game of baseball was a mission he took very seriously. He was genuinely honored and humbled by the interest and curiosity that fans showed when they discovered who he was, even when it came from those in his own fraternity.

The heady prestige of being a famous person would seemingly embolden most people, but on a scale of 1 to 10, Augie's confidence-meter was pinned on 11. It had nothing to do with baseball.

To add to his modicum of fame, Donatelli made his share of television and motion picture appearances, including a cameo in the 1968 film *The Odd Couple*, starring Jack Lemmon and Walter Matthau. He played the role of a first base umpire – a huge stretch.

The film also had cameos from fellow umpire Al Barlick, Maury Wills, Matty Alou, and Bill Mazeroski. Shot at Shea Stadium, the Mets were on the verge of blowing a one run lead with the bases loaded and no outs. Matthau, playing the role of sportswriter Oscar Madison, is diverted from the game by what he thinks is an emergency phone call. He soon discovers that the phone call is from his roommate Felix Ungar, played by Lemmon, who wanted to remind Oscar not to wolf down too many hot dogs at the game, because he was preparing franks and beans for dinner.

Donatelli laughing it up with Jack Lemmon between takes during filming
of *The Odd Couple* in 1968 . Photo courtesy The Donatelli Collection.

With impeccable timing, the Mets turn an around the horn triple
play to end the game, with Augie making a very authentic out call to
complete the triple play at first. Madison then instantly realizes that he
has missed one of the greatest defensive plays in baseball history. An
irate Oscar screams at his roommate over the phone, "Are you out of
your mind!?!"

Donatelli also appeared in a national campaign with Mets skipper
Casey Stengel. Naturally, the product they hawked was Bromo Seltzer,
a cure for upset stomachs. While on a flight from Los Angeles, Augie
ran into comedian Bob Hope, who seemed genuinely pleased to meet
Donatelli. Hope had become minority owner of the Cleveland Indians
when Bill Veeck acquired the team in 1946. A few minutes into the
conversation, Hope abruptly changed his tone and attempted to convince
Augie that he was headed for the wrong city.

"Hey, Augie," the comedian prodded, "the Dodgers aren't going to
New York. You'd better bail out."

"I suppose, in a way," Augie contemplated years later, "I was sort
of a celebrity myself, and the stars who met me thought that it was
exciting to meet a major league umpire. My wife said that fans always
wanted a piece of me, whether they wanted to just talk baseball or get
my autograph."

The 1962 All-Star game was a two game affair, held at a National
League and an American League venue. The first one was played in

Washington at District of Columbia Stadium, later renamed Robert F. Kennedy Memorial Stadium, and the second game was played at Chicago's Wrigley Field. The game in D.C., which was the home of the American League's Washington Senators, was played on a Tuesday afternoon on a warm, sunny day. Prior to the game, John F. Kennedy, a Red Sox fan, walked past the umpires' locker room. Augie brazenly stopped the entourage of officials and armed guards dead in their tracks. Kennedy was only the second president to attend an All-Star game and was scheduled to throw out the first pitch.

"Mr. President," Augie bellowed in his most confident umpire's voice as he beckoned to snag the President's attention. Kennedy looked at Augie and responded, "Hello, Mr. Umpire." According to Donatelli, he convinced the President of the United States to visit the umpires' locker room to sign autographs and meet the other members of the crew. Augie was a supporter of the young Commander in Chief and was elated that he had had captured his signature. He thought about how excited his family would be when he brought home proof of having met him. Kennedy spoke of a brief meeting he had with Stan Musial. He said to the perennial Cardinal All-Star, "A couple of years ago they told me I was too young to be president and you were too old to be playing baseball. But we fooled them." Musial had openly campaigned for the winning Kennedy / Johnson ticket "Mr. Kennedy was a real peach of a guy," recalled Augie. "It was the saddest day of my life when he was assassinated." Augie umpired first base, and after throwing out the first pitch, Kennedy sat through the entire game. In the sixth inning, with the game still scoreless, it was Stan Musial who delivered a pinch-hit single, which turned out to be his last All-Star hit. In 24 All-Star games, and 63 at-bats, Musial batted .317 and hit six homers. He won the 1955 game in Milwaukee with a 12th inning homer.

The connection between Augie and Stan Musial initially blossomed from the fact that the two men were raised within a few hours drive of each other. Musial, who grew up in Donora, a steel producing town near the Monongahela River and Donatelli in Bakerton. The Pennsylvanians shared other common threads. Donatelli worked a May 2, 1954 doubleheader in which Musial hit five home runs at Busch Stadium. The umpire was behind the plate for the first game in which the Hall of Famer hit three home runs. He was a base umpire for the nightcap in which Musial culminated his prolific day with a pair of home runs that landed outside the ballpark onto Grand Avenue. It proved to be an unforgettable seven hours of baseball for Donatelli. It also proved to be a memorable day for a young Cardinals fan who watched the game with his father. A kid by the name of Nate Colbert proclaimed to his dad that he would someday equal his hero's home run mark. As a member of the San Diego Padres 18 years later, Colbert hit five home runs in a doubleheader in Atlanta and collected a record 22 total bases – breaking Musial's record of 21. The first thing Colbert did after returning to the locker room was call his father. "Dad, remember the game we saw where Stan Musial hit those five home runs?" "Sure do," said his father. "Well, tonight I did it too!" answered Nate. His father replied, "I knew you could do it. It should have been you (to tie the record) because he was your favorite player"

Colbert's accomplishment was described in the *New York Times* by writer Sam Goldaper as one of the greatest hitting performances in baseball history. From Donatelli's point of view, Colbert's performance seemed even more remarkable because he was there in 1972 to see it first-hand, just as he had umpired the game in 1954 when Colbert's hero had accomplished the feat. Umpiring the only two five home run rampages in baseball history seemed to echo the fact that Donatelli's career had come full circle.

From the way Donatelli spoke of Musial, however, it was clear that "Stan the Man" was the player who impressed him most. Augie never uttered those complimentary words, but it seemed apparent by the way his face lit up when he spoke of the lifetime .331 hitter.

"Musial had a classy way about him," recalled Donatelli. "It wasn't only his great talent but his sportsmanlike attitude. He rarely disputed an umpire's decision. If there was a close play, he never said a word."

There was a wild incident during a 1954 game between the St. Louis Cardinals and Chicago Cubs that symbolized Musial's great class. The Cardinals trailed the Cubs 3 – 0 in the seventh inning with Musial at the plate and a runner on first with two outs. Pitcher Paul Minner had only allowed two singles when Musial stroked a ball into the right field corner that scored the runner from first. It appeared to be a possible turning point in the game, but first base umpire Lee Ballanfant signaled that the ball was foul. It was one of those plays in which the consensus of players thought the ball had landed in fair territory. The Cardinals' bench went wild over the call. Solly Hemus and manager Eddie Stanky were promptly thrown out of the game by Donatelli. Musial calmly walked over to Augie and asked, "What happened Augie, it didn't count, huh? Augie told him that the umpire had signaled that the ball had gone foul. Musial replied, "Well, there's nothing you can do about it." Musial stepped back into the batter's box and drilled the ball down the line once again, but this time Ballanfant called it fair. The hit sparked a six run rally and the Cardinals won the game. "Stan only had a harsh word for me one time, when I called him out on a third strike. He yelled something out from the bench, but I'm glad I couldn't make out what he said."

Augie Donatelli was behind the plate for Stan Musial's 3,000th base hit on May 13, 1958. Musial batted as a pinch hitter at Wrigley Field in Chicago and delivered a double to left that sparked a St. Louis victory. Copyright Bettmann/Corbis.

When Donatelli umpired first base during the 1962 All Star game, he stood only a few feet from Musial after he collected his final All-Star hit and trotted off the field. Coincidentally it was that very same All-Star game that Augie chose to make a point about umpire's compensation. Remarkably, umpires were not paid to work the All-Star game and only received gifts such as sterling silverware. Much to his dismay,

Donatelli recalled receiving a silver turkey platter, and vividly recalled a subsequent conversation with the assistant to the commissioner, Charlie Segar. "Charlie," he said, "I can't believe all we get for doing the All-Star game is a silly gift. It doesn't seem fair. He added, "Hell, any umpire worth his salt would like to work a great game like this, but he ought to be paid." Segar agreed to talk to commissioner Ford Frick about the matter. After the conversation, the umpires were awarded $500 each for working the '62 game.

Augie's youngest son, Pat was born in 1955 and it became increasingly difficult spending so much time on the road away from the kids. He recalled the time that he sat in front of the television set with Mary Louise, watching an All-Star game, when one of his daughters walked into the room with a friend. She was only six at the time, and she pointed at the home plate umpire on the television screen.

"That's my father!" she declared.

Her friend was duly impressed, and the two girls proceeded to walk out of the room. Donatelli was careful to remind his daughter a few minutes later that her father was indeed at home and not working the All-Star game on TV.

As the years marched by, paying closer attention to his family was of paramount importance, he decided that he would tote his son Pat with him to games at Forbes Field. Under age 10, Pat still recalled certain snapshot images deeply ingrained in his mind. It was a trip to the office to see how things were on the job. If your father happens to be a major league umpire, the observations become unforgettable. Pat recalled wandering around the Pirates locker room and a moment when Roberto Clemente looked him directly in the eyes. He remembered how his father asked him, "Where do you want to watch the game from?" Pat responded with a shrug of his shoulders and an innocent, "I don't know." "Okay, gimme your hand, let's go." They promptly walked into the Pirates dugout and Augie ambled up to manager Danny Murtaugh. "Hey Danny, keep an eye on my son, okay?"

Donatelli knew Murtaugh from his days as a player dating back to 1950. Like Donatelli, the Pirate skipper was also a World War II veteran who saw combat in Europe. The manager nodded nonchalantly and young Pat sat on the Pittsburgh Pirates bench as the game got underway. He marveled in wide-eyed wonderment as the game unfolded before his eyes. Then, he also recalled how Roberto Clemente and his father began a heated disagreement. Pat wasn't able to follow the gist of the conversation but soon noticed that Clemente was pointing in his direction. Could he be the cause of the dispute? Or was he a sidebar conversation to a baseball related dispute? Not long after, Donatelli marched towards his son. "Okay now," he said. "Ya gotta get going." The young Donatelli bravely wandered up the runway towards the locker room. He wasn't frightened, however, because he was trudging amongst his heroes. He only imagined, like a kid in a candy store, what sweet adventures lay ahead. Pat saw Pirates shortstop Gene Alley sitting on an inverted bucket chain smoking. The young Donatelli peered at Alley in amazement, as the slick fielding infielder puffed away. Then descending from above came the roar of the crowd. It echoed through the corridors, and served as a distant reminder that a game was going on. Not long after, a booming voice screamed from the vicinity of the dugout.

"Hey Gene, get a bat!"

"Gene hit a game winning home run," recalled Pat, "and the place went nuts. I think back on that moment often. How cool it was to be there. I often found myself in lots of cool places. I remember sitting with my pop in a car when he said,"let's go say hello to Maz. Then, there we were, visiting Bill Mazeroski." Years later, Mazeroski said, "Augie was one of the better umpires in my era. I enjoyed being around Augie and even visited him in his hometown of Ebensburg and enjoyed his company. He was just a down to earth type of guy from Pennsylvania and just about every player got along with him."

Bill Mazeroski, a Hall of Fame second baseman for the Pirates, became a national figure after hitting a dramatic game-winning home run in Game 7 of the 1960 World Series against the Yankees. Pat also recalled how Pirates announcer Bob Prince stopped by the Donatelli household to share a baseball story or two over a glass of wine. Prince broadcast Pirate games from 1948 to 1975 and was known for his rapid fire delivery. He gained the nickname "The Gunner." Pat loved listening to the announcer weave his stories with Augie at the kitchen table. Prince said, "I usually don't get to eat a hot dog until they're nice and green." The announcer's post-game dining experience eventually evolved into an inflatable green hot dog that fans used to spook opposing players.

The Donatelli kids often ran amuck around the household with their collection of inflated Green Weenies.

While Donatelli wasn't shy about fraternizing with players away from the diamond, he always managed to maintain total control of a ballgame.

Pittsburgh Pirates broadcaster Bob Prince with Augie Donatelli. Prince became a friend of the Donatelli family and often visited their home. Photo Courtesy of the Donatelli Collection.

Slugger Dick Allen recalled how Donatelli had a commanding presence. "When Augie umpired he had the game by the throat."

While he took no grief, the players maintained a certain comfort level knowing that Donatelli was in total control. Of course that wasn't the case with his son, who Augie occasionally brought on the road. The realization that for an umpire almost every game was a road game had a problematical effect on the family, and Donatelli desperately wanted to spend more time with his son. Yet this was clearly a more innocent era, before the game became over-scrutinized and off-beat highlights of mascots and other behind the scenes endeavors became the norm. A youngster randomly sitting in a major league dugout in the year 2011 would no doubt make every network's highlight package.

"During a game in Houston," said Pat, "I got to hang out in the runway behind home plate. It was great because I could see my father work and I wasn't getting in the way. I remember when Dick Allen stepped to the plate. He had his gold rim eyeglasses, white batting gloves, and a bright red jersey under his uniform. He was waving that huge 42 ounce bat."

Allen faced Astros hurler Jack DiLauro with the bases loaded and crushed a grand slam to centerfield, his 31st homer of the year and his sixth career grand slam. The blast helped St. Louis rout the Astros by a score of 14 to 7. The blowout came in the midst of a swirl of publicity surrounding Houston pitcher Jim Bouton, who was demoted to the minor leagues because of distractions surrounding his controversial book, *Ball Four.*

Pat Donatelli watched closely as Allen circled the bases. His eyes strayed from Allen to the ballboy as he picked up the slugger's bat.

"My jaw must have dropped to the ground as that ball sailed out," said Pat. Then I noticed that the bat was cracked. Sure enough I told the kid to hand the bat over to me."

"You sure?" the batboy asked, "it's busted"

"Yeah, pass it over."

The 15-year-old Donatelli cherished that bat for the entire summer.

"I stuck a nail in it to hold it together, and used it for months."

The umpire's son found himself thrust in the center of moments that might make any baseball fan green with envy. When the family moved to Florida, Pat was asked to assist Yankee legend Joe DiMaggio as he signed trays filled with baseballs at Al Lang Field in St. Petersburg, Florida.

"I helped hand the baseballs to Joe. He signed 'em and I would put them in the trays. I just happened to run into writer Joe Durso who recruited me for the job. I'll never forget when DiMaggio was done signing we walked out with all of the trays. We had to cross out in the open in a spot where a group of kids were camped out waiting for autographs."

One of the overzealous youngsters bumped into DiMaggio and the entire tray of signed baseballs fell to the ground and bounced in every direction. Pat shifted into emergency mode and coxed the kids to hand most of the baseballs back. "It was almost like a scene from some kind of comedy movie. There I was with the Yankee Clipper chasing after all of these baseballs that are probably worth a fortune today."

The Midsummer Classic always captured a great deal of attention across the country because of the great ball players it featured. Donatelli umpired his first All-Star Game at Crosley Field in Cincinnati in 1953. There were three National League umpires assigned to the game including Jocko Conlan and Bill Engeln. Among players, Johnny Mize, Mickey Mantle, Yogi Berra, Stan Musial, and Eddie Mathews participated.

Despite all of the offensive firepower, the game remained scoreless through the first four innings until Richie Ashburn and Pee Wee Reese both drove in runs with singles to give the National League the lead. The very next inning, right fielder Enos Slaughter raced after a line drive hit by Harvey Kuenn and made a diving, tumbling grab that ranked among the finest in All-Star history. By the eighth inning, the National Leaguers had a 3–0 lead. American League manager Casey Stengel brought in 47 year old Satchel Paige to pitch, who became the oldest pitcher to ever appear in an All-Star game.

Satchel played for the St. Louis Browns at the time, and was still an effective pitcher, but he was well past his prime. Enos Slaughter batted against Paige and swung wildly through the first two pitches that Satchel threw, but on the third pitch Slaughter lined a single that scored the fourth run of the game, then Satchel gave up another run-scoring hit to pitcher Murry Dickson.

"Satchel was great. But the amazing thing about Satchel, as far as I was concerned," said Augie, "was the fact that I saw him pitch in the Negro Leagues when he played for the Pittsburgh Crawfords in 1936, and in no way could I have imagined that 17 years later I'd be participating in a Major League All-Star game with him. He came back to pitch in 1965 for Kansas City at the age of 59. I liked his phrase,

'Don't look back…something might be gaining on you.' But not so good advice for a tail gunner."

The first 1959 All-Star game was played in Donatelli's home state of Pennsylvania at Pittsburgh's Forbes Field. The game took place in conjunction with the Steel City's bicentennial celebration, and it featured great talent worthy of the occasion. It was the second and final All-Star game played there. Vice President Richard Nixon threw out the first ball, and NBC covered the game nationally on both television and radio. 22-year-old Don Drysdale made his first appearance as an All-Star and pitched a tremendous game, striking out four batters in three innings while allowing no hits or walks. As usual he threw hard and maintained reputation of not being afraid to throw inside. Donatelli had forged a reputation as one of the finest arbiters of balls and strikes of all time, but ironically he never worked behind the plate during the Midsummer Classic. At the time, the players were selected by vote of league players. Commissioner Ford Frick announced the umpires: Barlick behind the plate, American League umpire Ed Runge at first, Donatelli at second base, and Joe Paparella at third. The foul line umpires were NL umpire Shag Crawford and AL ump John Rice. The rule required that the senior man from the league that was the home team to call the balls and strikes. Barlick worked behind the plate in Pittsburgh because he was the senior NL umpire. The other four games that Donatelli umpired were in American League ballparks.

"There were some years when I might have had a chance to work the plate," said Donatelli, "but at the time, umpires were paid absolutely nothing to work the game, and I valued time at home with my family more than working. But there was a lot of prestige involved in those games."

Forbes Field was the home of the Pirates from 1909 to 1970, and also the home of the Homestead Grays of the Negro Leagues, and Augie attended games of both teams as a fan. The ballpark was also the site of Babe Ruth's 714th and final home run in 1935. The most famous home run, however, was the one Bill Mazeroski hit to win the 1960 World Series for the Pirates.

In that 1959 All-Star game, Pirate reliever Elroy Face, who accumulated an amazing 12 and 0 record at the All-Star break and an 18 and 1 record by the end of the '59 season, gave up three earned runs in front of his hometown crowd in Pittsburgh. But the National League had a powerful lineup including Hank Aaron, Ernie Banks, Orlando Cepeda, Willie Mays; and 38-year-old Stan Musial, appearing in his 16th All-Star game.

"Mays was the best all-around ballplayer I ever saw," said Augie.

In that '59 game, Mays hit a triple off of Whitey Ford that scored the go-ahead run in front of a capacity crowd of 35,277 fans to give the National League All-Stars a 5 to 4 victory. Donatelli also worked the 1969 All-Star game in Washington and it turned out to be his last Midsummer Classic. He was slated to work first base during a night game, but it rained so hard that the game was postponed until the next afternoon. The scheduled starting pitcher for the American League was the Tigers' Denny McLain, but after the rainout McLain decided to fly to Detroit for a dental appointment. Since he didn't return in time, the Yankees' Mel Stottlemyre started for the American Leaguers. Johnny Bench hit a two-run homer in the second inning. McLain was inserted into the game in the fourth inning and gave up a run that put the National League ahead 9 to 2. There was terrific defensive play in the bottom of the sixth inning made by Boston's Carl Yastrzemski off the bat of Bench, robbing Johnny of his second home run of the game. Yastrzemski made a leaping grab at the fence with his glove at least three feet above the top of the barrier. Both Bench and Yastrzemski were inducted into the Hall of Fame together on their first ballot in 1989.

Donatelli was a bit of an iconoclast. He did things his own way. Umpires aren't taught to bend all the way down on one knee the way he did behind the plate, but it was a technique he developed with experience. He claimed that it gave him a terrific view of the strike zone, and it stabilized his vision. However, in getting down so low to call balls and strikes, he occasionally was prone to lose his balance, which made him place his hand on the catcher to maintain his stability. When a catcher complained about the umpire's touch by asking, "Is it legal for an umpire to touch a player?"

Augie replied, "It is now."

Donatelli even used an unconventional technique to elicit honest responses from players. During a game at Chicago's Wrigley Field, Frank Howard went back on a ball as it sailed towards the ivy-covered wall. Howard jumped in an attempt to snag the baseball, but just as he did a fan accidentally spilled some popcorn out of a giant bucket. He was jockeying for position and some of the popcorn landed on Howard as he attempted to make the grab. Howard missed the ball and two runs crossed the plate. Dodger manager Walter Alston ran out to the outfield and made the point that the fan's popcorn had interfered with the play. It seemed like a valid argument until Donatelli turned to the outfielder and asked, "Did the popcorn bother you?"

Frank responded, "What popcorn?"

Alston turned and marched off the field without saying another word. As American League umpire Ron Luciano once put it, "Nowadays people don't care how you make a call as long as you get it right. But back in the forties and before, there was only one way to make a call: very mechanical. Augie changed all of that. He put his hand on the catcher, put one leg way back, and was very demonstrative in his call."

Rumor had it that Donatelli inadvertently started umpiring balls and strikes on one knee because he was in physical pain after years of umpiring, others said that he did it because he was used to working that way in the coal mines. Miners were often accustomed to laboring in small spaces and had to swing their pick from that position. In actuality, he found the low angle gave him a better view of low, outside pitches. In his prime, Donatelli excelled at anticipating a play, and hustled into position quicker than most umpires. It gave him ample time to get what he deemed to be the best angle to make the correct call. His theory was that getting low to a play often gave him a better line of sight to the bag and the runner's foot. The better the angle, and the better the line of sight, the better chance he had of judging a play correctly.

The National League had a long history of picking umpires who were not tall but possessed a stocky frame. The American League leaned toward picking men of larger stature. As the years went by, size became less of a factor in grading potential major league umpires. After retiring, Donatelli and Al Barlick were employed by the National League as umpire supervisors under the direction of Ed Vargo. Just like Donatelli and Barlick, Vargo was a Pennsylvanian. He umpired from 1960 to 1983 and also earned a reputation for being an excellent judge of the strike zone.

These retired umpires were charged with the task of scouting potential major league umpiring prospects. The men employed a simple five-point rating system with five being the best and one the lowest score. "The only time I'd ever rate a man a five would be if I thought he graded out to be the best in his particular league," said Augie. Some of the criteria we are asked to consider when filing a report on a potential major league umpire include: judgment, consistency of the strike zone, hustle, decisiveness, and his or her ability to make rule interpretations under difficult circumstances. We were also asked to consider whether we thought an umpire had the ability to progress past the level he or she is currently in."

Other things umpires were graded on included: appearance, instincts on plays, and mobility. By the time the eighties rolled around, umpires were constantly being rated. Donatelli found that word invariably traveled fast when a crew found out they were being observed. He preferred that they didn't know he was on hand, because it added undue pressure. Augie watched games taking close notes on how umpires performed during close plays. If a bang-bang type of play didn't transpire in a game a major league umpire was being rated, then Donatelli felt he was responsible for following that umpire until he had a sufficient number of close plays to rate him. A bad report might jeopardize an umpire's career, so the supervisor had to be extremely confident in the score. If a minor league umpire rated highly, then they kept even closer tabs on him to determine his progress, and he or she were expected to get anywhere from four to six years of seasoning before it could be determined whether they were ready for a major league position. If they showed no potential of progress, they were terminated.

During his time grading umpires, Donatelli developed a friendly relationship with National League President Bart Giamatti. The two spent time together during spring training in 1988, when Giamatti was being touted as a possible replacement to Commissioner Peter Ueberroth. Giamatti was a strong advocate for umpires when he disciplined Pete Rose with a 30-day suspension for shoving umpire Dave Pallone after a disputed call in 1988.

The incident occurred during a heated game against the Mets that had already showcased a bench clearing incident in which Darryl Strawberry charged pitcher Tom Browning. Irate over a delayed ninth inning call on a close play at first base, Rose began pointing his finger at Pallone. The umpire pointed his finger back at Rose and brushed his face, causing Rose to push him. In addition to the suspension, Rose was fined $10,000. It was one of the severest penalties ever placed on a Major League manager. Giamatti believed that Rose's action nearly started a riot at Cincinnati's Riverfront Stadium.

During an interview with ESPN, the commissioner said, "There is a symbiosis between what goes on down on the field and in the stands. There is a circuit of energy and, by the nature of his job, a manager must be held responsible." Giamatti was also a stalwart advocate for umpires. While in high school, he admitted to not being skillful enough to be a player, so he became team manager, and was often asked by the coach to stand behind the backstop and check on the umpires. He became a self-proclaimed expert on fine umpiring, and clearly grasped its importance to the veracity of the game. Umpires are often criticized and verbally pounded on by the players, never complimented by anyone, and only noticed when they are perceived to make a mistake.

Bruce Weber wrote in *As They See 'Em*, "you are neither inside the game, as the players are, nor outside the game among the fans, but… the game passes through you, like rainwater through a filter, and your job is to influence it for the better, to strain out the impurities."

According to Donatelli, "Bart and I sat together for three games and Bart asked question after question about umpiring. His interest seemed genuine and sharp. I began to take a strong liking to the man. We had set a dinner date for him to stop by the house to talk baseball." Giamatti never made the dinner date as he died of a sudden heart attack in September of 1989, only six months into his term as Commissioner of Baseball.

Augie voiced a certain pride as he reminisced about the relationships he had forged with men like Giamatti. As he talked, a look of regret suddenly blanketed his face. He again mentioned the autograph he had procured from President John F. Kennedy. It had faded through the years and had all but disappeared. It was clear, however, that the memory of a chance meeting with the President was of lasting significance to him even some 30 years after the fact.

Family photo taken in December of 1954 in Ebensburg, Pennsylania near the family home. Augie Donatelli and wife ML pose with family, from left to right son David, with daughters Carol and Barbara. Photo courtesy of The Donatelli Collection.

ELEVEN

Toe to Toe with the Big Boys

Prior to 1964 major league umpires operated as individual contractors under the jurisdiction of the league presidents. Their contracts were renewed from year to year and they were paid to work from spring training through the end of the regular season. During the rest of the year, many of them sought alternate employment. Benefits for umpires were few and far between; no hospitalization, a meager pension plan, and raises were infrequent. By contrast, the Major League Baseball Players Association began to take formal shape a decade earlier in 1954 when the Association hired an attorney, J. Norman Lewis. The players downplayed the significance of the hiring, and Lewis went so far as to state publicly that the Association should not be thought of as a union. Lewis explained that there were no dues paid and that the newly formed Association was only an extension of the "Players Fraternity" which was formed in 1946. Lewis's initial assignment, however, was to help the players renegotiate their pension plan. Players were well represented, but umpires were looked upon as a necessary evil.

"If the players had a tough time negotiating a raise after a good year, imagine how tough a time an umpire had," Donatelli recalled. "An umpire doesn't have the luxury of pointing to any stats, besides the best umpires are the guys you don't notice too much."

Donatelli pointed out the then famed story of Hollis "Sloppy"

Thurston, a pitcher for the Chicago White Sox. In 1924, Thurston won 20 games, a fantastic accomplishment when you consider that Chicago won only 66 games that season and finished in last place. The following season Sloppy received a contract in the mail from owner Charles Comiskey for the same amount he earned the year before – $5,500. When he barged into Comiskey's office to complain, the owner shot back, "I'll tell you, son. We had bad attendance last year, and besides, we could have finished in last place without you."

Donatelli had a distant notion as far back as 1954 that the umpires should negotiate as a group; he sensed that if the players could organize then the umpires might also have an opportunity. "I had a lot of people tell me I was nuts," said Donatelli, "everybody said - they're not gonna let you start a union, but I had some experience with unions before."

He had firsthand experience with unions in his previous occupation. At the Barnes #15 mine in Pennsylvania, during the early 1930s, the coal miners refused to relent on the issue of allowing miners out of the mines before all the coal was weighed and accounted for. The experience was an important education for Donatelli, and formed the emotional foundation for his eventual and perpetual hard stance against Major League Baseball's hard negotiating executives. In his mind, if the issue was worth fighting for, he would most certainly stand up for fair treatment.

"Umpiring is a tough life," Donatelli would say oftentimes publicly, "but in the big leagues the salary compensates for the travel and the abuse you have to take. Look at it this way: I own my home and I'm raising four kids the way I want to raise 'em. It's a cinch I couldn't do it on a coal miner's pay."

But privately, the sentiment was often one of personal frustration. The time away from home was a challenge, and the compensation wasn't commensurate with the pressure that the profession generated. While he was grateful for the opportunity to make a living in the world of baseball, he felt the time was right for the umpires to make their demands. In 1963 Augie made the decision to spearhead an effort to organize National League umpires. Ford Frick was commissioner and Warren Giles was the National League president, and there was little doubt that both would fight tooth and nail to prevent its umpires from unionizing. One of the main issues that rankled Donatelli and prodded him into action was a lack of a respectable pension plan for umpires. Augie spent eight years working with legendary umpire Jocko Conlan, who by 1963 was nearing retirement. Conlan confided in Donatelli that he had decided to collect his entire pension in a lump sum in order to use the money to build a home.

"Hell's fire, Jocko," said Augie, "how do you expect to retire? You don't have a single cent."

"I know Augie, I know," Conlan replied shaking his head.

"We've got to start a union or an association," said Donatelli.

Jocko had planned on retiring in 1964 after 23 years of service. He anticipated that he would have no pension income. This disturbed Donatelli, who decided that the time was right to renegotiate the umpires' pension plan. At the time, the pension plan contributed only $200 for each year of service, so after a 25-year career an umpire's pension was worth $5,000 per year. Augie convinced Conlan, who was very highly respected, that the National League umpires should attempt to negotiate an increase collectively.

According to Donatelli, Conlan's initial response was, "What are you talking about? You can't do that, they'll never let you do it."

Conlan had umpired long enough to recall the events that transpired after the only previous time any sort of collaboration between umpires was attempted. The result was hardly successful. In 1945 American League umpire Ernie Stewart attempted to improve working conditions and benefits for umpires by reaching out to the commissioner of baseball. Acting on the request of the newly appointed Happy Chandler, Stewart was asked to survey every umpire and find out what their feelings were regarding their overall working conditions. Perhaps thinking that the umpires had found an ally in the new commissioner, Stewart wrote all of the umpires. When American League President William Harridge discovered that Chandler had asked the umpire to conduct a survey without his knowledge, Harridge decided to fire Stewart on the grounds of disloyalty. Umpiring had traditionally been the province of the league presidents, who were responsible for hiring and firing umpires. Oftentimes they did so with complete control and for whatever reasons they deemed significant.

During a pre–World Series meeting in October 1945, Chandler proposed that the salaries for umpires working the World Series should be raised from $2,500 to $4,000. Both Harridge and National League President Ford Frick voted down the proposal. When Stewart's name was brought up, Harridge reportedly informed Chandler that the hiring and firing of umpires was strictly league business and had nothing to do with the commissioner. Clearly, Stewart had fallen victim of a power struggle. The message to umpires was delivered with a clarion call, and the unfair treatment continued. Umpires repeatedly were dismissed subjectively, and prior to 1953, they had not received any type of salary increase in 15 years.

There were also incidents involving individual umpires that inflamed the relationship between owners and umpires. American League umpire Ed Runge heard that pitcher Don Larsen had been collecting unemployment checks during the off-season and made the assumption that he too was eligible. Both men lived in San Diego during the off-season and ran into each often during the winter months. Runge applied for unemployment, and the government approved the application but requested some paperwork from league president William Harridge. Harridge refused to sign the document and told Runge, "Don't worry, Ed. You don't need this. I'll take care of you when next season starts." Ed assumed that Harridge meant he'd receive a raise to tide him over during the winter months. At the time Runge was earning approximately $6,000 per year. When he received his new contract, it was for $6,500. The increase was one of nearly 10%, but the umpires were searching for something that might preclude them from working during the off-season. Stories like this circulated among the umpires and instilled bad blood.

The umpires approached representatives of the Players Association to suggest that the umpires might negotiate a new pension plan in conjunction with the players. Quite a few big name players supported the idea, including Ted Williams. Conlan decided to reach out to the National League player representative, Robin Roberts of the Phillies. Conlan knew that Roberts had developed the reputation of being a very tough negotiator.

"He was cold as ice," Phillies owner Bob Carpenter was once quoted in reference to Roberts's negotiating ability. Conlan wrote in his autobiography that he had cornered Roberts after a players' meeting and inquired whether the topic of helping the umpires had ever come up. According to Conlan, "He looked right through me with those blue eyes of his."

"What?" Roberts asked.

"I hear you talked about the pension plan," Conlan said.

"Why yes we did," said Roberts.

"Did you decide anything about the umpires?"

He gave Conlan one of the most disgusted looks he had ever seen in his life.

"We didn't even discuss you fellows."

The umpires were operating under a pension plan that was instituted in 1935 and was raised twice to $200 for each year of service, an amount that they considered unjustifiably low, considering the success that baseball was enjoying and the strides that the players had made. Expansion saw the game increase from sixteen to twenty teams and the game also captured a substantial increase in television revenue. By 1961 baseball had signed a five-year World Series/All-Star Game broadcasting package with NBC that was reported to be worth more than three million dollars a year. Televising games brought added attention to umpires and added scrutiny as well, since mistakes were more obvious than ever. In the age of television, umpires names and faces took center stage.

Umpires were unable to protect themselves from various inequities because they negotiated individually instead of as a group with the leagues. Donatelli later admitted that at the time he was unaware of the full details of the reasons behind Stewart's departure, after all he was still struggling for survival as a POW in war-torn Europe. However, he had recalled hearing that Stewart was caught acting alone. Donatelli was very conscious that he needed the full support of fellow umpires because it was dangerous ground they were treading. Supporting a large family, he had no interest in standing up to Major League Baseball alone, so he later admitted that he was very concerned about losing his job.

There was little doubt that both Frick and Giles would fight hard to keep its umpires from negotiating as a group. Donatelli wasn't one to take no for an answer and he scheduled a meeting of National League umpires on an off-day in Chicago at which five directors were elected: Donatelli, Conlan, Al Barlick, Tom Gorman, and Shag Crawford. Jocko arranged to find a lawyer to initiate the process. Conlan, who was well connected in the Chicago area since his days as a player for the White Sox, found a young Chicago attorney by the name of John J. Reynolds who met with the umpires and began formulating a strategy. There was strong support among umpires in forming the union. According to Donatelli, Ed Vargo, John Kibler, Chris Pelekoudas, Harry Wendelstedt, Dick Stello, and Vinnie Smith were among them. But it was Donatelli who had spurred the group to action, and it wasn't long after that he was demoted from his status as crew chief. Clearly the National League was intent on sending Augie and all the other league umpires a blunt warning. He was told that the demotion was due to his performance as an umpire, a charge that Donatelli refused to believe. Unlike players, umpires have no statistics to point to with regard to their competence. Augie had long been regarded amongst his peers as a great umpire. Not good – but great. Even more than a decade after his death, umpires still recall his prowess. Former National League Umpire Andy Olsen recalled Augie's ability on the diamond: "He was one of the best all around umpires. He was great on the bases and also behind the plate. You'd have to rank his as one of the great umpires."

Perhaps had Donatelli been regarded anything less than top rate, he too would have been fired. The demotion did not deter Augie, but only motivated him to pursue their goals with more fervor. Donatelli said that his experiences in the coal mines gave him the courage to never back down. When he was informed that he was being demoted from his status as crew chief, he later recounted that the move backfired for baseball.

"As it turned out," recalled Donatelli, "the National League office decided to assign me to Al Barlick's umpiring crew. We were able to plan very carefully." Joining two of the association's key members helped the cause in terms of communication and planning strategy.

Donatelli recalled that Barlick had his share of run-ins and bad blood with the league office and with Warren Giles in particular. He had a run-in with Giles in 1963 after the league changed the balk rule and let the umpires take all the heat for the uproar that ensued. Barlick was so enraged by the lack of support from the league office that he quit, went home, and refused to answer the telephone. Eventually he was convinced to change his mind and return.

In addition to improving the pension plan, some of the other basic issues the umpires sought included hospitalization and life insurance. The winter meetings after the 1963 season were held in Los Angeles. Reynolds was given an opportunity to speak to the league's executive board which included Buzzie Bavasi of the Dodgers, John Holland of the Cubs and Bill DeWitt of the Reds regarding their request which hardly seemed excessive. Reynolds was well received and it was recommended that he should be given an opportunity to present his case to the pension board. After Reynolds made the presentation, the sentiment among the umpires was very positive, as it appeared that the union was becoming a reality. In the months that followed Giles raised the pension an additional $50 for each year that an umpire spent in the league, but that was clearly a major disappointment, and the issues of hospitalization and insurance remained unaddressed. Subsequently, the union held a meeting to plot its strategy the following May at the Union League Club. Since all dialogue between the union and baseball had seemingly grinded to a dead halt, the umpires prepared an ultimatum; a strike date would be set if the executive board failed to negotiate with the union. Privately the umpires didn't want to strike but there was a growing sense of impatience. A majority of the 20 National League umpires had decided that it was time to play hardball with their employers. There was, however, a group of umpires who were against threatening to strike, including Jocko Conlan. He urged the umpires to be patient.

"Look, whatever you decide to do, I'll go along with it, because I'm an umpire and I'm all for the umpire getting everything that's coming to him. But you're doing it the wrong way. You're trying to bulldoze them. Why don't we send the lawyer down to talk to Giles again and explain our position?"

After union attorney Reynolds approached baseball's executive board with the ultimatum, baseball answered back that if they decided to hold any type of job action, and if they also continued the umpire's association, that every umpire would be fired. The threat was eerily foreshadowing the resolution to the Richie Phillips led negotiations that occurred many decades later. Phillips led the Major League Umpire's Association from 1978 through 2000 and oversaw huge pay increases, but in 1999 he recommended that all baseball umpires resign together in an effort to gain leverage in negotiating a new contract. The decision turned out to be a bad one as Major League Baseball accepted all of the resignations.

Swimming in unchartered waters in 1964, the umpires decided not to back down. In reference to the threat to fire all of the umpires, said Donatelli, "A lot of newspapers would have some great stories to print."

The umpires averted the walkout by only the thinnest of margins. Only some 15 minutes before Barlick and Donatelli's crew was to stage its walkout, they got word from Reynolds that the executive board would allow Reynolds to make a presentation during the All-Star break in New York. Donatelli and Barlick had felt they had won an important battle.

The next faceoff was at the bargaining table. Representing the owners was Warren Giles, Ford Frick, and two attorneys. The first point of negotiations was the pension plan and after Frick and Giles related what they thought was fair compensation. Donatelli, ever the bulldog, held the hard line and responded, "Your proposal is not even close."

"Well, how much do you want?" shot back a voice.

Donatelli said, "We want $500 per year for every year we put in. If a man puts in 20 years, then he gets $10,000 a year after he retires."

At the time the proposal was a reasonable amount of money in Augie's estimation, but baseball's representatives were shocked by it. Then Donatelli was quick to remind them that there were some umpires who had not received a raise in over a year.

"Whenever an umpire puts in a good year, he deserves a raise, and I don't mean $500 a year." According to Donatelli, the opposition was visibly bothered by his sharp comments. "Augie," shot back Ford Frick, "baseball can't pay umpires $50,000 a year!"

Although he was very outspoken during the negotiations, he was conscious not to stand out alone. Even though he paid for his outspokenness with a demotion, he felt that if he made enemies of the league president and if there were bad feelings that lingered after the negotiations were completed then they would look for any excuse to punish him. A few controversial calls on the field, and they would have an excuse to fire him. Often during the meeting, Augie made a point to turn to Barlick and Crawford. He would ask softly, "Are you satisfied with that offer?" He did this even if he thought the number offered was too low. Although Donatelli was the toughest of the group to please, he didn't completely get his way. The pension was raised to $300 for each year of service up to the age of 55. So an umpire with 20 years of active service would receive $6,000 a year upon retirement. And instead of paying five percent of salaries into the pension fund, they paid a flat $350 instead. They also attained the life insurance they sought as each umpire was insured for $20,000.

After their success in organizing, the American League umpires decided that they also wanted to form a union. The first initiative on organizing the union was taken by Al Salerno. In August of 1968, Salerno phoned Donatelli, who invited the young umpire to attend a September meeting at the Pick–Congress hotel in Chicago. There was a reluctant contingent of American League umpires who refused to attend the meeting, including Emmett Ashford, Ed Runge, and Cal Drummond. Salerno, who had umpired a 12-inning game in Oakland the night before, barely made the flight to Chicago. Salerno spoke in front of a nearly complete contingent of National League umpires. "The American League umpires are ready to organize a stronger group by having both leagues join together," said Salerno.

In the four years that had passed since the National League umpires formed its association, they had accrued substantial raises in pay and benefits and were earning substantially more than their American League counterparts. In 1968, Salerno was earning $12,000 a year. The top salary in the NL was $24,000 while the top AL umpire earned $17,000. The minimum was $6,500 in the AL and $9,500 in the NL. There were also substantial differences in terms of per diems. American League umpires also tried to begin organizing in 1965, but were intimidated by league president Joe Cronin's cold attitude to their proposal, which included the forced retirements of umpires Bill McKinley and Ed Hurley at age 55. Augie and the senior circuit umpires informed Salerno that they required letters from a minimum of 10 AL umpires to recognize their desire to organize. Salerno recalled being told at that first meeting that if any American League umpires were fired as a result of organizing, the National League umpires would back them by going out on strike.

Salerno mailed letters of agreement to all American League umpires and received signed letters back from most of the men. Only a month after the Chicago meeting, two American League umpires, Ed Runge and John Rice were meeting with AL Supervisor of Umpires Cal Hubbard at the American League office. According to Salerno, they told him that he and Bill Valentine were spearheading an attempt to organize the umpires. Minutes after receiving this information, Cronin phoned both men in their rooms at the Carter Hotel in Cleveland and fired them. The American League later claimed that both men were fired due to incompetence. Salerno, who was 37 at the time of the firing, had been umpiring for eight years in the AL while Valentine had been in the league for only six years. "They are just bad umpires, that's all," said Cronin. He stated that he had no knowledge of their organizing activities. He also claimed that his umpire-scouting people, who included Cal Hubbard and Charlie Berry had concurred with the decision.

"Interesting that I was deemed incompetent after umpiring 1,107 major league games," said Salerno many years later.

Most of the American League umpires were enraged by the action, and called for an emergency meeting in Chicago in which 18 of 20 American League umpires attended as well as National League umpires Barlick, Donatelli, Pelekoudas, Crawford, and Gorman. There was some serious discussion to strike during the 1968 World Series. However to their credit, both men made a plea not to 'deprive the American baseball fan of the annual Fall Classic.'

Reynolds also advised against the strike because he felt it would put public sentiment squarely against the umpires. In a public statement, Reynolds indicated that none of the umpires wanted to deprive the people of the fall classic due to the opinions of one man, referring to Cronin's decision. Yet had Valentine and Salerno not spoken out against the strike, Donatelli felt that there probably would have been enough votes to stage a strike of the World Series. At that meeting the association voted unanimously to form a single group called the National Association of Major League Umpires, and one of the newly formed groups' first actions was to demand the immediate reinstatement of Salerno and Valentine. The umpires also threatened a strike in spring training of 1969 unless the two umpires were reinstated. Some time later, the ousted umpires decided that they would sue the American League. They filed an unfair labor practice grievance with the National

Labor Relations Board. Armed with affidavit from one owner that stated that Cronin had told him that the umpires were doing a good job, but procedures, legal loopholes, and baseball's antitrust status all proved to lead to a dead end. At the time Donatelli thought the legal action was a mistake. He was of the opinion that the continued pressure that the umpires were applying would eventually reopen the door for Salerno and Valentine. After losing the suit, the umpires then decided to convene to discuss whether or not they should continue supporting their efforts to be reinstated. Augie recounted that meeting as emotionally charged. The conference was attended by 50 or so umpires, and at least 15 of them stormed out of the session because of heated discussion over the fact that Salerno and Valentine had filed an independent suit against the advice of the union and many of its members. The meeting was a firestorm that included much shouting, including from Donatelli.

"These guys made a mistake," screamed Augie, "but we said we'd back 'em and we should. We can't turn our backs on 'em cause they made a mistake!"

The meeting turned ugly when threats were made as emotions spilled over. It was Salerno, and not a veteran umpire, who stepped forward to reach out to Donatelli and who paid the price with his career. Donatelli was irate during his conversations with Fred Fleig, who was the NL umpire supervisor at the time. He bellowed over the telephone, much to his wife's chagrin.

Finally, the issue was put to a vote and the decision was cast not to support the two men. Years later, Augie admitted to feeling sorry about the outcome of the vote. Perhaps Donatelli sympathized with Salerno and Valentine so much because he felt equally stung by his demotion some five years earlier. Salerno looked back very bitterly at the final outcome of his efforts. He was originally scheduled to umpire the World Series that season and was not only out of a job, but he never had the opportunity to umpire a Fall Classic. Some time afterwards the league actually asked the men to umpire in the minor leagues for a few months before they might once again consider reinstating them. But both men declined. The bitterness and feelings of betrayal were too deep. Yet out of the extremely volatile experience emerged a single representative body for the umpires. The American League umpires subsequently had their salaries increased to the same level as the NL umpires.

"I don't believe for a single solitary second that the American League would have gotten any increased benefits at all without the union," Donatelli stated many years later. "Cronin was a good administrator, but if you're talking about taking care of the umpires – forget it."

While one storm settled another one was brewing in the not-so-distant future. In 1970, Donatelli told Giles that he wasn't doing enough to help the umpires. Even after Giles had awarded them a nominal raise, Augie was outspoken to a fault and his involvement with the umpire's union made him a focal point for trouble. The union was again involved in negotiating with baseball, and this time the driving force was postseason pay. Neither new National League President Chub Feeney nor Cronin felt that the umpires merited an increase. So in the days leading up to the strike deadline, Augie increased his public outcry. A headline in the *New York Times* stated, *"Umpire Assails Series Pay Offer. $500 increase is termed 'Peanuts' by Donatelli."* Donatelli told the Associated Press, "I know last time some of the fellows were a little shaky and they agreed to a settlement short of their demands. I don't think we're shaky anymore We have all the umpires behind us."

Feeney made his retort a public one as well. "If they choose to stay out, we can get umpires. We hope it doesn't come to this. But the series will go on." The umpires held out during the first game of the playoffs. Augie was in Pittsburgh carrying a picket sign outside of the ballpark while the game between the Reds and Pirates was going on with a crew of four minor league umpires.

Before the start of the second playoff game the Major League Umpires Association had garnered the support of Three Rivers Stadium employees, who were represented by two unions. The workers refused to cross the picket line that the umpires had established at 5 AM, which put the game at risk of postponement. By 11:15 that morning, Reynolds, Donatelli, Harry Wendelstedt and Shag Crawford were in serious negations with Feeney. It wasn't long after that the entire issue was settled since baseball had agreed to negotiate a settlement in good faith by the time the World Series started.

Asked if the umpires would strike again if no agreement were reached by the start of the Series in one week's time, umpire Doug Harvey replied, "It's an interesting thought, isn't it?"

The union received negative press for walking out and for holding a gun to baseball's head. To a man the umpires felt bad about walking out on the fans. After all, the umpires realized that the fans were the ones paying the salaries of everyone involved in baseball, but the decision was made that striking was the only course of action that might generate results. The day after the strike, Feeney met with Augie and the union representatives. It wasn't long before they were awarded their raises. Pay for the League Championship Series went from $2,500 to $4,000 while pay for the World Series increased from $6,500 to $8,000. The strike, the first by umpires in major league history, prompted the league presidents to recognize the Association and negotiate a labor contract that set a minimum salary of $11,000 and raised the average salary to $21,000.

According to retired umpire Jerry Crawford, the job action had a big impact and baseball subsequently frowned on any union-based businesses in their stadiums. "I was in the minors in the early 70s. From that point on there was a voice to be heard from the umpires. They were going to shut down the playoff game. That started a chain reaction where now there's no unions in the ballparks. Most of the workers at ballparks have no strike clauses."

It was only five years after Augie's retirement that the umpires made major advances under the new leadership of Richie Phillips, a Philadelphia lawyer who also represented National Basketball Association referees. Phillips was widely regarded by the umpires as a sharp negotiator and he guided the umpires to new heights. A second umpires' strike on August 25, 1978 lasted only one day, because of a court injunction against the Association. A third strike in 1979 earned big concessions for the union, including salaries that ranged from $22,000 to $55,000, based on years of service; annual no-cut contracts; $77 per diem while traveling; and two weeks midseason vacation. A fourth strike of seven of the eight 1984 playoff games was settled by the intercession of new Commissioner Peter Ueberroth, who gave the umpires a large increase for playoff and World Series games as well as starting a provision that pumped money into a pool that would be divided among umpires not working postseason contests. A fifth strike was averted in 1985 when an arbitrator – former President Richard M. Nixon – awarded umpires a 40 percent pay increase for the expanded best-of-seven playoff series.

Umpires also later negotiated a deal that earned them $2,000 a year for every year they put in and close to $100,000 cash after retirement.

Even Leo Durocher came to the umpires' support in 1979. "I'm for the umpires," the former manager said. "The umpires have the game in their hands. And they are the most underpaid men in baseball. No major league umpire should start for less than $25,000 now. Years ago Babe Pinelli or Beans Reardon, I forget which, told me the most they ever made was $23,000 a year. Isn't that awful. Pay the men who hold the integrity of the game in their hands. I had my ups and downs with them, my ins and outs, but every time I got thrown out, I deserved it."

With the newly generated money that had been negotiated, many of the umpires who had since retired, Donatelli included, felt somewhat hopeful that some consideration was awarded to retired umpires. Barlick, Conlan, Crawford, Donatelli, and others received modest additional benefits.

Jerry Crawford, who served as President of The World Umpires Association, retired in 2010 after a 35 year career, stated that the umpires never forgot the sacrifices of the previous generation of umpires. "We always tried to negotiate for the retired members. The fact is MLB doesn't have to negotiate for retired members. However, we were able to get some money for the retired guys. But baseball did it out of the goodness of their heart. The corporate bean counters look at it and the number of retired members and their wives is always being compounded. They're looking long range, and they tell us they can't budget for it. There's no bad guy here. When Augie was a supervisor in the National League after he retired I had this discussion with him. In Atlanta Georgia, we talked about the pensions. He had asked me about getting some money for the retired guys. A lot of other retired umpires made that point to me. I would say we're doing the best we can. There's not one guy who is umpiring today who wouldn't try to run through the wall to get a retired member money. But they wouldn't take a work action for that issue. Back in the '60s, I think it would be the same. I don't think the umpires would have gone on strike for a retired member."

Al Salerno attempted to make an appeal with regard to his lack of compensation. In 2006, he approached Major League Baseball with the hope that they might finally admit to treating him unfairly and offer him a pension. A league attorney denied his request. "You know, the attorney had the nerve to tell me to my face that baseball beat me fair and square."

As for Donatelli, he gained the legacy of being the man to initiate the battle to correct the lack of benefits and low wages for umpires. He was the lightning rod and the firebrand who initiated the first steps. At first, many of Augie's contemporaries, including Conlan, doubted the idea of an umpires' association was achievable but one by one he convinced them that they needed to act. There were many setbacks and travails that led to personal hardships for Augie because of his efforts. Some of them he probably never shared, but he pressed on with the resolve of a World War II tail gunner.

According to Goetz, "The union was Augie's idea and he did most of the hard work. Many umpires never properly thanked Augie, but if it wasn't for him they wouldn't be getting the salaries and benefits they have today. Most of us were satisfied with the little we got. Augie was always telling us we were wrong. He would always say, "They kick us around like a rubber ball because they know they can get away with it. A lot of people resented Augie because of this, but he was right. We got more respect and more money after we organized."

As Jim Enright, a writer for the old *Chicago Today* newspaper related in a published opinion piece for *Referee* magazine:

"Memo to Augie Donatelli, retired NL umpire and founding father of Major League Umpire's Association, "Look Augie, what they are doing to your union. The one you worked so hard and long to get off the ground. They said if you failed, you'd lose your job, especially if Warren Giles was still the NL president. Giles didn't see how unions would fit in baseball, and he opposed them vehemently."

With the formation of the union, the umpires had accomplished their goal. Years later, under the guidance of Richie Phillips, the Major League Umpire's Association enjoyed a 600% increase in pay for some umpires, and negotiated five weeks of paid vacation, and many other incredible benefits. In 1999 he recommended that all baseball umpires resign together in an effort to gain leverage in negotiating a new contract. The decision turned out to be a tactical disaster as Major League Baseball accepted nearly all of the resignations.

Said Crawford, "In 1999 we didn't stick together. Richie and I miscalculated. We didn't know the rules changed. We had been dealing with league presidents and suddenly we were dealing with corporate America. We didn't stick together. It cost 22 guys their jobs."

The umpires later voted to decertify the union, and replaced it with the World Umpires Association. Donatelli died more than a decade before that negotiating mistep unfolded. One can only speculate what he might have thought.

Crawford, who knew the Donatelli family since he was a little boy, had an inkling of how the originators of the union might have felt about how far the organization had evolved.

"My father (Shag Crawford) was amazed how far umpires have come. When they put the salaries in the newspapers, he was amazed. He never thought we would have come so far. He said 'hey, I made my bed and you guys are making yours. He said if you guys can get us some money that's great. If you can't, it's not like we don't know why.'

Despite the trials and tribulations he encountered during the formation of the union, Augie harbored no ill-will, and after his retirement he remained actively involved in the game he loved.

TWELVE

The Last Call

In April of 1973 it was announced that Augie, who was three years over the official retirement age of 55, was going to umpire in his 24th season. The National League added two rookie umpires that year, Art Williams, the first black National League umpire, and Terry Tata.

"There are a couple of other young umpires we really like," Chub Feeney said at the time, "but we didn't want to bring too many youngsters at once. We wanted a few of the senior umpires to stay with the league."

The league did retire Stan Landes, who claimed he wasn't retained because he has been "outspoken" in the past. The promising prospects that Feeney referred to were Paul Runge and Dutch Rennert. Paul was to follow in his dad's footsteps in what was eventually to be baseball's only three-generation umpiring family. Brian Runge made it to the major leagues in 1999. Dutch Rennert went on to have a 19-year career and, like Augie, was also known for his animated style.

Augie knew in his heart that 1973 was to be his last season. He wanted to end his career with as little ballyhoo as possible, and certainly no controversy. But the national spotlight found him on several occasions during that final season. As is always the case with umpires, it came as the result of controversial calls. In a May series in Houston between the Astros and Reds, Donatelli was criticized on a ball he called a home run. Bobby Tolan, who had hit the drive, stood at home plate as the ball hugged the foul line. He stood and waited with his eyes fixated on the umpire until he made the circling gesture to signify a home run. The call brought Augie's old nemesis Leo Durocher storming out of the dugout for a long rant, and the game was eventually played under protest. Then a few days after Donatelli had left town the Astros hosted the Braves, and there was another close play involving umpire Bruce Froemming, who got into a dispute after calling an Atlanta runner safe at second base in a potential double play situation. Astros' General Manager Spec Richardson ordered that a caustic message be put on the large center field scoreboard. There in big bright lights it read: "Umpires Froemming and Donatelli have blown decisions in two of the last three days." It was posted there as if it were a verifiable statistic. Some 11,000 angry fans gave the message a standing ovation, and some fans took matters into their own hands.

"You saw them start throwing things at us after they put that up," umpire Ed Vargo said. "We could've been hurt. So could the players. We've got wives and children, too. We have enough to do without worrying about fans throwing things."

Another umpire, Paul Pryor, simply called the message "bush," and Donatelli had a similar reaction. For the management of a major league team to decide that they wanted to help focus the fans' derision on umpires sent a bitter message to Augie. Perhaps it was time to step away from the game. League president Chub Feeney decided to fine Richardson $300 for his public pronouncement. Richardson showed no remorse. He later hinted in the press that several individuals had offered to pay the fine for him and that the statement flashed on the scoreboard was a matter of fact. Ultimately, Richardson was not known for his stellar judgment. In fact, he was better known for making some of the most unproductive trades in baseball history. He traded pitcher Mike Cuellar to the Orioles for Curt Blefary. Then he shipped 24-year-old Rusty Staub to Montreal in the winter of 1969. A few seasons later, he sent 22-year-old slugging first baseman John Mayberry to Kansas City, and subsequently he traded 27-year-old future Hall of Famer Joe Morgan to the Reds. Years later, sabermetric research concluded that had Richardson kept those players, the Astros would have been one of the better National League teams of the 1970s.

Donatelli experienced another bizarre incident in May of his final season during a game between the Giants and Cubs. With Doug Rader on first base, the Cubs' Milt Pappas threw a wild pitch that almost beaned opposing pitcher Jim Barr. Barr lurched towards Pappas in a threatening way. Some of the Cubs came out of the dugout and third baseman Ron Santo gravitated towards the mound just in case fisticuffs erupted. The ball, however, remained in play and continued to roll towards the backstop; Rader, whose nickname was the "Red Rooster" because of his reddish hair, never broke stride and raced towards third base. Cubs' catcher Randy Hundley finally chased the ball down and fired wildly towards third, but the ball sailed into left field. As he rounded third, Rader tripped over a Cub player who had left the dugout in anticipation of a brawl. Somehow, Rader got back to his feet and then crawled across home plate. An argument soon followed with the Cubs complaining that time should have been called. Augie, who was umpiring behind the plate, disagreed. He felt the play had not concluded. Not long after a verbal dispute, a brawl erupted and four men were thrown out of the game. Three others were sent to the hospital with injuries they had sustained during the fight. Rader's mad dash around the bases, and collision at third base with a player who wasn't even in the game would have made this play a leading highlight in modern-day television.

After reviewing the game, Feeney again came to the umpires' defense and said, "The play was continuous and no umpire had called time, nor did any Cubs' player request they do so."

Feeney supported Augie's decision in both these instances, but Donatelli and Feeney had encountered more than their share of disputes over the years, including the rough-and-tumble negotiations of 1970 that led umpires to stage their walkout. And as fate would have it, the two men would have one more tussle before Donatelli finally retired. Both men had come to baseball from opposite ends of life's spectrum. Feeney was the grandson of Charles Stoneham, principal owner of the New York Giants, and nephew of Horace Stoneham, who owned the Giants from 1936 to 1976. He attended Dartmouth College and at age 24 was appointed vice president of the Giants. Donatelli, never one to kowtow to men in position of power, or to anyone for that matter, felt obliged to give his opinion no matter how unpopular it might be. The source of their final disagreement occurred during the final series of the 1973 baseball season between the New York Mets and Chicago Cubs at Wrigley Field.

New York baseball was the bane of Augie's existence dating back to the start of his career when he umpired so many crucial and volatile ballgames involving the Brooklyn Dodgers and Giants. In 1973 the New York Mets became a prominent story. Managed by Yogi Berra, the team captured the city's imagination with a torrid season-ending comeback. Relief pitcher Tug McGraw's brilliant catch phrase, "You Gotta Believe!" is still uttered by Mets' fans many decades after the fact. At the end of August, they were a sub .500, last-place team, but their pitching was a notch above the rest of the division. New York had hard throwers Tom Seaver, Jerry Koosman, and Jon Matlack spearheading their pennant drive. McGraw proved nearly unhittable down the stretch. In his last 19 games, he collected 5 wins, 12 saves, and an ERA of 0.88.

The Mets' lineup featured Rusty Staub, Cleon Jones, Jerry Grote, and a 42-year-old Willie Mays. Mays, who broke into baseball in 1951, the year after Donatelli, was now retiring the same year as the umpire. Donatelli had tremendous respect for the "Say Hey Kid," and called him the "best fly hawk ever." He was Leo Durocher's star pupil. Durocher helped the young Mays early in his career by bolstering his confidence, and after a slow start, Mays hit his first career home run off of Warren Spahn in 1951 and never looked back.

On September 25, 1973, the Mets held Willie Mays Night at Shea Stadium. With 54,000 people on hand Mays spoke to the crowd.

"In my heart, I'm a sad man. Just to hear you cheer like this for me and not be able to do anything about it makes me a very sad man…

Willie, say good-bye to America."

The speech struck a chord with many who watched, especially Donatelli. He saw his own umpiring career flash in front of his eyes. He saw Mays break into the major leagues in 1951 at age 20. Some 22 years later, he retired from umpiring the same precise time that Willie Mays walked away from baseball. As fate would have it, both men walked off the baseball diamond for the final time after the 1973 World Series. It was well documented that Mays had lost most of his lauded skills, and it would stand to reason that Donatelli had lost a few steps as well. In his youth, he was known for getting into position quickly because of his exceptional foot speed for an umpire. Clearly he wasn't as nimble as he had been some two decades earlier. The question remained whether his judgment remained sharp, and he was faced with some critical decisions as the 1973 season came to a close.

One of the tightest divisional races ever featured four teams that were barely at the .500 mark. Heading into the final weekend of the season, the standings were so tightly packed that five of the six teams in the National League's Eastern Divison remained mathematically in contention. Donatelli was the senior umpire in rain-soaked Chicago, as the first place Mets prepared to take on the fifth-place Cubs. The second-place Pirates were at home playing against the fourth-place Expos. The third-place Cardinals were at home playing the sixth-place Philadelphia Phillies, the Phils being the only club that didn't have a shot at the division title. Because of the many convoluted possibilities involving potential ties and playoff scenarios, the league office conducted a conference call by telephone involving all five clubs in the race; discussed were the ramifications of a two-way tie, or even a five-team tie.

Meanwhile, rain fell on Friday in Chicago. After a long involved deliberation Donatelli decided to come onto the field at 2:30 PM, approximately an hour after the game was scheduled to begin. The decision had already been made. The rain had already abated, but the umpire had already spoken to both managers and NL President Feeney. He looked up towards the press box with a scant crowd of 2,000 fans at mist covered Wrigley Field. Without rain falling, Donatelli waved his hands with his palms facing downward to signal that the game was to be postponed.

He explained to the press after the decision, "Either way, we probably couldn't get in a full game, on a day like this, you can't see the ball after 4:30." At the time Wrigley was the only ballpark in the major leagues without lights. "Suppose one team was ahead after five innings and it got dark. We'd have to suspend the game, finish it tomorrow (Saturday) morning, then still play the scheduled doubleheader. And if one team was ahead after five and it rained, that would be a legal game and the championship might be decided by a five-inning game."

The result of Donatelli's decision was that the Cubs and Mets would have to play back-to-back doubleheaders on Saturday and Sunday, but the issue became even more nerve-wracking as rain fell on Saturday until ten after three. It had rained steadily for hours and Augie was ready to call the game. The Mets players were in the clubhouse focusing on a game of bridge when it stopped raining. The minute it stopped, Donatelli got a phone call from National League President Chub Feeney, asking him to start the game. They had waited 2 1/2 hours.

Donatelli told Feeney, "If we take the tarp off now, it won't be until four o'clock before we start playing, and then there's a good chance that it will get too dark before we can finish." Donatelli couldn't make him understand his point of view. Feeney insisted that Augie should start the game and get it in. Donatelli refused to budge. After getting off the telephone, Augie told his partners that he was going to call the game. They walked out of the dugout and gave everyone the signal that the game was canceled. He had called the game two hours and twenty minutes after the scheduled 11:30 AM start time.

When he returned to the clubhouse, an angry Feeney was waiting for him. "Why the hell did you call the game?" he demanded to know.

After a long and heated discussion, Donatelli had made his point, much to Feeney's chagrin. That same day in St. Louis, the Cardinals were making a strong case for overtaking the Mets by defeating the Phillies 7 to 1 to pull them to within one-and-a-half games of the Mets heading into Sunday.

On Sunday, the Mets split a doubleheader against the Cubs which assured New York of at least a tie for the division title in what amounted to one of the most complicated championship battles ever. The split knocked the Cubs out of the race. Also that day, the Pittsburgh Pirates defeated Montreal to eliminate the Expos. With the Pirates still in the hunt, the season was extended an extra day. Pittsburgh had to play a single makeup game against the San Diego Padres on Monday, while the Mets had to take on the Cubs in yet another doubleheader. The Cardinals were still mathematically alive, because if the Mets lost both games and the Pirates won its makeup game, then all three clubs would end tied for first; and a three-way sudden-death playoff would have to be played.

The Mets and Cubs began play at 12:30, the Cubs now hoping to play the role of spoiler. Only 1,913 fans came out to watch Burt Hooton face Tom Seaver. New York won the game 6 to 4 and clinched the title as Tug McGraw relieved Tom Seaver and pitched the final three innings. On August 30th the Mets had been in last place, and now they were division champs with their 82nd victory of the year. The second game of the doubleheader was cancelled because the Mets had clinched the division with the victory in the opener. It was a memorable win for New York, and it was Augie's last regular-season game.

The 1973 World Series was Donatelli's last assignment as a major league umpire. He knew that once the Series between the Mets and the American League champion Oakland A's was over that his 24-year stint in the majors was over as well. He was intent on leaving the game with his good name intact.

Donatelli worked behind the plate in Game 2 of the Series at Oakland. It turned out to be one of the longest World Series game ever played, lasting four hours and thirteen minutes. Vida Blue and Jerry Koosman were the starters. Both were scored upon early. As the game progressed, the shadows were getting longer, the outfielders were struggling with the harshly bright October sky, turning every fly ball into an adventure. The lights at the ballpark were turned on before the bottom of the ninth inning. It had been a very sunny day and in Augie's estimation the lights should not have randomly come on between innings without his okay. Someone had decided that the lights might help the A's hitters by lessening the shadows. Donatelli decided that he wanted the lights turned off, because the rules stated that if they were turned on during the course of a game, they had to be turned on at the start of an inning. Donatelli called Oakland manager Dick Williams out of the dugout.

"Who put the lights on?" he asked.

"It wasn't me," Williams answered. It was the answer Augie expected to hear.

"I'm going to threaten you," Augie said in about as direct a manor as he could.

"Because that's the only way to handle this. If you don't turn off the lights, I'm going to unload you, and then wait for them to turn the lights off anyway!"

"Hell, I told you I had nothing to do with it, Augie," screamed a perturbed Williams.

"Then why don't you tell me who the hell turned those lights on?" he asked.

Williams turned and pointed toward an area in the stands near the Oakland bench, "It's the guy behind the dugout!" The man Williams was pointing at was A's owner Charles Finley, who had his eyes glued to Donatelli from a distance. The umpire then turned and marched directly towards the flamboyant owner. Finley wasn't shy about getting into well-publicized disputes with his own players, including Reggie Jackson and Vida Blue, but this time he was going to clash with an umpire.

"Hey," Augie yelled while staring Finley straight in the eyes, "get those lights turned off, because if you don't, I'm going to have you thrown out of here!" Finley looked at Donatelli with an indignant expression. The fans sitting in the area around Finley thought it was funny. People chuckled and smiled. Donatelli repeated his command just to make certain that Finley knew he meant business. "Get those lights off!" he ordered.

The lights were soon turned off, and the game was heating up. New York was leading by a score of 6 − 4 in the ninth when pinch hitter Deron Johnson led off the inning with a high fly to center that Mays lost in the sun. It dropped in front of him for a double. The ballpark went wild and pennant flags were waving everywhere. Mays's misplay helped the A's storm back and tie the game at 6.

Mays entered the game as a pinch-runner for Rusty Staub in the top of the ninth. When John Milner singled, Mays missed second and had to go back to the bag instead of advancing to third base. Mets fans dreaded the thought that the aging legend might cost them a World Series game. Mays had contemplated walking away from the game after Willie Mays Night at Shea Stadium, but he was convinced to stay with the club through the end of the season. Little did he know at the time that he'd be playing his final games in front of a national audience. To make mistakes that he never might have otherwise made in his prime was a burden to Mays. A's star slugger Reggie Jackson, who rarely minced words, was open and less than nostalgic about the aging legend. "Willie Mays is the greatest player who ever played this game," said Jackson. "That's not Willie Mays out there. That's just Willie Mays in nomenclature. I mean, it was embarrassing to an extent."

Mays could only hope he would have an opportunity to redeem himself. With two runners on in the top of the 10th, Mets second baseman Felix Millan hit a fly ball to shallow leftfield. Bud Harrelson decided to tag up and try to score. Left fielder Joe Rudi fired the ball to home plate. It was a strong throw that arrived at the plate a split second before Harrelson did. Catcher Ray Fosse caught it and made a sweeping tag toward Harrelson's hip. The shortstop did not slide but instead tried to scamper past the tag standing up. Donatelli dropped as low as he could. He was flat on the ground when he saw Fosse's mitt graze Harrelson's hip as he flew past him without a slide. Donatelli immediately gave the out sign. Mays, who was the on-deck batter, was on his knees a few feet away and threw his arms up into the air in disbelief. Then within a matter of seconds, at least five men wearing Mets uniforms surrounded Augie, including manager Yogi Berra, Mays, Harrelson, and two coaches. Donatelli thought about throwing them all out of the game.

"You can't throw me out of the game because of your inadequacies," screamed Harrelson.

Berra kept repeating over and over, "It's a damn joke. It's a damn joke! Where did he touch him? Where did he touch him?" Finally Donatelli turned towards Yogi and gave him a slap on the hip. "Right here!" Augie bellowed. On NBC television, color commentator Tony Kubek, who had already positioned himself in the A's dugout to get a post-game interview overheard Fosse talking to his teammates. According to Kubek, Fosse said, "I think I brushed him." Years later Augie's opinion of the play remained the same. "I say Fosse tagged him, but even if he didn't, I doubt I could have positioned myself any better than I did. I rendered the decision based on my opinion after positioning myself as well as possible. The ball beat him by two steps and the catcher was ready for him. It takes superhuman judgment to call it, even when you have the angle." The replays were somewhat inconclusive, but an informal poll of New Yorkers would no doubt have concluded that the umpire had blown the call, while Oakland fans thought the exact opposite.

* * *

Pat Donatelli sat alone in his third floor dorm room watching on television some 3,000 miles away. He knew that this was his father's last game behind the plate, and he wanted to watch it in the solitude of his room. Pat couldn't attend the game because school was in session and he was the wide-receiver on the football team. After Augie had made the call, Pat thought to himself, *Great call, pop.* Not long after he heard a stampede of footsteps bearing down on his closed door. He instantly knew what it was about and mumbled under his breath, *Hell, they're comin.'* The door of his room slammed open and in came a group of angry classmates.

"Your pop screwed up the whole Series," they charged.

Two of the six students were teammates, both offensive linemen, much larger than Donatelli. There were also two members of the basketball team, one stood 6'10". They grabbed the umpire's son, overpowered him, and then hog-tied him with whatever they could find.

"Hey guys, it's just a game," Pat pleaded as he struggled to free himself. After binding his hands and feet, the irate group carried the umpire's son out into the corridor and towards the stairs. Donatelli struggled but was helpless against the six. The next thing he knew, he was being lifted down the stairwell. His head bumped against the railing. He screamed out for them to put him down. They obliged, and he tumbled down the landing.

"I was a second-team All-Conference wide receiver," recalled Pat. "So I was used to getting knocked around, but these guys were serious. They were angry." The twin doors at the front of the building burst open and seconds later Donatelli was flying through the air. He came to rest in a dirt pile. More grumbling and profanity came in his direction. Pat couldn't believe what had just transpired; he had sustained some bumps and bruises, but was thankful that he wasn't seriously injured. He never reported the incident, and was reluctant to tell his family until many months later.

* * *

In the 12th inning, Mays stepped to the plate. He pulled back out of the batter's box and asked Donatelli for time. Then the crafty Mays turned to catcher Ray Fosse and said, "Gee you know, Ray, it's tough to see the ball with that background. I hope he doesn't throw me any fastballs. I don't want to get hurt. Mays stepped back in and waited for a Fingers fastball. When it came, he hit a grounder over the pitcher's head and into center field. This time, Harrelson crossed the plate with the go-ahead run. "I just couldn't let the kids down," said Mays. It proved to be the final hit of Willie's career. In Augie's view, "I think most fans wanted to see Mays go out on top, and that base hit was certainly something that Mays fans and many baseball fans were glad to see. I broke into the majors a little before Mays and watched him throughout the course of his career. I was third base umpire for his most impressive performance, a four home run game in 1961. There certainly wasn't a player who had better baseball ability and instincts than Willie. In that last year with the Mets he wasn't the same player. To me, he looked hesitant in everything he did. His legs were worn out."

Perhaps Mays thought the same of Donatelli. In *Willie Mays, the Life, the Legend* author James S. Hirsch wrote that as the argument raged between the Mets and Donatelli, the thought that both men were soon to retire from the game flashed through Willie's mind. The question suddenly dawned on Mays. *What are we doing here?*

Willie Mays objects to Augie's decision when he called base
runner Bud Harrelson out at home plate in Game 2 of the
1973 World Series. Copyright Bettmann/CORBIS

The image of an older Mays on his knees pleading with Augie became symbolic of a star who had perhaps overstayed his welcome.

Mays however had played an important role for the Mets by playing in 66 games at the age 42, yet after being part of the game for two decades, both men were keenly aware that they were both past their prime.

Later in the 12th inning, New York's John Milner hit a roller towards second baseman Mike Andrews that skipped through his legs for a two-run error. Then, catcher Jerry Grote hit a bouncer towards Andrews, who threw the ball off the mark toward first base and yet another run crossed the plate. The Mets went on to win and Mike Andrews was later "fired" by Finley. The A's subsequently attempted to put Andrews on the disabled list, but commissioner Bowie Kuhn intervened and forced Kuhn to reinstate the humiliated Andrews. The never-relenting Finley forced Andrews to sign a false affidavit saying that he was injured. Other A's, manager Dick Williams and virtually the entire baseball community rallied to Andrews's defense. The Andrews fiasco escalated to a boiling point when some of the players threatened to stage a revolt and refuse to play the remainder of the Series. Kuhn later forced Finley to reinstate Andrews, and also fined the owner because of the lights being turned on without Donatelli's approval.

"The entire incident made me wish I had actually thrown him out because of the lights. Holy hell, it would have been interesting to see him escorted out of his seat." After the game, Donatelli was cornered by reporters, and questioned about the controversial call.

"How the hell do the Mets know if he was out?" Augie stated outside of the umpires' room in Oakland Coliseum after his controversial 10th inning decision prolonged the second game of the World Series by two innings.

"They were all behind the play," Donatelli said, "They couldn't see it. He was out and I called him out. That's it. It was a very difficult play but he was out." Donatelli was then questioned about lying flat on the ground while making the call. "You bet I was on the ground," Donatelli said, "I got a good look at it. But why doesn't the catcher make a good tag?" he asked. "If he really tags him hard, there's no question," and Donatelli slapped the arm of a reporter to show how a good tag should be made. Fosse concurred that it wasn't a good tag. "I just brushed him on the arm," he said. "Harrelson probably didn't feel it."

Two nights later when the umpires were going through the ground rules prior to Game 3, Dick Williams pulled Donatelli aside. According to Donatelli he said, "To me, Augie, you umpired the best game I ever saw."

Williams, who was elected to the Hall of Fame by the Veterans Committee, and inducted in 2008, led three franchises to the World Series, and was the only manager to lead four different teams to 90-win seasons. He played his first Major League game with the Brooklyn Dodgers in 1951. The manager was so upset by Finley's meddling with the team and his public humiliation of Andrews that he resigned and walked away from the A's after the Series concluded.

The Harrelson-Fosse play at the plate wasn't the only tough call Augie had to make in the Series. During Game 1, the A's Bert Campaneris bunted the ball down the first base line. Mets first baseman John Milner was playing in. He fielded the ball four or five feet inside the base line, and Donatelli called it fair. Campaneris slid inside the marked-off three-foot zone, which he was entitled to do, and Milner flew at Campaneris with the ball firmly in his glove. "I don't know how he managed to avoid Milner, but Campaneris did. I called him safe, and got more hell for it. That was a tough call to make, but the replays weren't as close on that play as they were on the Bud Harrelson play at the plate in Game 2. I also didn't have the luxury of having any help, because the home plate umpire hadn't moved from his position. After I gave a safe sign, I looked up at the home plate umpire and was surprised to see that he hardly moved. The man who made that mistake was Marty Springstead. Just to show you, even the best umpires have lapses in judgment. But the replay proved me right."

The Mets had a three games to two edge in the Series when it returned to Oakland, but the A's stormed back to win the Series in seven games. It ended with Wayne Garrett popping out to Bert Campaneris for the final out, the crowd erupted, and the World Series celebration took place.

Mays never played in Game 7.

"I got up seven times and I got two hits. I was very disappointed that Yogi didn't play me in the last game. It was in Oakland, and to me it would have been a storybook ending in front of fans in the Bay Area. But I didn't think of asking him."

As for Donatelli, the emotions were quite different. "I never felt a sense of sadness," said Augie. "It was more a feeling of relief that a tough job was complete, and the pressure was off my shoulders. I thanked the lord that I was able to get through it; 24-years as a big league umpire."

The Oakland A's celebrated their second straight championship on the field. As Sal Bando, Reggie Jackson, Gene Tenace, Ray Fosse and the rest of the A's celebrated; Donatelli looked back briefly to watch the celebration. Few acknowledged that the umpire's career had ended except for fellow umpires and Augie's family. Yet six months earlier, umpires had honored Donatelli when he was awarded the Al Somers School award as Outstanding Major League Umpire of 1972. Donatelli was deeply touched when he accepted the award in front of hundreds of people at St. Paul's Catholic Church auditorium in Daytona Beach, Florida. He was the third man to receive the honor after Al Barlick in 1970 and Nestor Chylak in '71.

Major League Umpires Harry Wendelstedt and Randy Marsh present Augie with the Outstanding Major League Umpire Award in 1972. Photo courtesy The Donatelli Collection.

Augie addressed the large gathering with a humble tone. "I've had a lot of awards," Augie said, "but I cherish this one most." He glanced at his wife ML and said, "How can ballplayers fans or anybody question my judgment? All they have to do is look at my wife. They'll know I don't make mistakes."

Some of Augie's contemporaries added praise in tribute of his outstanding career. Harry Wendelstedt: "This man's life truly has been dedicated to baseball. Nobody has given more back to baseball than he has. His courage and leadership in the formative days of the Major League Umpires Association made the life of all umpires better. And he paid dearly for this leadership, but he didn't quit, didn't back off." Hall of Fame umpire Al Barlick added: "Nobody has done as much to upgrade the standards and positions of umpires as Augie. He's a living proof in my book that a good major league umpire is synonymous with being a good citizen and person. You always try to do what is right." American League umpire John Stevens: "Augie is one of the all-time greats. Words can't describe his contribution."

When it came time to walk away, Donatelli knew that he would miss the people associated with the game more than anything. The thought of his mother crossed his mind. Back in 1951, the Pittsburgh Pirates honored Augie by giving him a pregame tribute at Forbes Field. It was the place that his boyhood heroes had played. He was honored on the very ground that they had played. It was a rarity for an umpire to be recognized, much less so early in his career. It was only his second season. Given his background as a Pennsylvania native and a former coal miner, the Pirates flattered Donatelli with a modest ceremony at home plate. Bakerton and Heilwood are less than 100 miles from the Steel City so the entire family sojourned to the ballpark, including Augie's mother, Vincenzina, who religiously followed baseball by listening to the radio broadcasts. She was a fan years before her son decided to become an umpire, and now she was mingling with her favorite team and her son. She met long time Pirates' broadcaster Rosey Rowswell, whose unique home-run calls always made her smile. Upon being introduced to the broadcaster she said, "Mr. Rowz-a-welt, Mr. Rowza-welt," Augie's mother exclaimed excitedly in her heavy Italian accent, "I am so happy to see you." Augie flashed back to that moment with a broad smile. The look he saw on his mother's face was something that touched a soft spot in the tough-as-nails umpire. It was her first major league game and she was there to see her son umpire. Also on hand to share in the celebration were 1,000 Cambria County friends. At the time, the Pirates were floundering and were 17 games out of first, so Bakerton's native son was as popular as he'd ever be at a ballgame. Pleasing his mom and the large contingent of family and friends filled the umpire with a heady pride. It was a show of support and appreciation for a local boy who had made the major leagues. Donatelli was then presented with an expensive set of leather luggage. He graciously accepted the gift and waved to the crowd in acknowledgment of their warm applause. Yet in the midst of his glory came a moment that brought him back to earth; a lone voice boomed out of the stands, "HEY DONATELLI, USE THE LUGGAGE TO TAKE A LONG TRIP!"

Augie followed the loud-mouthed Pirate fan's advice. He did go on a long trip. A journey that encompassed 24 years, six All-Star games, 10 no-hitters, and five World Series; and his tenure in the National League paralleled the careers of many legendary greats, including Willie Mays, Hank Aaron, Stan Musial, Sandy Koufax, and Bob Gibson.

The journey had come full circle, but the questions didn't stop. After the '73 World Series he was approached by reporters and asked whether instant replays on TV had harmed the game, considering how many times the controversial tag play in Game 2 had been played over and over again.

"Instant replay has done more good than harm," said Augie. It has proved that we are right 99 per cent of the time. It used to be that every time there was rhubarb, people would say we kicked another one. Now, since the replay, they wait and find out what it shows. Then they get an unpleasant surprise – it turns out we're right."

Regarding the Hall of Fame: "Even if I don't make it in, I still did good for a coal miner from Bakerton, P.A.. It's not an easy profession," said Augie. "It knocks the morale out of you. Mine stayed up because I was toughened by the war and loading coal." In his heart he knew that he was a Hall of Famer. He ranked highly on many lists, even decades after his death in 1989. Before a Cracker Jack old-timer's game in Washington, Hall of Famer Bob Gibson greeted Donatelli into the clubhouse by saying, 'Here he comes, the best ball and strike umpire I ever saw.'

Donatelli smiled whenever he told anyone that comment. He believed Gibson meant what he said. That was more than good enough for Augie.

Augie Donatelli speaking at a Pennsylvania banquet. Seated to the umpire's immediate left is Augie's mother Vincenzina and to her left is Augie's wife Mary Louise. Photo courtesy of the Donatelli Collection.

After retiring Augie remained close to the game he loved as an umpiring supervisor for the National League. He enjoyed sitting inconspicuously in the stands. Photo courtesy The Donatelli Collection.

Augie Donatelli World War II Medals, including the Purple
Heart, Gunner Wings, and his dog tag from Stalag Luft
6. Photo courtesy The Donatelli Collection.

THE BALTIC CRUISE

Written by an unknown World War II POW and excerpted
from "Our Last Mission" by Dawn Trimble Bunyak.

That sea of striken faces
That we saw down below
We can't express our feelings
But we won't forget I know

We climbed down the ladder
Below the water line
While Jerry was riding up on top
Where everything was fine

A prayer was on our lips we know
No Hypocrites were there
The sweat rolled off our bodies
All were stripped down bare.

Your husband, son, or sweetheart
Was maybe in there too
But did he complain? "No, Sir"
His thought(s) were still on you

If I can spare you torture
I won't say a word
Everyone must have thought the same
For not a sound was heard.

A little drink of water
Doesn't seem much to you
And a ray of fresh sunshine
Or a sky of velvet blue

But take them all away folks
And their value is very high
That's what happened on that boat
And we were all prepared to die.

Forty eight hours of hell on earth
We rode the stormy sea
Ten men were crowded in a space
Where one man ought to be.

We suffered torture and hunger
But we didn't hear a sigh
The stronger prayed for courage
The weaker prayed to die.

Although we're not complaining
We'll take it like a man
But we'll always remember
When we're back home again.

BALLAD OF THE MEN IN BLUE

An acknowledged fan of our National Game
(Dyed in the wool, as one might say)
I follow each star with a claim to fame
After the jerk has gone away
To warmer climes to make hay and pay,
Far from the chilly lands called hinter.
But the men in blue, ah, where are they?
What do umpires do in the winter?

Mays and Allen find life is tame
On the banquet circuit; it's rarely gay.
(Their managers don't quite feel the same:
December's pounds must melt in May.)
But what of the hams who call the play?
Does anyone care if their weight may splinter?
Who gives them a Ford or Chevrolet?
What do umpires do in the winter?

Do off-season umpires come aflame
And lead a life that is *toujours gai?*
(Heaven forbid that the blush of shame
Suffuse the red neck of an ump astray!)
Can Jackowski frug? Donatelli sway?
If they can, my name is Mary Miles Minter!
How fares the cat with no mice at bay?
What do umpires do in the winter?

Barlick, in dreams do the fans cry nay,
With slaty remarks that would shock the printer?
I await your answer next Opening Day;
What do umpires do in the winter?

- Howard Cushman

Acknowledgements

The following individuals made valuable contributions to the book, including Bob Smiley, Nargis Fischer, Dieter Artz, Steve Orlowski, Joan Rodriguez, and Augie's son Pat Donatelli.

Pat expressed these final thoughts, "I would like to thank those family and friends who shared Augie's life and career as a Major League Umpire. His dedication and love for umpiring was a reflection of his love for family, faith, and friends. My dad had an uncanny understanding of basic human nature; we were all touched by his humility and love for his fellow man. We salute you dad, always hustle."

Sources

Ayres, Travis L. *The Bomber Boys: Heroes Who Flew the B-17s in World War II*. Penguin Group, 2005.

Bergman, Ron. *Game 2 Belonged to Willie*, Oakland Tribune, October, 1973.

Broyles, William Jr. *The Vietnam Reader/Why Men Love War*. Routledge Great Britain, 1991.

Bunyak, Dawn Trimble. *Our Last Mission: A World War II Prisoner in Germany*, University of Oklahoma Press, 2002.

Conlan, Jacko and Robert Creamer, *Jacko*. J.B. Lippincott Company, Philadelphia, New York, 1967.

Dawson, James P. Cards in 2nd Place. The New York Times, 1952.

Donatelli, M.L. Author interview, 1988.

Donatelli, Augie. Author interview, 1988.

Donatelli, Pat. Interview, 1988, 2010.

Drysdale, Don with Bob Verdi. *Once a Bum, Always a Dodger*. St. Martin's Press, New York, 1990.

Dewey, Donald and Nicholas Acocella, *The Biographical History of Baseball*, Carroll & Graf Publishers, Inc. New York, 1995.

Evans, Billy. *Umpiring from the Inside*. Copyright by Billy Evans, 1947.

Falkner, David. *Great Time Coming*. Touchstone, 1995.

Fraley, Oscar. Burdette Toast of Milwaukee After Third Stirring Win. UP, October, 1957.

Gerlach, Larry R. *The Men in Blue, Conversations with Umpires*. The Viking Press, New York, 1980.

Gerlach, Larry R. *Total Baseball/The Umpires*, Editors John Thorn, Pete Palmer. Warner Books, 1989.

Gorman, Tom and Jerome Holtzman. *Three and Two!* Charles Scribner's Sons, 1979.

Gutkind, Lee. *The Best Seat in Baseball But You Have to Stand*. The Dial Press, New York, 1975.

Inzana, Mary Francis. *Bakerton Pennsylvania 1889 - 1989*. The A.G. Hallidin Publishing Company, Inc. Indiana, Pennsylvania, 1989.

Harvey, Doug. Author interview, 1988.

Hemus, Solly. Author interview, 1988.

Hirsch, James S. *Willie Mays: The Life, The Legend*. Scribner, 2010.

Jackson, Robert. The Encyclopedia of Military Aircraft. Parragon Publishing Book, 2002.

Kahn, Roger. *The Boys of Summer*, Harper & Row, 1972.

Kremper, Donald. Author interview, 2010.

Lewis, Jon E. *The Mammoth Book of Fighter Pilots*. Carol & Graf Publishers, UK, 2002.

Luciano, Ron. Author interview, 1992.

Maddox, Robert. *Annual Editons: American History*, Volume 2, McGraw Hill, 2002.

Mays, Willie with Lou Sahadi. *Say Hey, The Autobiography of Willie Mays*. Simon & Schuster, 1988.

Mead, William B. *Baseball Goes to War*. Contemporary Books, 1978.

Michrina, Barry P. *Pennsylvania Mining Families: The Search for Dignity in the Coalfields*, 1995.

Nogowski, John. *Last Time Out - Big League Farewells of Baseball's Greats*. Taylor Trade Publishing/edition 2005.

Mooshil, Joe. Leo Takes 'Koufax Tag' Out of Mothballs for Holtzman", Associated Press, 1969.

Neft, David S. and Cohen, Richard M. *The Sports Encyclopedia, 7th Edition Baseball*. St. Martin's Press, New York, 1987.

O'Hara, Dave. *Spahnie Calls Baseball Crazy, Wonderful Game*, Associated Press, 1961.

Olsen, Andy. Author interview, 2007.

Pinelli, Babe and Joe King. *Mr. Ump,* The Westminster Press, Philadelphia.

Rampersad, Arnold. *Jackie Robinson: A Biography*, Alfred A. Knopf, Inc, New York, 1998.

Salerno, Al. Author Interview, 2007.

Schoor, Gene. The History of the World Series: *The Complete Chronology of America's Greatest Sports Tradition*. William Morrow and Company, Inc. New York, 1990.

Shapiro, Milton. *The Don Drysdale Story*. Julian Messner, New York, 1964.

Smith, Curt. *Voices of The Game*. Diamond Communications, Inc., South Bend, Indiana,1987.

Solomon, Burt. *The Baseball Timeline*. A Stonesong Press Book, 1997.

Spahn, Warren. Author interview, 1988.

Stout, Glenn. The Dodgers - *120 Years of Dodgers Baseball*. Houghton Mifflin Company, *2004*.

Uecker, Bob and Mickey Herskowitz, *Catcher in the Wry*. Putnam Publishing Group, 1982.

NEWSPAPERS / MAGAZINES

Abramson, Jessie. (Special NY-HT) *Old Sal Maglie Spins No-Hit, No-Run Game*, September 26, 1956.

Anderson, Dave. *Guess Who's for the Umpires?* The New York Times, March 11, 1979.

Associated Press. *Astros GM Fined $300 by NL Boss*, May 18, 1973.

Associated Press. *Don Drysdale Breaks Major Shutout Mark,* June 9th, 1968.

Associated Press. *Fans 18 But mets' Lewis Homers*, June 15, 1965.

Associated Press. *Jackie Robinson Denies Door Assault Climaxing Season's Biggest Rhubarb,* September, 1951.

Associated Press. *Jackie Pays Fine, But Asks Hearing.* June 29, 1956.

Associated Press. *One for the Books, Durocher Praises Umpire.* April, 1951.

Associated Press. *Pappas Refused to Give Stahl Good Pitch to Hit.* September 3, 1972.

Associated Press. *Player, Ump Rhubarb After Giants Loss*, September 28, 1951.

Bock, Hal. (Associated Press) *Gee, Thanks A Lot Billy: Ken*, August 20, 1969.

Busch, Noel J. *Umpire School.* Life Magazine, March 10, 1947.

Carrol, Dink. *Playing the Field.* Montreal Gazette, October, 1949.

Chamberlain, Charles. (Associated Press) *Casey Stengel Mobbed by Fans*, October 2, 1957.

Dailey, Arthur. *Sports of the Times - Overheard at the Polo Grounds*, The New York Times, 1951.

Dailey, Arthur. *Sports of the Times - In the Bill Klem Image*, January 26, 1965.

Durso, Joe. *Club Can Win Title With Sweep and a Pirate Loss*, New York Times, Sept 1973.

Enright, Jim. *Referee Magazine*, 1973.

Holtzman, Jerome. *The Umpires Have Their Limits of Restraint*. Baseball Digest, 1991.

Koppett, Leonard. (Special to The New York Times) *New Spitball Rule is Eased, With Complications*, March, 1968.

Lemire, Joe. *Pappas supports Galarraga, keeps firing shots at Froemming, SI.com*, June 2010.

McGowen, Roscoe. *Dodgers Lose on Disputed Run and Lead Idle Giants by Half a Game*, The New York Times, 1951.

Rosenbaum, Art. San Francisco Chronicle, 1965.

The Desert News, Salt Lake City, Utah. *The Fanning Bee Hive*, 1946.

The New York Times. *American League Umpires Drop Plan to Strike Against World Series Work*, October 1, 1968.

The New York Times. *Umpire Assails Series Pay Offer: $500 Increase is Termed 'Peanuts' by Donatelli*. October 2, 1970.

Thompson, Jack. *Umpires Told: Don't Go to the Replay*. Chicago Tribune, June, 1999.

UPI, *Ump Insists Bud Was Out*, October 17, 1973.

UPI, *Astros GM fined $300 by NL boss*, May 18, 1973.

Young, Dick. Donatelli, *New NL Ump A Rickey 'Discovery'*, The New York Daily News, 1950.

Weiss, Don. *Typical Umpire Is 45, Big, Burly Family Man*, UP April, 1957.

Wilks, Ed. (Associated Press Sports Writer) *Warren (The Wonder) Spahn, Hurls No-Hitter.* April, 1961.

WEBSITES

Retrosheet.org/boxsetc/D/Pdonaa901.htm, 2010

Baseballreference.com

FILMS

Vintage World Series Films, DVD Oakland Athletics

INDEX

Colbert, Nate 156, 178
Coleman, Jerry 171
Coleman, Len 111
Comiskey, Charles 192
Conlan, Jocko 7, 115, 127, 143, 159, 163, 184, 193, 198
Connolly, Tom 7
Connors, Chuck 106
Cooper, Walker 126
Craft, Harry 128
Crawford, Jerry i, xiv, 8, 204
Crawford, Shag ix, 106, 185, 195, 203, 206

D

Daily, Elmer 96, 102
Dark, Alvin 110, 146
Dascoli, Frank 149, 159, 164
Davidson, Satch 3
Dean, Dizzy 29
DeWitt, Bill 155, 197
Dickson, Murry 184
Dietz, Dick 138
DiMaggio, Joe 46, 118, 183
Dixon, Hal 143
Donatelli, Mary Louise xiv
Donatelli, Pat 6, 7, 183, 216, 233
Dressen, Charlie 160
Dreyfuss, Barney 27
Drysdale, Don 136, 140, 185, 233, 235, 236
Dugan, Ed 41, 66
Dykes, Jimmie 115

E

Elliott, Bob 110, 131, 132, 148
Engel, Bob 132
Ennis, Del 113
Enright, Jim 206, 237
Erskine, Carl 144
Evans, Billy 7, 128, 233
Evers, Johnny 121

F

Feeney, Chub 202, 208, 209, 213
Feller, Bob 46
Fernandez, Nanny 106
Finley, Charles 215
Fitzsimmons, Freddy 131
Foli, Tim 3
Ford, John 94
Fosse, Ray 7, 216, 217, 221
Franks, Herman 131, 138
Frawley, William 113
Freese, Gene 137, 143
Frick, Ford 103, 106, 108, 125, 127, 180, 185, 192, 194, 198, 199
Froemming, Bruce 3, 156, 157, 163, 209
Furillo, Carl 113, 128, 131, 146, 164

G

Garcia, Rich i, x, xiv
Gardner, Billy 103
Gedeon, Elmer 46
Gehrig, Lou 99, 108, 171
Giamatti, Bart 188
Gibson, Bob 8, 173, 223
Giles, Warren 23, 109, 147, 164, 192, 196, 198, 206
Gilliam, Junior 168
Goetz, Larry 5, 142
Goldaper, Sam 178
Goodman, Benny 19
Gore, Artie 143, 144
Gorman, Tom 123, 131, 195, 234
Grim, Bob 168, 170
Groat, Dick 143

H

Hack, Stan 143
Haney, Fred 170
Harrelson, Bud ii, 6, 156, 216, 218, 220
Harridge, William 193, 194

Hart, Jim Ray 138
Hartsfield, Roy 103
Harvey, Doug 7, 115, 203, 234
Hatton, Grady 140
Hauser, Gus 38
Helfer, Al 29
Hemus, Solly 102, 130, 149, 179, 234
Hiatt, Jack 139
Hodges, Gil 113, 142, 147, 149, 168
Holton, John 12
Holtzman, Jerome xii, 5, 234, 237
Hornsby, Rogers 115
Houk, Ralph 46
Hubbard, Cal 7, 200
Hunt, Ron 139
Hurley, Ed 200
Hutchinson, Fred 138, 152

J

Jackowski, Bill 129
Jackson, Joe 105
Jackson, Randy 130
Jackson, Reggie 215, 221
James, Harry 19
Jansen, Larry 110
Javier, Julian 173, 174
Jones, Nippy 9
Jurges, Billy 129

K

Kahn, Roger 142, 148, 234
Kennedy, John F. 177, 189
Kessinger, Don 155, 156
Kibler, John 2, 196
Kiner, Ralph 143
Klem, Bill 4, 7, 124, 157, 237
Koosman, Jerry 6, 211, 214
Koufax, Sandy 136, 223
Kremper, Donald xiv, 54, 63, 73, 74, 89, 234
Kubek, Tony 170, 171, 216
Kuenn, Harvey 150, 184

L

Lamarr, Hedy 94
Lamont, Mary Louise 95, 101
Landes, Stan 152, 208
Landis, Kenesaw Mountain 28, 47
Landrith, Hobie 143
Lavagetto, Cookie 159, 160
Lewis, J. Norman 191
Lockman, Whitey 110, 146
Logan, Johnny 170, 171
Lombardo, Guy 19
Long , Dale 102
Lopata, Stan 114
Louis, Joe 60, 108
Lowrey, Peanuts 139
Luciano, Ron xiv, 121, 187, 234

M

Magerkurth, George 128
Maglie, Sal 236
Maloney, Jim 153
Mantilla, Felix 170
Mantle, Mickey 166, 167, 172, 184
Maris, Roger 172
Marshall, Dave 138
Martin, Billy 102
Mathews, Eddie 9, 10, 136, 170, 184
Matlack, Jon 6, 211
Matthau, Walter 175
Mature, Victor 94
Mauch, Gene 3, 139
Maxvill, Dal 174
Mays, Willie xiii, 7, 125, 146, 150, 151, 161, 186, 211, 215, 218, 223, 234
Mazeroski, Bill 175, 181, 185
McCarthy, Joe 108
McCovey, Willie 138, 150
McCullough, Clyde 129, 144
McDougald, Gil 168, 169
McGowan, Bill xii, 7, 97, 99
McGraw, Tug 6, 211, 214
McKinley, Bill 200

Steiner, Mel 154
Stello, Dick 155, 196
Stengel, Casey iv, 116, 169, 171, 176,
    184, 236
Stevens, John 222
Stewart, Ernie 112, 193
Stoneham, Charles 210
Stoneham, Horace 210
Stottlemyre, Mel 186
Strawberry, Darryl 188

T

Thomas, Frank 143
Torborg, Jeff 138
Townsend, Jim 99
Travis, Merle 12

U

Uecker, Bob 4, 236

V

Valentine, Bill 200
Vargo, Ed 5, 108, 151, 187, 196, 209
Vaughn, Hippo 143

W

Wagner, Honus 45
Waitkus, Eddie 113
Ward, Preston 143
Weatherly, Roy 106
Weekly, Johnny 153
Wendelstedt, Harry 5, 138, 157, 163,
    196, 203, 221, 222
Westrum, Wes 10
Wilhelm, Hoyt 46
Williams, Billy 154, 156
Williams, Ted 46, 194
Wilson, George 146

Y

Yastrzemski, Carl 186
Young, Cy 150, 151
Young, Dick 104, 237

Z

Zimmer, Don 168